AFTERMATH

ALSO BY JAMES RICKARDS

Currency Wars

The Death of Money

The New Case for Gold

The Road to Ruin

AFTERMATH

SEVEN SECRETS OF WEALTH
PRESERVATION IN THE COMING CHAOS

James Rickards

PORTFOLIO/PENGUIN

Portfolio/Penguin
An imprint of Penguin Random House LLC
penguinrandomhouse.com

Most Portfolio books are available at a discount when purchased in quantity for sales promotions or corporate use. Special editions, which include personalized covers, excerpts,
and corporate imprints, can be created when purchased in large quantities. For more information, please call (212) 572-2232 or email specialmarkets@penguinrandomhouse.com.
Your local bookstore can also assist with discounted bulk purchases using the Penguin
Random House corporate Business-to-Business program. For assistance in locating a participating retailer, email B2B@penguinrandomhouse.com.

Library of Congress Cataloging-in-Publication Data
Names: Rickards, James, author.
Title: Aftermath : seven secrets of wealth preservation in the coming chaos /
    James Rickards.
Description: New York : Portfolio/Penguin, [2019] | Includes bibliographical
    references and index.
Identifiers: LCCN 2019010409 (print) | LCCN 2019012464 (ebook) |
    ISBN 9780735216969 (ebook) | ISBN 9780735216952 (hardcover)
Subjects: LCSH: Investments. | Financial crises. | Finance—Forecasting. |
    Economic forecasting.
Classification: LCC HG4521 (ebook) | LCC HG4521 .R5154 2019 (print) |
    DDC 332.024—dc23
LC record available at https://lccn.loc.gov/2019010409

Printed in the United States of America
10 9 8 7 6 5 4 3 2 1

For Ann

Then I watched while the Lamb broke open the first of the seven seals, and I heard one of the four living creatures cry out in a voice like thunder, "Come forward." I looked, and there was a white horse, and its rider had a bow. He was given a crown, and he rode forth victorious to further his victories.

—Revelation 6:1–2

CONTENTS

INTRODUCTION

No Way Home

This book is about the aftermath of the 2008 global financial crisis and efforts by central banks first to prevent a complete collapse of capital markets, later to revive self-sustaining growth, then finally to withdraw from continual policy intervention. It also warns that the crisis never really ended and offers a path to preserve wealth in the next phase. Like the *Odyssey*, this ten-year journey cannot be understood without reference to the struggle that preceded it. We consider the before, the after, and the future of the greatest financial crisis since the Great Depression.

In Homer's epic poem the *Odyssey*, Scylla and Charybdis confront the hero, Odysseus, sailing home after the Trojan War. Scylla and Charybdis were the most feared women of Greek mythology. They lived in caves, a bowshot apart on each side of a narrow strait. Although female in nature, they were monsters. Scylla had six heads. Each mouth had rows of razor-sharp teeth that made the shark in *Jaws* seem tame. Her waist was shrouded with heads of baying dogs. She swam and walked on twelve snaky legs and devoured all within reach.

Less is known about the look of Charybdis, yet her powers were as daunting as Scylla's. Three times a day Poseidon's daughter would swallow the sea and spew it out, creating a whirlpool fatal to ships and sailors.

Odysseus is faced with a terrible choice. He must guide his vessel through the strait. Avoiding one peril needs put him in reach of the other. Odysseus orders the crew to steer clear of Charybdis, taking his chances with Scylla. He reasons that a whirlpool portends complete loss, while Scylla is a more selective threat—an ancient exercise in risk management. The gamble pays off. Scylla devours six of the crew. Still, Odysseus and the remnant survive, their vessel intact, to continue their journey home to Ithaca.

This hero's dilemma, known in modern idiom as "being between Scylla and Charybdis," is a perfect metaphor for the state of the global economy today and the choices confronting policymakers. Odysseus could coolly calculate his choice based on the nature of the horrors he confronted. Policymakers face similar tough choices now, with no way to gauge which is worse. The history of central bank policy since 2008 is an odyssey back to normalized interest rates and balance sheets. In the original *Odyssey*, the hero eventually arrives home, despite the dangers. In 2019, central bankers are still wandering, their travels far from over.

This twenty-first-century central bank odyssey was preceded by its own version of the Trojan War. In 2000, Federal Reserve chairman Alan Greenspan faced four challenges in quick succession that caused near deflation. The first was the bursting of the dot-com stock bubble beginning in March 2000. Second was a cyclical recession beginning in the United States in March 2001, part of a global slowdown in developed economies. Third were the 9/11 attacks, which, in addition to their historic geopolitical consequences, caused $40 billion in insurance losses and a one-day 7.1 percent stock market decline. This decline followed the longest trading suspension, September 11–14, 2001, since 1933. Finally, China's accession to full WTO membership in December 2001 opened world markets to the greatest agglomeration of cheap labor and abundant capital in history. China's emergence put downward pressure on prices that has not abated.

The result was a flirtation with deflation, a central banker's worst nightmare. The consumer price index, or CPI, rose 1.55 percent in 2001, the lowest reading since 1986, and before that, 1964. After a slight increase to 2.38 percent in 2002, the CPI dipped again to 1.88 percent in 2003. In response, the annualized Fed Funds effective rate plunged from 6 percent in January 2001 to 1.8 percent by the end of that year. Greenspan then held the Fed Funds effective rate below 2 percent until November 2004 in an effort to slay the deflation dragon.

Deflation is a central banker's greatest fear because it increases the real value of debt, which leads to defaults that jeopardize bank solvency. Similarly, an increase in the real value of debt shines a light on the growing burden of government debt and calls U.S. solvency into question. Price deflation also produces gains in citizens' real standard of living that governments cannot effectively tax. Deflation makes cash more valuable, which discourages consumption, the linchpin of economic growth. Worse yet, deflation is a trap that central bankers cannot escape with existing policy tools, what John Maynard Keynes called a liquidity trap.

Greenspan succeeded in defeating deflation. In 2005, his last full year as Fed chairman, the CPI was back up to 3.42 percent, a comfortable cushion above zero. Yet Greenspan scored a Pyrrhic victory. That three-year stretch of sub-2 percent Fed Funds from 2001 to 2004 was rightly criticized as "too low, for too long." Low rates gave rise to the housing bubble and subprime mortgage crisis that exploded in 2007. The following year saw the global financial crisis and near destruction of the banking sector and the international monetary system.

What ensued was a more extreme version of Greenspan's antideflation medicine. The CPI was 0.09 percent in 2008, the year of the crisis, even lower than the 1.55 percent rate that spooked Greenspan in 2001. Greenspan's successor, Ben Bernanke, took the Fed Funds target rate to 0 percent in December 2008 where it remained until another Fed chair, Janet Yellen, raised the rate to 0.25 percent on December 17, 2015. If Greenspan's three-year experiment with sub-2-percent rates gave rise to the global financial crisis, what was the world to make of the Bernanke-Yellen policy of 0 percent for seven years?

The zero-interest-rate policy was not the only extraordinary measure taken by Bernanke's Federal Reserve. Bernanke also engaged in a completely unprecedented money-printing binge called quantitative easing, or QE. The money printing was executed through Fed purchases of long-term securities from bank primary dealers. The purchases were paid for with money from thin air that the Fed simply deposited with the banks through accounting entries.

Quantitative easing came in three rounds. The first, QE1 ran from November 2008 through June 2010. The second, QE2 began in November 2010 and lasted until June 2011. The third round of money printing, QE3, started in September 2012 and lasted until October 2014. As a result of these three rounds of money printing, the base money supply, M0 in Fed parlance, increased from $800 billion to $4.1 trillion. The offsetting asset on the Fed's books was a $4.1 trillion mountain of U.S. Treasury notes and mortgage-backed securities.

The effects of QE are still debated. Most observers grant that QE1 was a proper central bank response to a liquidity crisis that had reached an acute stage with the Lehman Brothers bankruptcy in September 2008. However, QE2 and QE3 were more like a Bernanke-bred science experiment with no historic precedent.

Critics of QE quickly claimed that money printing on this scale would produce a wave of inflation. The inflation never came, because inflation has little to do with money supply per se. Inflation is a psychological phenomenon based on expectations and a form of adaptive behavior described mathematically as hypersynchronicity. Money supply can be like dry kindling, but inflation will not burst into flames without a catalyst. From 2008 to 2018, that catalyst was missing because consumers were saving, paying off debt, and rebuilding their balance sheets. The velocity or turnover of money plunged after 2008, the continuation of a decline that began in 1998. The psychological scars left by the 2008 market collapse had not healed. Still, the kindling was there. Ten years after the crisis, the risk that saver psychology might shift quickly and cascade into lost confidence in the dollar and rapidly rising inflation as it had in the late 1970s was nascent.

Supporters of QE defended Bernanke by asking rhetorically, "What choice did he have?" In late 2008, the United States was facing the most severe financial and liquidity crisis since 1933. Bernanke's academic reputation was grounded in his study of the Great Depression, in particular the pivotal year of 1933, when Franklin D. Roosevelt succeeded Herbert Hoover as president. When I met Bernanke in Seoul in 2015, he expressed his admiration of FDR's role in alleviating the Great Depression. He told me that FDR rarely knew exactly what impact his policies would have and he often made mistakes. Still, in a crisis, FDR felt it better to do something rather than nothing. Hippocrates would disagree, but Bernanke was an economist, not a physician. Like FDR, he was determined to do something to fend off a depression.

There is an academic theory behind Bernanke's QE, called the portfolio balance channel. The idea is that investor money has to go somewhere. By purchasing long-term Treasury securities, the Fed lowered their total return and made them less attractive to investors. In turn, this made stocks and real estate more attractive on a relative basis. As investor funds flowed to equity and property channels, those assets would be worth more. Higher asset values would provide collateral for more borrowing. The higher asset values would also create a wealth effect that would encourage consumption, as everyday Americans felt richer and more willing to spend freely. In combination, more borrowing and more spending would push inflation to the Fed's 2 percent target, facilitate normalized interest rates, and drive real GDP growth to its former self-sustaining trend above 3 percent.

None of these results emerged. Inflation measured by the Fed's preferred yardstick, core personal consumption expenditure, or PCE, year-over-year, remained below 2 percent for six years through 2017. The Fed Funds target rate was still 2.0 percent as late as mid-2018; well below the hoped-for 3.5 percent. Real GDP growth from June 2009, the end of the last recession, through the first quarter of 2018 was less than 2.2 percent, materially below the long-term trend. As academic research on the QE experiment arrived after 2014, the best scholars could say was that it did no harm. There was no consensus that it had done any good.

By 2015, the QE and the zero-interest-rate policies ended. Critics were wrong about inflation; it never arrived. The Fed was wrong about stimulus; trend growth never arrived either. The ten-year episode of low rates and bloated balance sheets did not live up to the worst fears of critics or the great expectations of policymakers.

However, QE and zero rates did have one effect. It was the same effect Greenpsan produced on a smaller scale at the start of the century—asset bubbles. The difference was that Greenspan's bubble was confined to mortgages, although the ensuing panic knew no bounds because of leverage, derivatives, and the dense interconnectedness of the global banking system. In contrast, by late 2018, the bubbles were everywhere—stocks, bonds, high-end real estate, emerging markets, and Chinese credit. The interconnectedness was greater also. And if the damage in 2008 was caused by low interest rates from 2001 to 2004, now the potential damage was the fruit of low rates *and* swollen securities holdings of central banks. Indeed, these central bank blunders were not confined to the Fed, but were a signal characteristic of central banks around the world.

By late 2015, central banks were desperate to normalize rates and balance sheets. The definition of "normal" for this purpose was speculative, since there was no precedent for highly abnormal rates and QE policies to begin with. Even the Bank of Japan, which has been experimenting with extreme remedies since 1990, including negative interest rates and asset purchases of equities in addition to government bonds, has given hints of a desire to reverse course. In the case of the Federal Reserve, normal might be a balance sheet of $2.5 trillion, and a Fed Funds target rate of 3.5 percent, both a far cry from the Fed's position in early 2019.

If 1998 to 2008 was a financial Trojan War, and 2008 to 2018 was an odyssey back to financial normalcy, where are we now? Unhappily we are nowhere near home. In fact, we are now in sight of Scylla and Charybdis. Like Odysseus, Fed chairman Jay Powell must choose a course. Scylla is a global recession and stock market decline of 60 percent; severe, but manageable. Charybdis, the vortex, is a new global liquidity crisis that the international monetary system will not survive.

Outwardly the Fed purports to be sanguine about the prospects for monetary normalization. Both former chair Janet Yellen and new chair Jay Powell have said that interest rate hikes will be gradual. In practice, this means four rate hikes per year, 0.25 percent each, every March, June, September, and December, with occasional pauses prompted by strong signs of disinflation, disorderly markets, or diminution in job creation.

Balance sheet normalization is even more on autopilot than rate hikes. The Fed will not dump its securities holdings. Instead, it refrains from rolling over maturing securities. When the Treasury pays the Fed upon the maturity of a Treasury note, the money received by the Fed simply disappears. This is the opposite of money printing; it's money destruction. Instead of QE, we now have QT, or quantitative tightening. The Fed has been transparent about the rate at which they will run off their balance sheet this way, although transparency should not lead to complacency. The balance sheet reduction tempo as of early 2019 is $600 billion per year, equal in impact to four 0.25 percent rate hikes per year. The annual combined impact of the Fed's rate policy and QT is an annual 2 percent increase in interest rates. For an economy addicted to cheap money, this is cold turkey.

The Fed would have investors believe that the rate hikes are already priced in to capital markets, and QT is a nonevent, running on "background," in the Fed's words. The Fed pretends it's like running an Excel spreadsheet on your laptop while you watch a film from Netflix. That assumption is not correct. The conceit that rate hikes are priced in ignores the complexity of global capital markets. Will other countries whose currencies are pegged formally or informally to the dollar raise rates in lockstep with the Fed to maintain the peg? If so, will those same countries later be forced to break the peg, close their capital accounts, or devalue their currencies? Will disorderly stock markets derail Fed tightening plans, as happened in September 2015, when the Fed postponed the "liftoff," or in December 2016, when the Fed finally raised rates to save face? These questions limn just a few of the negative outcomes from rate hikes that Fed models cannot resolve.

The view that balance sheet normalization can run on background without disruptive effects is even more flimsy than the rate-hike conceit. The Fed printed almost $4 trillion of new money over six years from 2008 to 2014 to inflate the value of risky assets. Now, the Fed would have investors believe that destroying $2 trillion in even less time will have no negative impact on the value of those same risky assets.

Why is the Fed raising rates and destroying money? Despite the absence of any empirical support, Fed governors and staff economists persist in their reliance on the Phillips Curve, which predicts that low unemployment leads to rising inflation. Unemployment in the United States at 3.7 percent in early 2019 is at fifty-year lows. The Fed, despite occasional pauses, insists that the time to tighten monetary conditions is now, before the inflation emerges.

Yet the Phillips Curve bears no correspondence to reality. The 1960s were characterized by low unemployment and rising inflation. The late 1970s were characterized by high unemployment and high inflation. The 2010s have been characterized by low unemployment and low inflation. There is no correlation between inflation and unemployment, just as there is no correlation between inflation and money supply. Inflation is always and everywhere a psychological phenomenon. When citizens lose confidence in a form of money, velocity takes off. Reliance on the Phillips Curve for Fed policymaking is false science.

The other ostensible reason for Fed tightening is official confidence that the U.S. economy is on a solid growth path. As with the Phillips Curve, there is no evidence for this belief. The U.S. savings rate plunged to 2.1 percent by late 2017, a fraction of the 6.3 percent rate that prevailed from 1970 to 2000. The combined impact of the 2017 Trump tax cuts, bipartisan congressional repeal of discretionary spending caps, and rising student loan defaults will push U.S. budget deficits well past $1 trillion per year beginning in 2019 and continuing indefinitely. This added dissaving will push the U.S. savings rate to zero. This means the United States must either reduce investment or borrow savings from abroad. Both courses hurt growth. Other headwinds to growth include Trump's trade war, impediments to immigration, and higher real rates as the U.S. Treasury tries to attract buyers for the $10 trillion of new debt it must sell in the decade to come. These specific headwinds are of recent vintage and come on top of the preexisting secular stagnation due to demographics, de-leveraging, and declining productivity.

The hoopla about higher growth associated with the Trump tax cuts is hokum. This growth expectation is rooted in the Laffer Curve, which posits that lower tax rates produce higher growth, which leads to higher tax collections that offset the rate cuts. Prominent supporters, including the eponymous economist Art Laffer, Larry Kudlow, Steve Moore, and Steve Forbes, point to the Reagan Revolution (of which they are all veterans), during which tax cuts enacted on August 13, 1981, were followed by robust real growth beginning in the first quarter of 1983 that continued through the decade. True enough.

What the Reagan Revolution myth leaves out is that from the second quarter of 1980, late in the Carter administration, through the third quarter of 1982, well into the Reagan administration, the U.S. economy suffered six quarters of negative real growth in the form of back-to-back technical recessions, including the worst recession since the Great Depression, a record that held until 2008. By 1983, the U.S. economy was primed for a strong cyclical recovery with or without tax cuts. Compare that to the U.S. economy in early 2019, which is over nine years into an expansion, the second longest in U.S. history, with little in the way of unused capacity on a scale that existed in 1982.

The other factor left out of the Reagan-Trump tax-cut comparison is that Reagan enlarged the U.S. debt-to-GDP ratio from 35 percent to 55 percent during his administration, a near 60 percent increase in the ratio. Reagan was a closet Keynesian, as David Stockman, Reagan's budget director, pointed out then and has reminded citizens ever since. The Trump administration came into office with a debt-to-GDP ratio of 105 percent, nothing at all like Reagan's starting line. A 60 percent increase à la Reagan would put the U.S. debt-to-GDP ratio at 170 percent, just slightly lower than Greece at 180 percent. Of course, the United States would suffer a crisis of confidence in the dollar and a global monetary collapse long before the U.S. debt ratio got that high. Worse yet for the growth thesis, extensive and convincing research by Harvard professors Carmen Reinhart and Kenneth Rogoff shows that once a nation's debt-to-equity ratio passes 90 percent, the stimulative impact of added debt, including debt from tax cuts, is negative.

Initial conditions of debt and the business cycle confronting Trump are unlike those that Reagan enjoyed. Reagan had a once-in-a-century chance to jump-start growth with debt, and he did it successfully, to bury the Soviet Union and win the Cold War. Trump is not so lucky. Trump's tax cuts will bury economic growth under a mountain of debt and shake world confidence in the U.S. dollar.

The Fed understands these impediments to growth, although they cannot publicly pivot away from the rosy scenario. This begs the question, why is the Fed tightening if the economy is so weak? The answer is that the Fed is preparing for the *next* crisis. The evidence is clear that it takes 4 percent in rate cuts to pull the United States out of a recession. The Fed cannot cut rates even 3 percent when the Fed Funds rate is less than 2.5 percent. So, the Fed is in a desperate race to raise rates before a recession arrives, so they can cut rates to cure the recession.

How does balance sheet normalization fit in? Reducing the balance sheet is a precautionary step in case a recession arrives before rates reach 4 percent. In that case, the Fed would cut rates as far as they could, until rates hit zero, and then revert to QE. (The Fed has shown no inclination to use negative rates, and the evidence from Europe, Sweden, and Japan is that negative rates don't work anyway). Contrary to the leanings of modern monetary theorists like Professor Stephanie Kelton, the Fed does not have an unlimited capacity to monetize debt. The constraint is not legal, but psychological. There is an invisible confidence boundary on the size of the Fed's balance sheet. The Fed cannot cross this boundary without destroying confidence in the central bank and the dollar. Whether that boundary is $5 trillion or $6 trillion is unknowable. A central bank will find out the hard way instantaneously when they cross it. At that point, it's too late to regain trust. Having pushed the balance sheet to $4.5 trillion in the last crisis, the Fed needs to reduce the balance sheet now so they can expand it again up to $4.5 trillion in QE4 if necessary.

In short, the Fed is tightening monetary conditions now so they can ease conditions in the next crisis without destroying confidence in the dollar. The Fed's conundrum is whether they can tighten monetary conditions now without causing the recession they are preparing to cure. The evidence of the past ten years shows the answer to that question is no. The Fed's odds of accomplishing their task without harm to markets are near zero. Tightening monetary policy in a weak economy is steering a course between Scylla and Charybdis. Here are the likely outcomes.

In one scenario, call it Scylla, the double dose of tightening from rate hikes and QT slows the economy, deflates asset bubbles in stocks, strengthens the dollar, and imports deflation. As these trends become evident, disinflation tips into mild deflation. Job creation dries up as employers rein in costs. A stock market correction will turn into a bear market with major indices dropping 50 percent or more from 2019 highs. All of these trends would be exacerbated by a global slowdown due to the trade war, concerns about U.S. debt levels, and reduced immigration. A technical recession will ensue. This would not be the end of the world. It would be the end of one of the longest expansions and longest bull markets in stocks ever. The Fed would respond to this recession with rate cuts back to zero, the end of QT, and a new round of QE that would take the Fed balance sheet back up over the $4 trillion mark. As was the case with Odysseus, the costs would be high, yet the economic vessel and crew would (mostly) survive.

The other scenario, call it Charybdis, is a more complex process with a far more catastrophic outcome. In this scenario, the Fed repeats two historic blunders. The first blunder occurred in 1928, when the Fed tried to deflate an asset bubble in stocks. The second blunder was in 1937, when the Fed tightened policy too early during a period of prolonged weakness.

Until December 2017, the Fed rejected the idea that it could identify and deflate asset bubbles. This policy was based on the experience of 1928, when Fed efforts to deflate a stock bubble led to the stock market crash of October 1929 and the Great Depression. The Fed's preference since then is to let bubbles pop on their own and then clean up the mess with monetary ease if needed. This policy preference was followed in the aftermath of the emerging-markets bubble of 1997, the dot-com bubble of 1999, and the mortgage bubble of 2007.

However, the popping of the mortgage bubble in 2007 was far more dangerous and the policy response far more radical than the Fed expected going into that episode. Given the continued fragility of the financial system, the Fed began to rethink its cleanup policy and chose a more nuanced stance toward deflating bubbles. This new view (really a reprise of the 1928 view) emerged in the minutes of the Federal Open Market Committee, the Fed's rate policy arm, for October 31–November 1, 2017:

> In their comments regarding financial markets, participants generally judged that financial conditions remained accommodative despite the recent increases in the exchange value of the dollar and Treasury yields. *In light of elevated asset valuations* and low finan-

cial market volatility, several participants expressed concerns about a potential buildup of financial imbalances. They worried that a sharp reversal in asset prices could have damaging effects on the economy. (Emphasis added.)

This view was echoed in the public remarks of Fed officials in the days following this FOMC meeting, and in the FOMC's decision to raise rates at their December 13, 2017, meeting despite continued concerns about disinflation. As if to validate the concerns expressed, U.S. stock markets soon suffered a sharp 11 percent correction from February 2 to February 8, 2018—a mild preview of what happens when the Fed tries to deflate asset bubbles. Still, the Fed persisted in its rate hikes throughout 2018. Given the proliferation of passive investing strategies, algorithmic trading, and hypersynchronous reaction functions, the Fed's attempted finesse in financial markets will ultimately result in a market crash as bad or worse than 1929.

The impact of such a market crash will not be confined to the United States. In fact, a stronger dollar resulting from tight monetary policy could precipitate a crisis in emerging markets dollar-denominated debt that morphs into a global liquidity crisis through now well-known contagion channels. Turkey is a good candidate to play patient zero in such a contagion, with over $400 billion in external debt and deteriorating relations with its NATO allies. Such a debt debacle would not be entirely the Fed's fault. Chronic trillion-dollar deficits in the United States created by Congress will require higher interest rates to induce investors to purchase massive amounts of Treasury notes. With the Fed no longer a buyer, those purchases must come from private sources here or abroad. In turn, those sources will sell U.S. stocks or foreign debt to raise cash to buy Treasuries. That's a dangerous dynamic that could cause compression in prices of risky assets and catalyze a crisis.

The second historic Fed blunder was an effort to normalize rate policy in 1937 after eight years of ease during the worst of the Great Depression. Today's policy normalization is almost an exact replay. Economic performance from 2007 to 2019 is best understood as a depression, not in the sense of continual declining GDP, but as Keynes defined it, "a chronic condition of sub-normal activity for a considerable period without any marked tendency either towards recovery or towards complete collapse." In other words, a depression occurs when actual growth is depressed relative to potential growth, even without outright declines.

It is understandable that the Fed wishes to resume what it regards as normal monetary policy after the better part of a decade of abnormal ease. The difficulty is that the Fed has painted itself into a corner from which there is no easy exit. When the Fed tried to normalize policy in 1937 they triggered a second severe technical recession following the 1929–1933 recession and helped to prolong the Great Depression until 1940. Reverting to monetary ease does not allow an escape from Charybdis. More ease merely reinflates asset bubbles and increases systemic scale, insuring a crash of unprecedented magnitude.

Internally, the Fed has congratulated itself on their fine-tuning and market finesse. They shouldn't have. All the Fed proved in recent years was that they really couldn't exit extraordinary policy intervention without disruption. The Fed has been storing up trouble for another day. That day is here.

We Are Not Helpless

History's a hard mistress. Her judgments are unsparing, seldom those we expect. Leaders laughed at in their day are deemed heroic by later generations. Harry S. Truman was viewed as unfit and lacking in stature while president, particularly in comparison with his predecessor, FDR. Today Truman is ranked by historians as one of the ten greatest presidents, ahead of icons such as Thomas Jefferson and Ronald Reagan. Ike had a like re-appraisal. President Eisenhower was considered an avuncular, golf-playing figure while in office, not particularly prescient or engaged in policy. Today he ranks fifth among U.S. presidents, ahead of Truman and just behind the big four—Lincoln, Washington, FDR, and Teddy Roosevelt.

In a similar way, history will elevate Gerald R. Ford. President Ford was set apart as the only commander in chief never elected to national office. Most in the baby-boom generation never forgave Ford for his 1974 pardon of the villainous Nixon. After stumbling on the Air Force One staircase, Ford was relentlessly ridiculed as clumsy by *Saturday Night Live* comedian Chevy Chase. Ford served only fifty-four months in office. He lost his first and only national election contest in 1976. Today, Ford is ranked by historians at twenty-fifth among forty-four past presidents, the bottom half of the class.

The reality was that Ford was a handsome college athlete who played on two championship teams and was named a college all-star. His academic record includes Phi Beta Kappa at the University of Michigan and a law degree from Yale. Ford was the Republican leader in the House of Representatives. As president, Ford's pardon of Nixon is widely viewed as a healing act of forgiveness, even if many will not forgive Ford. In a speech at Tulane University on April 23, 1975, Ford declared the war in Vietnam "finished as far as America is concerned." By closing the door on Watergate and Vietnam, two of the bitterest episodes in U.S. political history, Ford allowed America to mend and move on. In 1976, he led the nation in a joyous celebration of its bicentennial.

Yet these accomplishments, all well known to historians, will not advance Ford's place in presidential annals. Ford's lasting legacies, ones that history will smile upon, are his twin contributions to individual freedom—the Helsinki Accords and the legalization of gold.

The Helsinki Accords were signed on August 1, 1975, by President Ford; Leonid Brezhnev, general secretary of the Communist Party of the

Soviet Union; and leaders of thirty-three other Western and Eastern-bloc states. The accords were an odd mix of ostensibly pro-Soviet and pro-Western pledges.

References to "territorial integrity" and the "nonuse of force" seemed to solidify Soviet claims to control of countries behind the Iron Curtain. Brezhnev said the accords ratified post–World War II boundaries from the Baltics to Berlin. Ford was bitterly criticized by Americans of European descent and others who considered the accords a sellout of Baltic and Polish aspirations for freedom.

Yet the accords also called for respect for human rights, and freedom of thought, conscience, and religious belief. The accords insisted on equal rights, self-determination, and peaceful resolution of disputes. For the first time since the Cold War began, people behind the Iron Curtain had a legitimate standard for freedom that the Soviet Union had agreed to in writing. This led to the creation of watchdog groups and regular progress reports on adherence to the accords.

The objective criteria established by the Helsinki Accords provided a legal framework for movements such as the June 1976 protests in Poland, a precursor to the formation of the Solidarity labor union in September 1980. In time, and with support from Ronald Reagan and Pope John Paul II, Solidarity and other movements led to the breakdown of the Communist order, the destruction of the Berlin Wall in 1989, and the dissolution of the Soviet Union in 1991. This is not a marginal view. As recently as July 2018, the establishment journal *Foreign Affairs* wrote:

> In Helsinki in 1975, the United States, the Soviet Union, and various European powers devised a security architecture for Europe that was controversial at the time but ultimately crucial to the Cold War's peaceful end. Without the Helsinki Accords, which fostered agreement on Europe's borders and enshrined a nominal commitment to human rights in the Eastern bloc, the revolutions of 1989

may never have come and almost certainly would not have been as peaceful as they were.

Ford's courage and foresight in supporting the Helsinki Accords in the face of elite skepticism abroad and popular opposition at home was a world-historic achievement.

Ford ushered in another kind of freedom on August 14, 1974, just five days after becoming president. He signed Public Law 93-373, which legalized ownership of gold by American citizens for the first time in over forty years. FDR declared gold to be contraband by Executive Order 6102 on April 5, 1933; Ford's signature reversed FDR's ban. The new law went into effect on December 31, 1974. Since then, Americans have been free to own physical gold bullion or coins.

Freedom to own gold means freedom from inflation, freedom from banks, and freedom from digital surveillance and hacking. America is not on a gold standard. Still, Americans can create a personal gold standard thanks to the emancipation from fiat money afforded by Gerald Ford.

Ford's two great liberating acts—facilitating freedom from Communism and freedom from fiat currency—are why history will favor Ford in the fullness of time.

In fact, gold is one way out of the Fed's conundrum. The Federal Reserve and U.S. Treasury acting in concert could create a one-time inflation shock by devaluing the dollar against gold and defending the new parity with the Fed's printing press and the Treasury's gold hoard. The Fed could conduct open-market operations in gold as it currently does in bonds to keep the dollar price of gold in narrow bands near the parity. A reasonable nondeflationary price for gold would be required. This price is estimated at ten thousand dollars per ounce, given exiting monetary aggregates and the current gold hoard. Discretionary monetary policy would exist side-by-side with gold; the money supply could be expanded by buying private gold and adding it to the hoard. Citizens who presciently purchased gold would see their wealth preserved. Social security indexation would offset the inflationary impact for current and future retirees. The real value of the national debt would be greatly diminished, saving the United States from a crisis of confidence. The dollar would become the soundest currency in the world, making the United States a magnet for foreign capital. Growth could rebalance from consumption to investment, insuring another century of American greatness. The ship of state would sail smoothly past Scylla and sister Charybdis.

Aftermath is a closer look at these themes. The reader will journey through geopolitical rivalries, nationalism and trade wars, debt and deficits, behavioral economics, robo-investing, income inequality, systemic risk, and the rise of a new international monetary system. Some of the content of this book will shock the most seasoned readers; yet readers can take comfort knowing that once prepared, they will not be shocked as events unfold in the years ahead.

It should not be lost on readers that *Aftermath* is the fourth volume of a quartet on the international monetary system, along with *Currency Wars* (2011), *The Death of Money* (2014), and *The Road to Ruin* (2016). What may be less apparent is the resemblance of these volumes to the four horsemen of the Apocalypse from the book of Revelation.

Few can name the four horsemen, although most believe they can and will gladly give it try. War and Death come easily to mind; those two answers are correct. War rides the red second horse, and Death the pale green fourth. Beyond that interlocutors lapse into "plague" and "famine," which are incorrect guesses. Those misfortunes are described as instruments of Death, not separate riders.

The third rider, on a black horse, has no specific name but holds a scale and is heard to say, "A ration of wheat costs a day's pay." Scholars have determined that a day's pay, one silver denarius for a soldier of Rome or a common laborer, was an unusually high price for a day's ration of wheat, about one quart. The admonition of the third rider is either scarcity or inflation. I chose the name Ruin to encompass both conditions.

The name of the first rider, on a white horse, is also unclear, a subject of scholarly contention as to the meaning of the original Greek writings. Some translations say "Conquest," with a malignant connotation, while other translations say "Victory," with a benign connotation. Rather than wade into this struggle between Antichrist and Christ, I'm content to say the struggle itself points to a conclusion and an Aftermath.

Metaphors and prophesy have their place, yet we live in the real world. These volumes are intended as a clear-eyed look at the recent past and not-distant future of the international monetary system—the real system as distinct from the one elites would have you believe exists. Writing these books has been a joy. I hope the reader delights in reading them as much as I have delighted in the writing.

CHAPTER ONE
SCATTERGOODS

From November 1918 down to the present day, no frontal challenge to state power has ever succeeded in any Western state.

—Adam Tooze, *The Deluge* (2014)

HISTORY IS THE FIRST CASUALTY OF MEDIA'S MICROSECOND ATTENTION span. An army of pseudo-savants saturate the airways to explain that tariffs are bad, trade wars hurt growth, and mercantilism (the art of accumulating reserves) is a throwback to the seventeenth century. These sentiments come from mainstream liberals and conservatives and tagalong journalists trained in the orthodoxy of so-called free trade and the false if comforting belief that trade deficits are the flip side of capital surpluses. So what's the problem?

The problem is that perpetual trade deficits have put the United States on a path to a crisis of confidence in the dollar. Capital surplus is a euphemism for excessive debt issuance by corporations and the Treasury. Zero tariffs are an invitation to outsource manufacturing and destroy high-paying U.S. jobs. Mercantilism makes China the fastest-growing major economy, while free trade leaves the United States to languish with depression-level growth. The cherished verities of liberal economics are mostly junk science; a thinly veiled stalking horse for the real goal of global governance and taxation in the name of globalization.

A visit to the history section of a library reveals liberal hero Alexander Hamilton was a staunch protectionist who nurtured U.S. industry with bounties, tariffs, and other obstacles to free trade. Progressive icon Teddy Roosevelt supported the gold standard and a strong dollar. Our first globalist president, Woodrow Wilson, wanted globalism not based on integrated supply chains, but on U.S. hegemony over authoritarian Germany and Russia and imperialist France, Japan, and the U.K. Wilson's way of achieving this was not with arms but with gold, dollars, and Wall Street credit. Conservative champion Ronald Reagan imposed such high tariffs on Japanese cars that they moved their factories to Tennessee and South Carolina, where the factories remain today. In fact, America's greatest periods of prosperity were associated with tariffs and mercantilism until the 1990s, when debt and war became all-purpose substitutes for investment in U.S. factories. Now the debt boom is dying, a day of reckoning approaches, and false economic nostrums won't save us.

This conundrum between what works in practice (protection and mercantilism) and modern miseducation (free trade and globalism) must be solved to secure the future strength and stability of the United States. There is ample room for smoothing the rough edges off mercantilism, but only if clear-eyed and historically trained negotiators are assigned to the task. Soft-power globalists are happy to see the United States in relative decline as long as "the world" is better off. The problem is that most of the world is violent, authoritarian, unethical, and inimical to U.S. values. Enriching China at U.S. expense is not just a weak globalist trade-off; it finances concentration camps and industrial slavery. Globalist champions such as Jeffrey Sachs and Mike Bloomberg are in deep denial on this, yet it's true.

Resolving this conundrum requires talents that range far beyond economics. The quandary can be addressed only by combining experts in geopolitics, history, sociology, law, and complex dynamics. This kind of high-level expert integration with a view to national security is an unsung strength of the Central Intelligence Agency. In this fashion, we turn to the CIA for an inside look at how the United States is using centuries-old tools to meet the twenty-first-century threat from globalization.

A House in Langley Woods

CIA headquarters is a secure compound, with admittance tightly restricted. Yet the location is not secret. The main entrance is on Virginia Route 123, also called Dolley Madison Boulevard, about a mile off the George Washington Parkway, not far from the Potomac River's south bank.

As if to confound the casual inquirer, most guideposts around headquarters seem to have three names. Dolley Madison Boulevard is shown on some maps as Chain Bridge Road. Reporters frequently refer to CIA headquarters as "Langley," yet there's no such town in that part of Virginia; headquarters is located in the town of McLean. The initials "CIA" do not appear in the official headquarters name, the George Bush Center for Intelligence. These double and triple namings seem in keeping with the CIA's main mission of deception.

Any driver can turn off Dolley Madison Boulevard onto the CIA headquarters access road, yet you won't make it far without an official badge in hand or a visitor's badge waiting for you at the security building near the main gate. If a visitor, you'll be heavily screened before you even get to the gatehouse to pick up your badge.

Once inside, the CIA campus has an open, airy feel not unlike a lot of large corporate campuses located in suburban bands around major cities. The architecture is decidedly midtwentieth century; not at all like the twenty-first-century dome and starship designs adopted by Amazon in Seattle and Apple in Silicon Valley. The two main buildings, Original Headquarters Building, OHB, and New Headquarters Building, NHB, are connected at ground level by glass corridors that frame a small park contained between them.

Beginning in 2003, I was on the front lines of global financial warfare working at CIA headquarters and in the field. My projects involved insider trading in advance of terror attacks, predictive analytics using market data, and national security implications of foreign investment in the United States, among others. One of the pleasures at headquarters was to wander through the CIA Museum on the main floor of OHB. This could be relaxing during snowstorms when scores of staff were no-shows. As a long-time New Englander, I never considered snow a reason to miss work, yet a lot of Virginia colleagues were paralyzed. Senior management sympathized with the locals and routinely granted snow days just like in elementary school. These days meant canceled meetings, which gave me downtime to explore the hidden treasures in headquarters that most staffers rushed by on their way from one vault to another. Former CIA director Mike Hayden called the CIA Museum, "the best museum you'll probably never see," a reference to the fact that it's not open to the public.

The museum is a collation of contributions from private collections, captured items from foreign intelligence services, and the CIA's own resources. One highlight is an ENIGMA machine invented by a German engineer and used by the Nazi regime in the Second World War to send encrypted message traffic to the German military. Polish, French, and U.K. cryptographers eventually cracked the ENIGMA codes, a feat memorably portrayed in the 2014 Oscar-winning film *The Imitation Game*. Few of the original machines survive; one of the scarce ENIGMA machines in private hands was sold at auction by Christie's for over five hundred thousand dollars. I have been fortunate to see two of the originals, one at CIA headquarters and one at the Imperial War Museum in London.

My favorite display in the CIA Museum is a lipstick gun, also called the Kiss of Death. It's a small-caliber, single-shot pistol disguised as a tube of lipstick. A woman spy in a tight spot could casually reach into her purse, remove the tube of lipstick, and kill her target at close range.

Near one end of the museum is an exhibit that doubles as a lesson in tradecraft. It's a large black-and-white daytime photograph of Washington, D.C., taken from a high-altitude spy camera. The photograph is about 20' long x 5' wide, embedded in the floor. An inattentive visitor could walk over it and not even notice. A more fun approach is to turn to a guest, point out the photograph, and ask them to tell you the exact date and time of day the photo was taken.

The usual first response was "I have no idea." Then the visitor would start to think. The photo shows the trees are bare, so you can narrow it down to the October to March time frame. The parking lots are empty, so you can narrow it down further to weekends and holidays. Right there, you're down to sixty days, which eliminates 85 percent of the calendar. A good start.

Next you can look for certain buildings with known construction dates. The Kennedy Center is visible in the photograph, so you can be sure it was taken after 1970, and so on. A more expert analyst with access to public records of building permits in Washington, D.C., could go block by block and narrow down the date to a particular year based on the presence or absence of certain buildings.

As for the time of day, once you have narrowed down the possible dates and have an azimuth of the sun on those dates, the shadow of the Washington Monument is the world's largest sundial. Your visitor leaves the museum feeling like they just finished a day shift analyzing imagery at the National Geospatial-Intelligence Agency.

Of course, lipstick guns and black-and-white photos seem primitive compared to the digitized, miniaturized, spectroscopic technology available to spies today. That misses the point. The ingenuity on display in the CIA Museum is impressive on its own and conjures up the romance and deadly seriousness of Cold War espionage. Interestingly, old-school tools and tradecraft are suddenly new again. Sophisticated hacking tools and flash drives have made even the most advanced digital systems highly vulnerable. Intelligence agencies are reverting to nondigital devices to avoid intrusions. Recently the Russian FSB intelligence service, successor to the KGB, ordered typewriters for use in preparing internal reports and memos. Typewriters cannot be hacked and leave no digital trails. The brush pass, dead drop, and one-time pads are all back in style among spies and case officers.

The inverse of intelligence is counterintelligence, the search for spies aimed at your own organization. The best counterintelligence tool is compartmentalization. Access to intelligence is broken into compartments or cells within the intelligence community. These cells typically consist of small groups of individuals working on a discrete problem. A top secret security clearance including special access programs beyond top secret is not enough to gain access to a wide array of classified information. It is also necessary to have a "need to know," which is demonstrated by a written or verbal application to a security officer. Once the need to know is established, a cleared person would still have to be "read in" to a project by a project director or team leader. Even when these hurdles are cleared, the person seeking access may still have to work with IT administrators to open up the necessary links or pages in the CIA's internal secure servers. This process is repeated every time a new topic is addressed or a new assignment given.

CIA personnel are trained to be wary of "social engineering." That's a technical term for simple friendliness to strangers. If you were in line to buy a cup of coffee in a Starbucks, it might not seem unusual to start a polite conversation with the person next to you in line about the weather or slow service or anything else, for that matter. The CIA has a Starbucks located on the main floor of OHB, near the cafeteria. It's reputed to be the world's busiest Starbucks, because it's open 24/7 and has plenty of caffeine-addicted customers with nowhere else to go. It's bad form to chat up a stranger while waiting in line. The object of your inquiry is trained to ask herself, "Why is he talking to me? What does he want? Is he trying to glean information out of his lane?" and so on, as if you were a new Aldrich Ames. This lends an all-business air to daily encounters; not the friendliest workplace environment, yet the social distance serves its purpose.

Compartmentalization can be cumbersome and slow, but it works well. The most damaging leaks of classified information in recent years involving Chelsea Manning and Edward Snowden did not come from CIA files. Manning released State Department information, and Snowden's information came from the National Security Agency, or NSA. The CIA has been victimized by internal moles in the past, and will be again, but on the whole, it has done a better job of protecting secrets that some of its sister agencies in the intelligence community, or IC.

The darkest agency I ever worked with, and the one most directly involved in counterintelligence, is the NCIX, or National Counterintelligence Executive. That agency is the successor to the work of legendary mole hunter James Jesus Angleton, who headed CIA counterintelligence from 1954 to 1975. NCIX staff are spy hunters who not only look for foreign spies but also look for moles, traitors, and leakers inside the IC. NCIX also hunts down supposed double agents (American spies pretending to be Russian spies who are actually loyal to America) who are really triple agents (American spies pretending to be Russian spies who really are Russian spies). This ontology of deceit and deception is called the wilderness of mirrors.

My first visit to NCIX included a tour of the Hall of Shame—a gallery of framed 8" x 10" photos of the most notorious traitors to the United States since the Second World War. The gallery begins with Klaus Fuchs, the German physicist who worked on the Manhattan Project and leaked atomic bomb secrets to the Soviets, which accelerated the Soviet race to become a nuclear power. The gallery continues in chronological order with about one hundred headshots in all, including the infamous spies Julius Rosenberg, Aldrich Ames, Robert Hanssen, John Walker, and Ana Belén Montes. The headshot photograph of Ana Montes, a spy for Cuba who worked at the Defense Intelligence Agency, is especially memorable because it's a cropped version of a 1997 photograph in which she is seen receiving a Certificate of Distinction from former CIA director George Tenet.

The damage caused to U.S. national security by the traitors in the Hall of Shame is incalculable. This devastation included not just the release of technical information, but exposure of U.S. assets working in Russia and other IC designated denied areas. When those individuals were later executed or imprisoned, the United States lost access to the future stream of invaluable intelligence they would have provided. The losses also made future recruitments more difficult. The Hall of Shame is chilling and stays with you long after you walk past the gallery into the nerve center of U.S. counterintelligence operations.

My most memorable encounter with Russian spies was serious, with a heavy dose of farce. It took place on January 26, 2009, at the Fontainebleau Hotel in Miami Beach. I was there to give a keynote speech titled "The Geopolitical Special Address" at 9:00 A.M. to an audience of about a thousand hedge fund and alternative asset managers. It was one of the year's most high-profile investment conferences, taking place immediately after the 2008 financial panic, but before markets hit bottom. The conference program listed my subtopics as "China and Russia" and "Tensions with Iran and North Korea," among others.

The Fontainebleau Hotel, opened in 1954, is an icon of American architecture, designed by the celebrated architect Morris Lapidus. Its best-known feature is the gently arching main building that forms a bright white semicircle overlooking the hotel pool and Atlantic Ocean. The Fontainebleau was ground zero for Frank Sinatra and the Rat Pack when they visited Miami in the late 1950s.

It was my first time at the Fontainebleau. The hotel had loomed large in my imagination for over forty years, since I saw the opening scenes of the classic 1964 James Bond film, *Goldfinger.* In those scenes, Bond, played by Sean Connery, breaks up a card-cheating operation being conducted at the hotel by Goldfinger. The sequence made a lasting impression. I decided I should stay at the Fontainebleau someday just for fun. In 2009, I got my chance. The Fontainebleau was the place to see and be seen in Miami Beach that winter.

After my keynote address, I went back to my room to relax and enjoy the view. The red message light on my bedside phone was blinking. I retrieved the message and returned the call.

The male caller had a deep voice and a distinct European accent. He said, "I saw your presentation this morning. Very interesting. The parts about financial warfare were new to me. I'd like to meet you to discuss these topics further. I may have some consulting opportunities for you also." Geopolitical consulting was one of my pursuits at the time, along with intelligence work and public speaking. It seemed worth finding out what this caller had in mind.

"Okay, thanks. I'm just here for the day. I could meet at three in the lobby bar. We'll chat about it then," I said. There were several bars in the hotel. I gave him my cell phone number so he could locate me. I planned to hit the lobby bar anyway, so meeting the caller there was not inconvenient. I don't usually drink on workdays, but it seemed a shame to stay at the Fontainebleau and not visit the bar to absorb the ambience.

"Thanks," the caller replied. "I'll be with my associate. We'll see you then." Click.

I arrived at 2:45 at the bar in Gotham Steak, a lobby restaurant since closed, so I could enjoy a drink before my visitors arrived. I ordered my usual Mount Gay Rum and tonic with lime. Then I relaxed and took in the scene.

My visitors found me easily enough; the bar was mostly empty that time of day, and they knew me from my presentation. They walked over to my table and introduced themselves but didn't sit down. I looked at them and couldn't believe what I saw.

The man was stout, swarthy, and short, about five foot four, wearing a suit and shirt with no tie. His associate was a woman, a head taller in high heels, with straight black hair and a long silk dress that displayed her dé-colletage. She was Asiatic, not especially Han; more central Asian.

I thought to myself, "This is unbelievable. It's Boris and Natasha."

Growing up in the early 1960s I was a devoted fan of a TV series called *The Rocky and Bullwinkle Show*. The show was originally broadcast by ABC after *American Bandstand* in the late afternoon. That was my break time between classwork and homework. I was usually glued to the screen.

Among the recurring characters on the show were a pair of Russian-like spies named Boris Badenov and Natasha Fatale, who reported to a dictator named Fearless Leader. The show was popular at the height of the Cold War during the post-Sputnik hysteria about Russia over-taking the West. Boris and Natasha may have been caricatures, yet they seemed the epitome of nefarious, scheming Russian agents despite their comedic incompetence. My interlocutors were dead ringers but for the absence of Boris's black trilby and moustache. I was staring at cartoon spies in real life.

I asked if they wanted a drink. Boris said, "No," they wouldn't be long and preferred to stand. He came straight to the point.

"Your presentation this morning showed a lot of knowledge about fi-nancial warfare and sanctions on Iran, Russia, and North Korea. You're clearly an expert. I have clients who would pay a lot of money to meet with you. They'd like to know what you know."

"Big money," added Natasha for emphasis.

"Who are these clients? Where are they located?" I asked.

"They're in Russia," Boris said, without being more specific. "You'd have to travel there to meet with them."

"Big money," repeated Natasha. Perhaps she was concerned I hadn't heard her the first time.

At the time of this encounter, I was deeply involved planning the Pen-tagon's first-ever financial war game. This was scheduled for March 2009, and was to be conducted with participation from the military, CIA, Trea-sury, Fed, and a host of think-tank denizens and subject-matter experts at the top secret Applied Physics Laboratory near Washington, D.C. By January 2009, the game design team was well along in forming financial scenarios to be played out in the war game. These scenarios inevitably involved Russia.

The approach by Boris and Natasha was clearly a recruitment. They knew I knew a lot more about financial warfare than I was able to disclose in my public remarks. Their clients back in Russia were willing to pay me to share those secrets. Boris and Natasha made no bones about their proposition. It was money for secrets delivered to Russians, as simple as that. I knew I would report them to CIA counterintelligence, but decided to string them along to collect all the information I could.

"Well, I'll need to think about that," I said to Boris. "I can't give you an answer today. Do you have a business card, or some way to reach you?"

He reached in his pocket and handed me his card. As if to complete the caricature, the card was printed on red paper, the color most closely associated with Russia.

"Thanks, I'll be in touch," I said.

"Thank you for meeting us. Our client would really like to meet you. We'll wait to hear."

I half expected Natasha to say "big money" one last time, but they both left the bar; that was the end of the rendezvous.

All CIA assets are required to report contacts with foreigners immediately. The extensive paperwork associated with maintaining a security clearance makes the status slightly less glamorous than it may seem to outsiders. Still, the reporting requirements serve a purpose and are taken seriously. I put details of the encounter in a foreign contacts report, including physical descriptions, and dropped the red business card off with my security officer. That was that. Now it was in the hands of counterintelligence officers.

I never heard more; no follow-ups or postreport interviews. That didn't trouble me; it was all part of the compartmentalization that one learns to live with inside the intelligence community. One thought did gnaw at me, though. What if Boris and Natasha were not Russian agents? What if they were actors sent by U.S. counterintelligence to test my loyalty? This is not as bizarre as it sounds given the sensitivity of some of my work, and my unusually public profile. If so, I passed the audition. Welcome to the wilderness of mirrors.

CIA headquarters structures and ancillary buildings are surrounded by several hundred acres of trees and a tracery of trails used by staff for morning and lunch-hour jogging or a walk in the woods. A college campus atmosphere was precisely the goal of legendary spy Allen Dulles, the CIA's director from 1953 to 1961, who spearheaded the move of CIA headquarters from its original location at 2430 E Street in Washington, D.C.'s west end to its current McLean, Virginia, locale. Dulles wanted the best of both worlds—a bucolic setting without nosy officials from other agencies nearby, yet close enough to the White House so that the CIA director could be in the Oval Office within minutes if needed.

Within this expanse of woods and trails, sculptures and museums, and glass offices, there exists one architectural anomaly. It's a white, three-story, wood-frame farmhouse on the CIA campus rarely entered by more than a handful of agency personnel, even those with the highest security clearances. It's a building that predates the CIA by decades, part of an estate that witnessed the Revolutionary War, the Civil War, and every major turning point in U.S. history since. The formal name of the structure is the Scattergood-Thorne residence, known to CIA insiders as Scattergoods.

I spent many days at Scattergoods over a seven-year stretch from 2006 to 2013. I was not there to greet visiting intelligence chiefs or for ceremonial occasions. While most CIA officers barely knew the house existed, and even fewer had been inside, a group I organized made the house our main venue for some of the most politically sensitive work ever conducted by the CIA. This work involved a government bureau few Americans have ever heard of—a body called CFIUS.

The Dirty Dozen

In my years of intelligence work for the U.S. government, I rarely met such quizzical looks as when I mentioned my involvement with CFIUS (pronounced "SIFI-us"). Of course, the name sounds funny. Wits would ask, "Does it itch or burn?" No one I encountered outside the intelligence community had ever heard of it.

CFIUS is an acronym for Committee on Foreign Investment in the United States. The committee was created under Executive Order 11858, issued by President Gerald Ford on May 7, 1975. Interestingly, Ford's executive order cited the Gold Reserve Act of 1934 as one of the bases for the committee's legal authority. Reference to the Gold Reserve Act was used because CFIUS operations were funded with the U.S. government's insider trading profits from FDR's 1933 gold confiscation.

The original committee consisted of the secretary of state, secretary of the treasury, secretary of defense, secretary of commerce, and several White House officials. The committee has expanded greatly since 1975, and now includes the secretary of homeland security, secretary of energy, and the attorney general.

CFIUS is the gatekeeper that decides whether sensitive foreign acquisitions of U.S. target companies are allowed to go forward. The committee tries to strike a balance between benign foreign investment, which the United States encourages, and malign penetrations of critical infrastructure. Broadly speaking, critical infrastructure includes telecommunications, internet, and cloud computing, the electric grid, hydroelectric plants, finance, transportation, ports and waterways, defense and space, and natural resources; in short, any network that keeps America safe and keeps the lights on. CFIUS guards against foreign penetration of these sectors by adversaries.

The intelligence community is not a member of CFIUS. Instead, the

IC is tasked by CFIUS with determining if a potential foreign acquisition of a U.S. company is a threat to U.S. national security based on the identity and intentions of the buyer. The IC gathers intelligence on possible connections of the foreign acquirer with a criminal cartel or with the military or intelligence apparatus of a U.S. rival.

There is a dynamic tension in CFIUS decisions. On the one hand, the United States maintains an open economy and welcomes foreign investment. Some of the best-known brands in the United States are manufactured by foreign companies such as SONY and Samsung. Lenovo, which makes a laptop computer formerly called ThinkPad, is based in China, but acquired its laptop business from IBM. German-engineered BMW automobiles are made in plants in South Carolina. Foreign investment in the United States brings jobs, technology, and growth to the U.S. economy. Still, the United States has corporate crown jewels, enterprises that no foreign investor is allowed to touch without strict scrutiny from a national security perspective.

If a Russian firm with Kremlin connections bought NASDAQ, it could program order entry systems to flood the market with fake sell orders on Apple, Amazon, Facebook, and other American business icons. This could trigger a crash and destroy Americans' savings in a market meltdown worse than the panic of 2008. Russia would wipe out more wealth with a rigged stock market than with a well-placed nuclear bomb. A Russian acquisition of NASDAQ would certainly be refused by CFIUS. Still, many CFIUS cases are more opaque and less obvious. Raw intelligence needs to be gathered and the dots connected.

To do this, IC members including the CIA and DIA use case officers, secret agents, and technical means to penetrate layers of legal obfuscation that bad actors use to disguise their role. This may involve risky operations in IC designated denied areas such as Moscow, Beijing, and Tehran. Once the intelligence collections are made, the raw reports are delivered to analysts at CIA headquarters in Langley. The analysts connect the dots by comparing collections with other sources of information, including data

gathered by technical means, of which the human collectors may be unaware.

The entire file is turned into a big picture mosaic that IC senior management uses to assess whether the buyer is a threat. Often the result is not
black or white, but may still raise concerns for CFIUS to consider. That
assessment is delivered to the Treasury on behalf of CFIUS. After further
consideration by the full committee, CFIUS makes a final recommendation to the White House. The Treasury Department acts as the coordina-
tor and home agency for CFIUS, but it does not have the last word; the
White House does. Consensus among the member agencies is usually
achieved. In cases where there is no consensus, the matter is passed up the
chain for a final decision by the president.

My involvement with CFIUS began in 2006, shortly after the infamous Dubai Ports fiasco. That was a deal in which a Middle-Eastern
company planned to buy the operator of the largest port facilities in the
United States, including those in New York, Philadelphia, Miami, Balti-
more, and New Orleans. The ports handled imports and exports of a significant part of U.S. food and energy supplies, as well as cruise ship
operations. These ports constituted some of America's most sensitive
critical infrastructure. Prior to the proposed deal, the ports were owned
by the Peninsular and Oriental Steam Navigation Company, P&O, a British firm, clearly from a friendly jurisdiction.

The proposed buyer, DP World, is owned by the Emirate of Dubai, part
of the United Arab Emirates, or UAE, controlled by Dubai's ruler, Sheikh
Mohammed bin Rashid Al Maktoum. Despite its location in a rough
neighborhood, the UAE is assessed by the intelligence community to be
a good friend of the United States. The UAE has been an active ally of
the United States in fighting terrorism, ISIS, and the ruthless Assad regime in Syria.

DP World knew the deal was sensitive from a U.S. national security
perspective and approached CFIUS in October 2005 for clearance. United
States Coast Guard Intelligence, the relevant IC agency with regard to port

security, raised concerns. DP World addressed those concerns through a process called mitigation, in which concessions are made with regard to governance, compartmentalization, and transparency to alleviate government concerns. Based on a mitigation agreement, CFIUS and the White House green-lighted the deal. Stockholders of P&O approved the port sale to DP World in February 2006.

What came next was a political blow-up bigger than Krakatoa.

When a rival port operator saw the public deal announcement, they hired lobbyists to persuade Senator Chuck Schumer to oppose it. Schumer leapt at the chance and denounced the deal in borderline racist terms, referring to an "Arab" takeover, ignoring the difference between regional friends like Dubai and regional enemies. Schumer did this while grandstanding at a press conference with families of 9/11 victims. The frenzy of opposition was bipartisan; Dennis Hastert, a Republican, planned legislation to block the acquisition by DP World. Democratic senators Hillary Clinton of New York and Robert Menendez of New Jersey joined Schumer in his opposition to DP World and planned their own legislation opposing it. In the face of this rank politicization of a nonthreatening ports acquisition, President George W. Bush doubled down on his support. On February 22, 2006, the White House threatened to veto any legislation that would stop the deal.

At the height of this political firestorm, DP World hired former president Bill Clinton as their CFIUS adviser. This created the curious spectacle of Bill Clinton helping the deal while Hillary Clinton opposed it. The Clintons were working both sides of the street.

Left out of the media and political frenzy was the fact that as part of its mitigation, Dubai secretly agreed to allow the CIA to position assets in other DP World port facilities. These postings would constitute an invaluable source of intelligence from ports in Africa, the Middle East, and South Asia otherwise difficult to access. By blowing up the deal, Schumer and Hillary Clinton were damaging the IC's ability to help keep America safe.

DP World went ahead with the acquisition of the P&O ports in late February 2006, but in the face of the political fiasco, immediately agreed to sell the contested U.S. port operations to an acceptable operator. Once that agreement was made, Congress withdrew its threat to nullify the deal. In December 2006, DP World fulfilled its pledge by selling the U.S. port operations to a division of the U.S. insurance giant AIG.

This fiasco was a major embarrassment for CFIUS and the White House. In terms of national security considerations, the supporters of the deal had done everything right. The U.S. Coast Guard assessed the risks. DP World offered mitigation. The United States would have all the over-sight and transparency it needed to insure the ports were operated safely. The intelligence upside from Dubai's cooperation in other areas was con-siderable. Still CFIUS had shown a blind spot when it came to outside perceptions. An alarm sounded inside the national security community about the need to avoid humiliations in future.

In response, the intelligence community turned to Major General John R. Landry, a highly decorated West Point and Harvard graduate with warfighting experience from Vietnam to Desert Storm. General Landry had the position of national intelligence officer (NIO) for military affairs, a position he held from 1993 until his retirement in 2013. The NIO-military reports to the director of the National Intelligence Council, and is the highest-ranking intelligence official charged with assessing military mat-ters. General Landry wasn't a logical choice for CFIUS damage control because his brief was military, not economic. Still, he possessed an invalu-able trait—he was known at Langley as a "can-do" officer who did not suf-fer fools. Landry cut through red tape and completed critical tasks faster than typical bureaucrats. CFIUS needed a quick fix, and Landry was the ideal choice to lead the way.

In May 2006, just weeks after the Dubai Ports deal disaster, one of my CIA points of contact asked if I could meet with General Landry as quickly as possible. I agreed and arranged to be at headquarters within days. On arrival, I was ushered into General Landry's office. He was short, muscular, handsome in a tough-guy way, with silver-hair and the blunt, bulldog-type demeanor one expects from a fighting general.

Landry got to the point. "Jim, we've just come through a firestorm on this Dubai Ports deal. I'd like you to recruit and organize an expert team who can help us avoid being blindsided. The intelligence on that case was fine, but we need outsiders, real-world perspective. If we add that dimension, we'll see political landmines in advance. We want Wall Street's take on these deals. Can you put a team together for us?"

Of course, I accepted the mission. I had done a lot of recruiting on Wall Street beginning in 2004, to help the CIA on Project Prophesy. That was a post-9/11 strategic study related to insider trading ahead of the attacks. Project Prophesy used Wall Street expertise to build and test predictive analytic systems that could foresee new terror attacks using market data. One of the most gratifying parts of that project was that when I called Wall Streeters to volunteer I was never turned down. Everyone I recruited, from major bank investment chiefs to hedge fund billionaires, dropped what they were doing to help us any way they could. I welcomed the chance to enlist volunteers again for the CFIUS mission.

Over the next few months I recruited one of the best possible teams. I tapped deal lawyers, risk arbitrageurs, subject-matter experts, and private-equity players who knew their way around those emerging markets most likely to be the source of threats, especially China and Russia.

As I identified each recruit, we made arrangements for that person to visit General Landry at CIA headquarters before making a formal offer to participate in the project. My favorite interview story involves a blond, blue-eyed investment banker from Connecticut with strong Middle-East connections. Like most of my recruits, he was a first-time visitor to Langley. Landry knew how to turn on the charm. We escorted our visitor through a special headquarters tour, including the director's seventh floor office suite. Landry had his run of the premises due to longevity and the respect of his peers.

When we got back to Landry's office we completed the interview. The candidate was clearly a strong choice. Landry was pleased to welcome him aboard. As we were wrapping up, Landry reached in his desk and pulled out a gold-plated CIA challenge coin stamped with the agency logo. He handed it to our recruit and said, "Here's a souvenir of your visit; something to show your kids when you get home." Our recruit placed it in his pocket and said, "Thank you, general." At that point, Landry turned serious and said, "Good. Because once you put that coin in your pocket we have you in our pocket." The recruit blanched.

I had to keep myself from laughing out loud. I wondered how often the general had used that line on newcomers. Landry gave me a sideways glance and a slight smile at the inside joke he had just pulled. The recruit smiled nervously. At CIA, nothing is ever quite what it seems. In any case, our Connecticut banker had just joined the team.

When I was done and my recruits had all received their engagement letters, we were officially organized as an advisory panel to the intelligence community's CFIUS Support Group. Unofficially we were the "dirty dozen" helping to keep America safe from foreign financial threats.

We operated for seven years with good success. In early 2007, when the IC was worried about telecommunications takeovers, we warned that financial institutions would be the next battlespace. That proved prescient. In late 2007, during the financial panic, Wall Street ran to sovereign wealth funds in China, South Korea, Singapore, and Abu Dhabi for fresh cash to prop up insolvent banks like Bear Stearns, Lehman, Citi, and Morgan Stanley. Those deals raised exactly the types of national security threats we warned about. The dirty dozen's work was so successful that a Pentagon official took me aside at Langley one day and asked if I could set up a similar body for the Defense Department. This new panel would assist them in conducting their own CFIUS intelligence, and other matters including export controls on U.S. weapons systems.

Beginning in mid-2013, our group was quietly phased out in stages. We got word that our regular October 2013 meeting was postponed due to the threat of a government shutdown at the time. That meeting was never rescheduled. We received a formal termination notice in January 2014. We didn't know it at the time, but our last meeting had been in April 2013, because of the subsequent cancellation and termination. The dirty dozen were disbanded, our services no longer needed. I carried on with other missions for the intelligence community; my CFIUS days were done.

We were told the advisory board's termination was for budget reasons, but that never rang true. We were mostly volunteers who got paid travel reimbursements and little in the way of fees. We even passed the hat during meetings at Langley to pay for our buffet lunches. We were probably the best value for money the government ever saw. Still, orders were orders. General Landry had retired, and sadly passed away in June 2015. I was informed privately that another general, James Clapper, the director of national intelligence in 2013, wanted our operation shut down. I never knew why, yet always suspected there was a reason other than lunch money and a few plane tickets.

Clintons, Russians, and Uranium One

While our advisory board was helping the IC with foreign threat assessments, CFIUS principals, based in the U.S. Treasury Department, were wrestling with the strange case of Uranium One. Over the course of 2016, Uranium One became the most publicized and politicized CFIUS case since Dubai Ports in 2006. The Uranium One deal is a twisted saga with roots dating back to 2005. That backstory is crucial to understanding how the Uranium One deal later became politically toxic for CFIUS.

In 2005, a wealthy Canadian entrepreneur, Frank Giustra, with a background in gold mining penny stocks and film production, made a foray into uranium mining. Uranium is a scarce, silvery-colored element, atomic number 92, that is used both for peaceful generation of electricity in nuclear power plants, and for military purposes, to power vessels and for nuclear weapons. It is one of the most strategically sensitive natural resources on the planet.

Giustra and his associates formed a company called UrAsia Energy with a view to acquiring uranium mining rights in Kazakhstan in Central Asia. Giustra enlisted Bill Clinton to assist his efforts. As Giustra put it, "All of my chips, almost, are on Bill Clinton. He's a . . . worldwide brand, and he can do things and ask for things that no one else can." On September 6, 2015, Giustra and Bill Clinton visited Almaty, the capital of Kazakhstan. On that visit, Clinton met privately with the ruthless Kazakh dictator, Nursultan Nazarbayev. UrAsia and Giustra got the Kazakh uranium mining rights over stiff competition from larger, more seasoned mining companies in Australia, Russia, and other producing countries. In the following years, Giustra orchestrated hundreds of millions of dollars in contributions to the Clinton foundation.

Once the Kazakh uranium mines were secured, UrAsia embarked on a dizzying round of dealmaking. In November 2005, UrAsia shares were listed on the Toronto Stock Exchange. With listed shares now available as currency to fuel further deals, UrAsia announced on February 12, 2007, its plans to merge with Uranium One, another major uranium producer based in Canada and South Africa. After that merger was completed, the combined company, now called Uranium One, with Giustra and the other UrAsia shareholders in control, began to acquire uranium mining assets in the United States. In just over two years, UrAsia Energy moved from the ranks of junior miners to the ranks of major global uranium producers under the banner Uranium One.

During this period, Hillary Clinton was actively seeking the presidency of the United States and was deemed by the media to be the inevitable winner. Bill Clinton continued to meet with Nazarbayev. The Kazak dictator was named head of a human rights organization, the Organization for Security and Cooperation in Europe, OSCE, despite his atrocious record on civil rights and opposition from senior senators such as Joe Biden. Nazarbayev was invited to attend the Clinton Global Initiative in

New York City in September 2007 and was a featured participant. Giustra announced a new pledge to give over $100 million to the Clinton Foundation. The web of mutually beneficial payments, appointments, and accommodations among Bill and Hillary Clinton, Frank Giustra, and the dictator Nazarbayev grew densely interconnected.

Then Giustra commenced his endgame—a sale of Uranium One, including U.S. uranium mines, to the Russian State Atomic Energy Corporation, Rosatom. On June 15, 2009, Rosatom, operating through its mining arm Atomredmetzoloto, or ARMZ, announced it had acquired a 17 percent stake in Uranium One. Just a few months earlier, on January 21, 2009, Hillary Clinton had become the U.S. secretary of state in the administration of newly elected president Barack Obama. As secretary of state, Hillary Clinton immediately became one of the most powerful voices on CFIUS.

In a succession of follow-on acquisitions, Rosatom announced plans to acquire 51 percent control of Uranium One in June 2010. That transaction was approved by CFIUS, with Hillary Clinton's support, on October 22, 2010, and was closed by year end. In January 2013, Rosatom acquired complete control of Uranium One and took the company private. Today Rosatom owns the substantial U.S. uranium assets of the former Uranium One.

Facets of this deal are curious. The timeline of the Uranium One story runs from 2005 to 2013, which overlaps almost perfectly with the work of the dirty dozen from 2006 to 2013. The deal fits squarely in the realm of deals typically denied, where an adversary, Russia, is buying a sensitive asset, uranium. Strangest of all, this deal never came to our attention. Not once in any meeting, classified or unclassified, was Uranium One ever mentioned in our full advisory board sessions or one-on-ones. It's as if the deal were being handled inside the intelligence community on a special track, precisely to avoid the analysis our group was formed to provide. Uranium One was the dog that didn't bark.

Although the deal attracted contemporaneous news coverage as Giustra's plan progressed, it did not become a political scandal until the 2016 presidential election cycle and the publication of the book *Clinton Cash*, an exposé by Peter Schweitzer that covered the Uranium One story in detail. At that point, Hillary Clinton surrogates rushed forward with red-herring defenses of her conduct that do not withstand scrutiny.

The first defense is that Hillary Clinton was just one of nine votes on CFIUS and could not have single-handedly influenced the outcome on the Uranium One case. It is true that CFIUS has nine votes (eight Cabinet-level departments plus the president's science adviser), and that the Uranium One deal was approved unanimously. So, this Clinton defense has superficial support.

But, this defense bears no relationship to how CFIUS works in practice. In fact, there are only four votes that count—the secretaries of state, defense, energy, and treasury. The Treasury has the most important role because they chair the committee and set the agenda. "Downtown" principals meetings, as the IC calls them, are held in the main Treasury building. The secretaries of state and defense have the main equities on national security. Everyone else is a bystander. The Commerce Department is considered a proinvestment cheerleader and is not taken seriously. The Office of the U.S. Trade Representative and the president's science adviser can chime in but are little more than rubber stamps for what the big four want. The Departments of Justice and Homeland Security contribute intelligence from the FBI and other collectors. This is added to collections produced by CIA, DIA, and NSA, yet those agencies seldom voice a strong view on the merits of a deal.

CFIUS is a consensus-driven group. If the secretary of state pushed hard for Uranium One, the secretaries of defense and treasury would go along because their equities, weapons systems and terrorist finance specifically, were not infringed. Other members would remain mute. If the White House did not oppose the secretary of state, then her strong support for a deal could single-handedly carry the day.

The second defense of Hillary Clinton's role was summed up as "the uranium isn't going anywhere." The U.S. uranium mines controlled by Uranium One (and ultimately Russia) are located in Wyoming. It is true that the mine cannot be moved and none of the uranium produced there will be shipped abroad to adversaries such as Iran. Yet this is another defense with only superficial substance.

What this defense misses is that uranium, usually in the form of the low-enriched concentrate, U_3O_8, called yellowcake, is a fungible commodity with a worldwide market. Uranium One has mines in Kazakhstan, the United States, and Tanzania. It has customers, directly and indirectly via parent Rosatom, around the world, including Iran, Russia, and China. Prior to the acquisition of Uranium One by Rosatom, a U.S. nuclear power plant could have been supplied from mines in Kazakhstan. After the acquisition, Rosatom could assign that supply contract to Uranium One, a U.S.-to-U.S. deal, and the Kazakhstan output would be available for shipment to Iran. In effect, the Wyoming uranium is supplying Iran through a simple substitution of suppliers in a three-party structure.

Rosatom could also shut down the Wyoming mines temporarily. Taking the Wyoming production off the market would be costly in the short run, but the sudden shortage could increase the world price and benefit other mines owned by Rosatom. This is a price manipulation strategy that a global, government-owned player such as Rosatom could execute that would never be tried if the U.S. mines were owned by a smaller independent player.

Spotting market strategies such as supply substitution and price manipulation are exactly the kind of guidance our advisory board was expected to bring to the table. These techniques and others are not second nature to most bureaucrats, who focus solely on first-order export license issues.

In the end, the Uranium One deal went through because the secretary of state and the White House wanted it to go through. The position of this deal in the category of deals typically denied was ignored. The perspective of our advisory board, which was set up precisely to contribute expertise on sensitive deals, was never sought. The dirty dozen, formed to do damage control after Dubai Ports, were sidelined by General Clapper on the most politically explosive deal of all. All that remains is Russian control of U.S. uranium by a classic Clinton obfuscation.

Today, the Uranium One story lives on. On November 16, 2017, Reuters reported the case of William D. Campbell, a lobbyist and FBI informant. Campbell claimed to have information pertaining to corrupt efforts by Rosatom to influence the CFIUS approval of the Uranium One acquisition. Campbell was also linked to a separate case in which Vadim Mikerin, the head of U.S. operations for a Roastom subsidiary, Tenex, pleaded guilty to bribery and was sentenced to four years in prison. The bribery charge involved contracts to ship Russian uranium to the United States. Expectations are that as more facts emerge, the Clinton role in CFIUS will be viewed in a harsh light.

Nationalism and Globalism

The threads I weaved while working on CFIUS and other matters for CIA in the early 2000s exploded into headlines by 2015. Donald Trump's presidential campaign, launched on June 16, 2015, was the most explicitly nationalistic campaign by a major party candidate since Pat Buchanan's run for the Republican Party nomination in 1996. As the result of his successful campaign, Trump was sworn in on January 20, 2017, as the strongest nationalist since Theodore Roosevelt. For the first time in over one hundred years, a committed nationalist was sitting in the Oval Office.

Obama, both Bushes, and Bill Clinton were globalists, defined as those willing to trade off or compromise U.S. interests for the sake of a stronger global community from which the U.S. benefits. Even conservative hawks like Ronald Reagan and John F. Kennedy were firmly in the globalist camp, as they relied on NATO, the UN, and the IMF, among other multilateral institutions, to pursue their Cold War goals. Richard

Nixon's famous opening to China, Lyndon Johnson's willingness to wage war half a world away in Vietnam, and Gerald Ford's 1975 triumph with the Helsinki Accords were all milestones in the history of a robust American engagement with an international system of allies and adversaries, in which American interests were sometimes subordinated to a greater good.

What sets Teddy Roosevelt and Trump apart is not isolationism but unilateralism. American presidents can never be truly isolationist; America is too big and too rich to stand apart from the world, nor should it want to. The distinction among presidents is whether the United States works with allies and in a multilateral framework, or whether she works on her own initiative, unilaterally at first, but with cooperative allies only as the American direction becomes clear.

Teddy Roosevelt was an unabashed unilateralist and imperialist. Trump is an equally unabashed unilateralist and nativist who is happy to defund U.S. contributions to the UN at the slightest offense from the General Assembly. Roosevelt supported tariffs in his race against Woodrow Wilson in 1912; Wilson called the tariffs "stiff and stupid." Trump is actively imposing new tariffs today.

Trump's slogans—"Make America great again," and "America first"—are echoes of Roosevelt's "Speak softly and carry a big stick," and the ebullient "Bully!" Roosevelt even invented the term "muckraker" as a name for unethical journalists. Roosevelt wrote that this kind of journalist "speedily becomes, not a help to society, not an incitement to good, but one of the most potent forces of evil." This was more than a century before Trump leveled the charges of "fake news" and "enemy of the people" to make the same point.

Roosevelt was and Trump is nominally Republican, but both fought hard against their own party. Roosevelt stormed out of the Republican Convention in 1912 and labeled Republicans as a party of thieves. Trump routinely excoriates Republicans on Twitter. Both Roosevelt and Trump can be said to have hijacked the Republican Party from the hands of established figures and a wealthy donor class.

A Trump-Roosevelt comparison cannot be taken too far. Roosevelt was a distinguished scholar, voracious reader, author of eighteen books, and Nobel Peace Prize recipient. Trump shows little inclination to read books and is not well versed in history or international affairs.

Yet their political instincts are eerily similar. In 1912, Roosevelt ran as a third-party candidate for president on a program he called the New Nationalism. This program attacked cronyism and political corruption on the part of Democrats and Republicans. One of the main planks of Roosevelt's platform declared that "to destroy this invisible Government, to dissolve the unholy alliance between corrupt business and corrupt politics is the first task of the statesmanship of the day." Trump was slightly less articulate when he yelled, "Drain the swamp." Still, there was no mistaking the shared sentiment.

The point of this historical comparison is that Trump is not a unique figure, he's a type, the true nationalist, that Americans have not seen in the White House in over a century. Before Roosevelt there were other presidents, James Knox Polk (1845–49), and Andrew Jackson (1829–37), who fit the nationalist mold. President George Washington (1789–97) would arguably have no objection to an "America first" motto. It's as if America needs a jolt of pure nationalism once a century or so to maintain her identity and destiny against the multilateral lure. Trump is that jolt for the twenty-first century.

Today's most potent political divide between nationalists and globalists is on the matter of borders. This goes beyond clichés about Trump's border wall with Mexico and stepped-up immigration enforcement. Borders can be physical, legal, or psychological. Trump and the globalists are fighting over all three.

The touchstone of globalism is a borderless world. This means a free flow of capital, people, goods, services, and ideas around the world without regard to national boundaries, national source, or national destination. The globalist vision treats the nation-state as at best an inconvenience, and at worst a threat to the full realization of their vision.

Unspoken in the rush to a heroic new world of free capital flows, free trade, free-floating exchange rates, and frictionless migration is the fact that national governance will not be diminished, it will be displaced. National parliaments and congresses will be little more than town meetings called to deal with parochial issues. The momentous issues involving capital, labor, applied technology, and fiscal and monetary policy will be decided globally by various institutions such as the IMF (for monetary policy), OECD (for tax policy), UN (for climate change), and the G20. This leadership is mainly unelected and self-perpetuating. Some G20 leaders occasionally have to run in national elections, yet these are orchestrated so the globalist agenda wins regardless of which party leader is selected. Globalists know how unpopular their agenda is when starkly stated. So, the globalists resort to spurious arguments regurgitated by a press that shows no interest in examining underlying premises.

The globalist case for "free trade" is putatively based on the early-nineteenth-century theory of comparative advantage articulated by David Ricardo, the preeminent classical economist. Ricardo's theory began with a view that countries should not try to be self-sufficient in all aspects of manufacturing, mining, and agriculture. Instead, countries should specialize in what they do best, based on advantages in labor, capital, or natural resources, and let others also specialize in what they do best. Then countries could simply trade the goods they make for the goods made by others. All sides would be better off because prices would be lower as a result of specialization in goods where one trading partner has a natural advantage.

Yet the factor inputs that make up comparative advantage are not static. What happens if Country A attracts capital from Country B with tax and other incentives, then builds high-tech robotics side by side with basic manufacturing and cheap labor? Now Country A has all the jobs and technology, and Country B has no jobs, a trade deficit, and retains only its direct foreign investment or portfolio investment in Country B.

This may seem like an extreme example, but it bears a close resem-

blance to the relationship between China and the United States, where the
U.S. advantage in capital formation was siphoned off by China, so that
China ended up with the comparative advantage in labor *and* capital and
a huge bilateral trade surplus.

Comparative advantage is not only mobile, it is created from thin air.
Taiwan had no comparative advantage in semiconductor manufacturing
in the 1980s. Yet the Taiwanese government made a political decision to
create the state-sponsored Taiwan Semiconductor Manufacturing Company. The Taiwanese government nurtured Taiwan Semiconductor with
tariffs and subsidies in its early days when it was most vulnerable to foreign competition. Today, Taiwan Semiconductor is a publicly traded company and the largest semiconductor supplier in the world. The company
would never have attained that status without government help. This is a
good illustration of why comparative advantage is not static. If the theory
of comparative advantage were static, Taiwan and Japan would still be
exporting rice and tuna fish instead of cars, computers, TVs, steel, and
semiconductors.

Free-floating exchange rates, a flawed legacy of University of Chicago
professor Milton Friedman's early-1970s faux–free market prescriptions,
are another globalist scheme. Floating exchange rates were originally intended as a substitute for the pre-1971 gold standard that Friedman de-
spised. Friedman liked the idea of elastic money to give central bank
planners the ability to fine-tune the money supply to optimize real growth
and price stability. Gold was considered inelastic and not suitable for the
fine-tuning discretionary monetary policies needed.

Friedman's hope was that gradual changes in exchange rates would
raise or lower relative prices between trading partners, and these changes
in terms of trade would reverse trade deficits, mitigate trade surpluses, and
restore equilibrium in trade without shock devaluations of the kind the
United Kingdom experienced in 1964 and 1967. Friedman's laboratory approach ignored the real-world behavior of financial intermediaries, such as
banks and hedge funds, that create leverage and derivatives. Financializa-

tion dominates and amplifies the smooth exchange-rate adjustments Friedman envisioned. What followed was borderline hyperinflation in the late 1970s, and a succession of asset-bubble booms and busts in Latin American debt (1985), U.S. stocks (1987), the Mexican peso (1994), Asian debt (1997), Russian debt and derivatives (1998), dot-com stocks (2000), mortgages (2007), and derivatives again (2008). On two of those occasions, 1998 and 2008, global capital markets came to the brink of total collapse.

If free trade, open capital accounts, and floating exchange rates are empirically deficient ideas, why do the Davos elite embrace them? The answer is that these theories serve as a smokescreen for the elites' hidden agenda. That agenda is to promote global growth at U.S. expense, to diminish the power of the United States in world affairs, and to enhance the power of rising nations, especially China.

America historically prospered with high tariffs to protect its industries. From Alexander Hamilton's plan for infant manufacturing to Henry Clay's American Plan, the United States has always known how to protect its industries and create American jobs. Trump is returning to that American tradition. Trump refrained from imposing tariffs in 2017, his first year in office, based on the advice of his then national security team, including National Security Advisor General H. R. McMaster, Secretary of State Rex Tillerson, and Secretary of Defense James Mattis. The national security team urged President Trump not to start a trade war because the U.S. needed Chinese help to avoid a shooting war in North Korea. However, China did not do all it could to apply pressure on North Korea. Solid intelligence showed that China helped North Korea to cheat on sanctions imposed by UN resolutions. As if to rub salt in the wound, China's 2017 trade surplus with the United States was $275 billion, the highest ever.

Once China's lack of cooperation on North Korea became clear, Trump saw no harm in confronting China on trade, a policy he's advocated since the summer of 2015, during the early days of his campaign. As a result, a trade war Trump has been planning since his 2015 campaign erupted in full force in early 2018.

In the midst of this new trade war, CFIUS returned to center stage as a potent weapon. On January 18, 2018, Reuters reported a decision by CFIUS not to approve acquisitions of U.S. target companies by privately owned Chinese conglomerate HNA until HNA provided more detailed information on the true identities of its shareholders. HNA had earlier acquired material stakes in Hilton Hotels and Germany's giant Deutsche Bank. HNA did disclose that over half its shares were owned by two charitable foundations, based in China and the U.S. respectively. Yet the beneficiaries and controlling parties of those foundations remain opaque.

Then on March 12, 2018, in one of the most aggressive applications of CFIUS ever, the White House vetoed a hostile takeover of U.S. semiconductor giant Qualcomm by Singapore-based Broadcom, a deal valued at $117 billion. This action was usual in two respects. It was a hostile takeover, so there was no agreement in principle between buyer and seller for CFIUS to consider, and therefore no opportunity for mitigation by the parties. And the U.S. Treasury's public statement said that its reasons for rejecting the deal were "in significant part . . . classified," but made reference to the fact that Broadcom's Singapore base was largely under the control of "third-party foreign entities" understood to be Chinese. Now, the Trump administration had weaponized CFIUS, which became a frontline weapon in a burgeoning trade and financial war between the United States and China. This was a far cry from the doormat role CFIUS played in the Uranium One case.

On August 13, 2018, President Trump signed into law new legislation designed to strengthen the role of CFIUS and to force it to give greater weight to national security considerations compared to the prior open borders approach to direct foreign investment. This new law was the Foreign Investment Risk Review Modernization Act, FIRRMA, co-sponsored by Republican senator John Cornyn and Democratic senator Dianne Feinstein. FIRRMA greatly expands the types of transactions requiring CFIUS approval and introduces new categories subject to review, including "critical materials," and "emerging technologies." FIRRMA creates a white list of "identified countries" that would not be subject to the new strict scrutiny due to their friendly relations with the United States, including parties to mutual defense treaties. Ironically, this is just a more stringent and legally enforceable version of the analytic approach the dirty dozen introduced to CFIUS ten years ago. That approach was brushed aside when CFIUS approved Uranium One.

Investment Secret #1: Tariffs and trade surpluses are back in style. Prepare for a more mercantilist world.

Investors should prepare for a more mercantilist world in which trade surpluses and gold accumulation are ends in themselves. This means that tariffs, demands for reciprocity, and tax provisions that favor domestic production will be the norm. This makes a stark contrast with the multilateral free-trade regimes favored by globalists since the end of the Second World War and pursued vigorously since the end of the Cold War.

Major powers never completely abandoned mercantilism; it was always just below the surface, as developed economies paid lip service to free trade. A global trading system always required some constraint on surplus countries in addition to the financial pain typically inflicted on deficit countries. John Maynard Keynes made this point emphatically at Bretton Woods in 1944, but his proposed mechanisms for surplus adjustment were ignored by the United States.

China and Germany are the worst trade offenders. Germany exploited the euro and the European Central Bank to run surpluses with its trading partners in the Eurozone periphery. This amounted to a kind of vendor finance scheme that lasted until Spain, Italy, and Greece almost went broke in 2010. Germany then refinanced its Eurozone customers with IMF and U.S. help, at the expense of social spending in the southern tier, to restart the game. China used cheap labor, a cheap currency, low-cost domestic finance, and wasted investment to gin up its own surpluses with the United States. What is new is that the United States under Donald Trump is refusing to play the free-trade game any longer. The United States will match China, Germany, South Korea, and other surplus giants tariff for tariff and subsidy for subsidy.

American investors should look for new domestic champions in steel, autos, renewable energy, and transportation. Global growth may slow, but profits at companies such as Boeing, SolarWorld, Mission Solar, Nucor, U. S. Steel, and General Motors all benefit from a protected U.S. domestic market, still the largest in the world.

Accumulation of physical gold and silver is the hallmark of mercantilism. American and Canadian gold and silver mining companies will be bolstered by continued strong global demand driven by China and Russia. Their stock prices will also be bolstered by a wave of merger and acquisition activity, as large miners absorb juniors to achieve economies of scale.

The emerging neomercantilist world is one that would be congenial to Alexander Hamilton and Henry Clay. America will play to its strengths even as China, Russia, and Germany play to theirs.

CHAPTER TWO

PUTTING OUT FIRE WITH GASOLINE

It appears to have been the common practice of antiquity to make provision, during peace, for the necessities of war, and to hoard up treasures beforehand as the instruments either of conquest or defence; without trusting to extraordinary impositions, much less to borrowing, in times of disorder and confusion. . . . We have always found, where a government has mortgaged all its revenues, that it necessarily sinks into a state of languor, inactivity, and impotence.

—David Hume, "Of Public Credit" (1752)

THE CHOIR OF DIRE DEBT ADMONITIONS HAS GONE SILENT FOR NOW. THIS is strange. Beginning in the 1980s and continuing through the Tea Party victory in 2010, no political debate was complete without one party or the other warning of damage to confidence in U.S. debt and the dollar itself due to profligate spending and increasing debt-to-GDP ratios. These warnings were bipartisan, albeit with varied timing and targeting depending on which party was on offense.

In the 1980s, Democrats and some Republicans (David Stockman comes to mind) railed against the Reagan deficits. Reagan was a big spender who did run up deficits, yet one suspects the real objection was that new spending went to defense rather than entitlement programs favored by the Democrats. During the 1990s, the out-of-power party routinely complained about spending by the in-power party, while in truth both George H. W. Bush and Bill Clinton did a creditable job keeping the debt-to-GDP ratio under control. In the 2000s, Democrats complained about George W. Bush's trillion-dollar war spending, and Republicans complained about Obama's trillion-dollar stimulus that did nothing to stimulate a return to long-term trend growth. Yet now the damage was serious. Bush 43 doubled the national debt and Obama doubled it again from a higher level. When Trump was inaugurated in January 2017, the Bush-Obama team handed him a 105 percent debt-to-GDP ratio, worse than most of Europe and not far behind debt dandy Italy.

Despite changing parties and changing fortunes, the critique of excessive spending never stopped. Until Trump. Now, both parties have gone silent. Trump has not attacked the favored Democrat entitlements so they have no cause for complaint. Trump has expanded military spending so Republicans are content. Removal of discretionary spending caps and the return of earmarks for pork-barrel projects has cheered both parties. Trump has revived the age of trillion-dollar deficits, last seen in the first Obama term. Entitlements and defense both get to gorge at the trough, so there's no dissension in D.C.

The only loser is the country. The slow growth of the debt-to-GDP ratio can be compared to a fatal tumor or a termite infestation. The initial stages may go unseen and unnoticed. Still, there comes a time when the damage is irreversible, complete, even fatal. The United States is near that point. Understanding the history of U.S. debt is a starting place for comprehending where we are today and why the present debt situation is not "business as usual," but an entirely new state of affairs that threatens the centuries-old foundations of democracy and national security.

A Brief History of U.S. Debt

It's wondrous that simple economic concepts are stretched by economists and pundits to the point of incomprehension by everyday Americans. So it is with deficits, debt, and the debt-to-GDP ratio. No economic metrics are more certain to put citizens into a deep trance of indifference, yet none are more important to the perpetuation of liberty. In fact, these concepts *are* simple once stripped of jargon.

The deficit is simply the excess of spending over revenue. The United States keeps its books on an annual basis, so if revenue for a given year is $3 trillion and spending is $4 trillion, the deficit that year is $1 trillion. Debt is the sum total of all prior deficits minus the occasional surplus. The United States has not had a surplus since the fiscal years 1999 and 2000, and before that, 1969. Today the U.S. national debt is $22 trillion. The debt-to-GDP ratio is merely national debt divided by national output calculated in the form of gross domestic product, or GDP. If the national debt is $22 trillion and GDP is $21 trillion, then the debt-to-GDP ratio is 105 percent ($22 trillion ÷ $21 trillion = 1.05). That's it. With a grasp of these three concepts—deficits, debt, and debt-to-GDP—tendentious debates over fiscal policy, monetarism, Keynesianism, and central bank machinations come clearly into focus.

A naïve view of U.S. national debt assumes the United States started with a clean slate in 1789, began accumulating a small amount of debt in the nineteenth century, and saw debt grow exponentially in the twentieth century, until reaching its current nonsustainable stage early in the twenty-first century. This view is incorrect.

The history of the U.S. national debt is less linear and more nuanced than the naïve view suggests. The United States had national debt before it was even a nation. The subsequent history of that debt shows a pattern of alternating deficits and surpluses, depending on exigencies of the day. In general, the United States borrowed to finance wars and paid down debt during peacetime. As a result, the U.S. debt-to-GDP ratio rose and fell repeatedly, yet only moved to extremes on rare occasions. Consequently, it's troubling that in the past ten years the U.S. debt-to-GDP ratio moved to extreme levels with no plausible plan to mitigate the trend. This debt crisis is the result of high baseline spending combined with the policy preferences of three presidents: Bush 43 (war spending), Obama (social spending), and Trump (tax cuts). Bush 43 added $5.85 trillion of debt, Obama added $8.59 trillion of debt, and Trump will add $8.28 trillion of debt through his first term, based on Treasury projections. That combined $22.72 trillion of debt in twenty years is a 300-percent increase in U.S. debt over the $5.8 trillion at the end of the Clinton administration. Simply put, after 230 years of prudent debt management, the U.S. national debt is now off the rails.

When the United States began as a nation under the Constitution in 1789, it faced the handling of Revolutionary War debt incurred from 1775 to 1783 by individual states and the Continental Congress. Under a plan devised by Alexander Hamilton in 1790, the United States agreed to assume these debts. Hamilton issued new Treasury bonds to pay off the Revolutionary War debt and financed the new bonds with tariffs, which also protected infant U.S. industries against U.K. competition. These new bonds marked the beginning of the U.S. Treasury securities market. With U.S. credit now established, Hamilton and his successors issued new bonds to pay off maturing bonds, in effect rolling over the debt.

Starting with the election of John Adams, the second president, until the beginning of the Madison administration, the U.S. ran budget surpluses in fourteen of sixteen years from 1796 to 1811. Adams held public debt constant at $83 million, while Jefferson reduced the debt to $65 million during his two terms, despite borrowing to finance the Louisiana Purchase. Adams and Jefferson did not eliminate the national debt, yet they kept it manageable, and gave the United States a higher credit rating than any country in Europe. Jefferson also established the first of two pillars of prudent U.S. debt management—debt declined in a time of peace.

In the last two years of Madison's administration, during the War of 1812, the nation exhibited the second of two pillars of U.S. debt management—debt increased in a time of war. Public debt almost doubled from $65 million to $127 million under Madison. Jefferson and Madison together established the signal attributes of U.S. national debt. The debt does not go up continuously; debt rises in war and declines in peace. Budget surpluses achieved during peace, even if they do not eliminate debt entirely, serve as a rainy-day fund so the United States has ample borrowing capacity during war. Borrowing capacity is financial dry powder, no different in purpose than gunpowder or ammunition stockpiled for unforeseen yet inevitable strife.

The administrations of James Monroe (1817–25), and John Quincy Adams (1825–29) continued this accordionlike pattern. Together they reduced the national debt from $127 million to $67.5 million, an almost 50-percent decline. John Quincy Adams's successor, President Andrew Jackson (1829–37), took this pattern to its logical conclusion by eliminating the national debt entirely. The United States was practically debt-free in 1836. Jackson also eliminated the Second Bank of the United States, which acted as the central bank. Jackson's last year in office was the only time the United States was debt-free in its history. Coincidentally, starting with Jackson, the United States did not have a central bank for seventy-seven years, until the creation of the Federal Reserve in 1913. Jackson's legacy was no debt and no central bank.

The national debt soon returned. Debt was $4 million at the end of Martin Van Buren's term (1837–41), and rose steadily to $65 million by the time of Abraham Lincoln's election in 1860. The most notable increase in this period was a rise from $33 million to $47 million during the single term of James Knox Polk (1845–49). Most of this debt arose in connection with the Mexican-American War (1846–48) waged by Polk. These war costs were money well spent, since the United States acquired all or part of present-day California, Nevada, Utah, Wyoming, Colorado, and Arizona. Texas previously agreed to annexation by the United States in 1845, yet the borders with Mexico were not settled. Texas definitively became part of the United States as a result of Polk's war. Despite war spending, national debt by the end of James Buchanan's term (1857–61) was $65 million, exactly where it was when Jefferson left office in 1811, a half century earlier. The United States had no increase in its debt in fifty years despite two major wars, the War of 1812 and the Mexican-American War, and numerous lesser conflicts. This was the result of budget surpluses and prudent spending in times of peace.

Abraham Lincoln's single full term—he was assassinated six weeks into a second term—saw both America's bloodiest war, measured in total casualties, until the Second World War, and the first exponential increase in America's national debt. During the Civil War (1861–65), national debt rose from $65 million to $2.7 billion, a 4,000-percent increase. This increase is in keeping with the history of debt during existential wartime crises. If the borrower loses the war, debt is irrelevant; it is repudiated or extinguished, perhaps replaced with reparations. If the borrower wins the war, there is enough gain through havoc or reconstruction to reduce the debt. Either way, citizens in general and domestic financers in particular rarely question a government's need to borrow during war—creditors stand or fall with the nation itself.

America's Civil War debt was extinguished in stages. From $2.7 billion at the end of the Civil War, the national debt dropped to $1.6 billion by 1893, a 41-percent reduction by the end of President Benjamin Harrison's single term (1889–93). Since the period from 1865 to 1893 was one of enormous economic growth in the United States, the debt-to-GDP ratio dropped even more dramatically than the debt itself. Debt increased again during William McKinley's term in office (1897–1901) to $2.1 billion because of the Spanish-American War (1898), another illustration of the yin and yang of U.S. debt and the dogs of war.

This pattern continued in the twentieth century. The U.S. national debt rose modestly from $2.1 billion to $2.9 billion during the combined administrations of Theodore Roosevelt (1901–9) and William Howard Taft (1909–13), despite Roosevelt's robust big-stick diplomacy and $50 million spent to acquire land and rights for the construction of the Panama Canal, a transaction in which J. P. Morgan acted as fiscal agent for the U.S. Treasury.

The second exponential increase in U.S. debt after the Civil War occurred during the Woodrow Wilson administration (1913–21) in connection with financing U.S. participation in the First World War (1917–18). National debt exploded from $2.9 billion to $27.4 billion, an increase of 845 percent. This debt was partly financed by the issuance of Liberty Bonds to the general public. Previous wars were financed by wealthy private financers beginning with Philadelphians Robert Morris (Revolutionary War), Stephen Girard (War of 1812), Nicholas Biddle and Jay Cooke (Civil War), and later New Yorkers J. P. Morgan ("Pierpont"), and his son, Jack Morgan (First World War). Salmon P. Chase, secretary of the treasury during the Civil War, financed the Civil War in part with a popular issuance of small denomination, non-interest-bearing demand notes initially exchangeable for specie, although redemption was later suspended. These notes, called greenbacks because they were printed with green ink on the reverse, were more like proto-money than true securities and circulated as legal tender. Liberty Bonds issued in the First World War marked an innovation in war finance—they were U.S. Treasury debt. For millions of Americans, a Liberty Bond purchase was their first experience investing in securities. Liberty Bonds made the linkage between patriotism and war finance explicit in the minds of everyday American citizens.

Following the U.S. and Allied victory in 1918, the national debt once again declined. The Harding and Coolidge administrations produced eight consecutive surpluses from 1921 to 1929, reducing the national debt to $17.6 billion, a 36-percent decline from the postwar spike. The national debt increased only slightly under Herbert Hoover (1929–33), despite the demands of the worst years of the Great Depression. When Hoover left

office, the national debt was $19 billion, still 31 percent below where it
stood when Wilson left office twelve years earlier. The pattern of expanding then contracting debt that prevailed since 1787 remained intact.

The first two terms of Franklin D. Roosevelt's administration, 1933–
1937, and 1937–1941, marked a decisive turning away from the then
nearly 150-year old pattern of expanding debt only in time of war. FDR
did indeed expand the national debt from $19 billion to $42 billion, a
120-percent increase. Still, there was no war. Instead there was a continuation of Hoover's Great Depression, including a severe technical recession
in 1937–1938. In his first two terms, FDR was not fighting a war against a
foreign enemy; he was fighting a "war" at home against unemployment,
malnutrition, deflation, and rural underdevelopment. Federal deficits were
enlisted in this war in part on the advice of the U.K.'s John Maynard
Keynes. Yet FDR's impact on the national debt in his first two terms goes
far beyond typical increased spending in peacetime. His response to the
exigencies of the Great Depression ended the small government era forever. It was in 1935 that FDR and Congress enacted Social Security, one of
the earliest and still the largest entitlement program, which created off-
budget contingent liabilities in the form of promises to retirees. The political sales pitch that Social Security is "insurance paid for with payroll
tax contributions" was false in 1935 and remains false today. Social security has always been a pay-as-you-go scheme in which younger workers
pay retiree benefits, with no particular lifetime relationship between payments and benefits, as with true insurance. The difference between then
and now is that Social Security was cash-flow positive for decades as the
postwar baby-boom generation grew and entered the work force beginning in the 1960s. Today, Social Security is cash-flow negative as the
boomers hit retirement age beginning in 2008. The fault cannot be laid at
FDR's feet, since entitlement programs have been mismanaged by Congress and the White House in recent decades. Still, the fuse on today's
fiscal time bomb was lit in 1935.

Notwithstanding FDR's two-term deficit without war prior to 1941,

FDR or his successors might have reduced the deficit based on an anticipated economic recovery in subsequent years. This vision was shattered by the instigation of a real war—the Second World War—and America's involvement from 1941 to 1945.

Roosevelt was elected to a fourth term in 1944, but died on April 12, 1945, less than three months after being sworn in. Roosevelt's third term (1941–45) overlapped America's fighting in the Second World War, which saw an unprecedented expansion of the U.S. national debt in the face of an existential threat to U.S. national security from Nazi Germany and the Empire of Japan. In Roosevelt's third term, the U.S. national debt grew from $42 billion to $245 billion. Over the same four-year period, the U.S. debt-to-GDP ratio grew from 50 percent to almost 120 percent, the highest in U.S. history. This $203 billion increase in the national debt from 1941 to 1945 dwarfed the $23 billion increase in FDR's first two terms. FDR's fiscal policy ran parallel to that of his predecessors since 1789. America expands its debt as needed to win wars, and then mitigates the debt postwar. America's bloodiest war in history, measured in casualties, required the greatest expansion of the U.S. national debt in history, measured in dollars. This debt expansion in time of war was consistent with U.S. fiscal policy since the founding.

The next four administrations, Truman, Eisenhower, Kennedy, and Johnson, in cooperation with Congress and with explicit and implicit assistance from the Federal Reserve, engineered an extraordinary reduction in the U.S. debt-to-GDP ratio from 120 percent at the end of the Roosevelt administration to 38.6 percent in January 1969, the end of Johnson's term. This was accomplished through a combination of occasional budget surpluses (1947–49, 1951, 1956–57, and 1969), strong real growth (after a prolonged postwar recession from 1945–47, the economy had a series of outstanding growth years, including 8.7 percent in 1950, 8.1 percent in 1951, 7.1 percent in 1955, 6.5 percent in 1965, and 6.6 percent in 1966; an analyst need only compare those growth rates to annual average real growth of only 2.2 percent for the nine years from June 2009 to June 2018 to see why strong real growth is the best cure for high debt-to-GDP ratios), and the Federal Reserve's financial repression policy (holding nominal interest rates slightly below inflation for extended periods to reduce the real value of nominal debt). There were two major U.S. wars during this period—Korea and Vietnam—yet the debt-to-GDP continued to decline because the Korean War was paid for with tax increases and the Vietnam War was made affordable by the strong real growth of the Kennedy-Johnson years.

The steady melting away of the postwar debt-to-GDP ratio continued through the Nixon, Ford, and Carter years (1969–81) for different reasons. Real growth was not nearly as strong in the 1970s as the 1960s (there were recessions in 1974–75 and in 1980), yet high inflation especially after 1976 had the same impact as financial repression in the 1950s. Inflation ran ahead of interest-rate increases until Paul Volcker slammed on the brakes with 20 percent interest rates in 1980. As long as nominal GDP increases faster than the deficit plus interest expense, the debt-to-GDP ratio declines even if real GDP growth is weak.

A parlay of design in the 1950s, good fortune in the 1960s, and inflation in the 1970s ultimately reduced the U.S. debt-to-GDP ratio to 32.5 percent when President Jimmy Carter left office in January 1981, about the same ratio as in 1790 during George Washington's first term and the lowest ratio since the 1930s. Through seven presidential administrations, from 1945 to 1981, Democrat and Republican, the looming tower of postwar debt was whittled down to a sustainable, even enviable, level. It was a moment for fiscal hawks to savor, yet it was fleeting. The debt-to-GDP ratio would never be that low again.

With this economic history in mind, we turn to the story of the past four decades, during which spending became unmoored from national security or existential threats and the sequential expansion and contraction of national debt was replaced by one long expansion, to the point of national humiliation.

The Breaking of America from Reagan to Trump

Absent higher growth, which is elusive due to demographics and declines in productivity, the only ways to escape America's new debt dilemma are default, inflation, asset sales, an IMF world money bailout, or some combination. Default imposes immediate losses on unpaid government bondholders and mark-to-market losses on other bondholders as interest rates spike to account for increased default risk. Inflation mitigates the government's debt burden by spreading losses indiscriminately to holders of all forms of fixed-dollar claims, including bank deposits, money market funds, annuities, insurance policies, pensions, and long-term contracts. Asset sales are a humiliation, as Greeks would attest after their sovereign debt crisis from 2010 to 2015. American assets such as parks and highways are worth little to foreign investors, since they cannot be removed, exploited, or used to generate cash-on-cash returns. An IMF bailout requires the United States to give up partial control of its economy to an unaccountable globalist institution, a politically unpopular prospect. It would also result in unforeseen consequences, including displacement of the dollar by the IMF's special drawing right, or SDR, as the benchmark global reserve currency, at China's insistence.

At least one of these dire outcomes is inevitable. To see why, begin with consideration of the U.S. debt-to-GDP ratio. Debt itself cannot be analyzed in isolation; it must be compared to the income available to support that debt. Comparing debt and income is no different for a country than for an individual. If you owe $25,000 on a MasterCard that may or may not be a problem depending on your income. If you earn $20,000 per year, the $25,000 credit card debt overwhelms you with interest payments and penalties, possibly causing you to file for bankruptcy. On the other hand, if you earn $500,000 per year, you can probably pay off the credit card debt with ease, using the cash in your bank account. The point is, you cannot determine whether $25,000 is a high or low debt load without looking at the income available to service the debt.

Countries are the same. The United States today has $22 trillion in national debt. Is that high or low? If U.S. GDP were $60 trillion, analysts would treat the $22 trillion in debt as low and easily manageable. The U.S. debt-to-GDP ratio would be 37 percent ($22 trillion ÷ $60 trillion = 0.37), about where it was in 1790 and 1981. Conversely, if GDP were only $21 trillion, then the debt-to-GDP ratio would be 105 percent ($22 trillion ÷ $21 trillion = 1.05). Of course, the United States is in the latter situation. The debt-to-GDP ratio is 105 percent, a dangerous and nonstable level. To see how America came to this pass, one needs to review almost forty years of fiscal policy under presidents Reagan, Bush 41, Clinton, Bush 43, Obama, and Trump. Fiscal policy for the period 1981 to 2019 can be summed up in a curious phrase: *Feed-the-beast, starve-the-beast.*

The beast is the U.S. government with its voracious appetite for taxpayer funds. Feeding the beast refers to huge deficits to support expanded spending. Starving the beast refers to spending cuts and fiscal prudence. These alternating bouts of spending increases and spending cuts amplified by tax increases or tax cuts make deficits larger or smaller than they would be based on baseline spending alone. The problem is that feed-the-beast, starve-the-beast strategies were used by successive administrations to tie the hands of their successors, with ruinous results. This recurring and destructive dynamic combined with the simple math of growth and deficits has led the United States to the dolorous debt condition it finds itself in today.

When Ronald Reagan was sworn in as fortieth president of the United States in January 1981, the U.S. debt-to-GDP ratio was 32.5 percent, a level last seen in the 1930s. Reagan faced other challenges when he assumed office, including 20 percent interest rates, 15 percent inflation, and a major recession, the worst since the Great Depression, which consumed his first two years in office. Still, the debt level was low and American credit was sound.

After Fed chairman Paul Volcker eradicated inflation in 1982, interest rates fell, the recession ended, and a period of strong growth began, which lasted from 1983 through 1990. This was the "King Dollar" sound money era. Contrary to popular mythology, Reagan was not a fiscal conservative; he was a big spender. Reagan saw the low debt ratio he inherited as a tool to help win the Cold War. He set out to win with the same determination as previous wartime presidents Lincoln and FDR.

The Cold War was as much an existential conflict as the Civil War or World War II. Reagan used fiscal deficits and borrowing power to finance a huge military expansion, including the Strategic Defensive Initiative (the so-called Star Wars) antimissile technology, and a six-hundred-ship navy. By the mid-1980s, the Kremlin leadership realized they could not keep pace with the U.S. militarily or financially.

Mikhail Gorbachev became head of the Soviet Union in 1985 and engaged in negotiations with Reagan designed to de-escalate the military buildup, open up Soviet society, and give the Soviets space to modernize their economy. The negotiations were successful. Yet the Soviet opening process, called *glasnost*, combined with guarantees included in the Helsinki Accords, spun out of control and led to liberal resistance in Central Europe and the Soviet Union's eventual collapse in 1991. In addition to massive new Cold War spending, Reagan also pushed through major tax cuts early in his administration, which put added pressure on debt and deficits. During the Reagan years, the U.S. debt-to-GDP ratio grew from 32.5 percent to 53.1 percent, the highest level seen since the early 1960s.

To Reagan's credit, he won the Cold War. The Soviet Union's demise occurred on December 25, 1991, while Bush 41 was president, yet historians rightly credit Reagan's military and technology policies with impelling the victory. Reagan had reason to believe America would follow its historic pattern of running up the debt to win a war, then reducing debt once the war was over.

Yet a new dynamic was in play. The early years of the Reagan administration were an example of a feed-the-beast approach consisting of tax cuts and big spending increases. Resulting deficits would force later administrations to cut spending, the strategy called starve-the-beast. The dynamic was that tax cuts deprive the government of revenue and the high debt ratio forces the government to reduce deficits. The only way to reduce deficits in a low-tax regime is to cut spending. That's exactly what fiscal conservatives around Reagan wanted.

The Reagan administration's big-spending, tax-cutting policies were highly successful at growing the economy and winning the Cold War. A deficit day of reckoning would fall on subsequent administrations, which would have to pursue unpopular measures such as tax increases or spending cuts. Original feed-the-beast politics would morph into starve-the-beast and tie the hands of subsequent administrations. Over the course of the next two administrations, one Republican and one Democratic, that's exactly what happened.

By the summer of 1988, the Reagan administration was winding down and the next presidential election campaign was in full swing. The 1988 campaign pitted Reagan's vice president, George H. W. Bush, against Democrat Michael Dukakis. The Democrats were already calling for tax increases to offset the Reagan deficits.

At the Republican nominating convention on August 18, 1988, in New Orleans, Bush declared, "The Congress will push me to raise taxes and I'll say no. And they'll push, and I'll say no, and they'll push again, and I'll say, to them, '*Read my lips: no new taxes.*'" That pledge was intended to shore up Bush's support from the conservative wing of the Republican Party, which favored spending cuts and opposed tax increases. It worked. Bush easily obtained the nomination and just as easily defeated Dukakis in the general election. The no-tax pledge was the most memorable line Bush ever said on economics, and the American people remembered it.

Unfortunately, the deficit numbers did not buttress Bush's pledge. Midway through Bush's term, the debt-to-GDP ratio crossed the 60 percent threshold. Economists consider this a red line. The 60 percent level is the one used under the Maastricht Treaty, which governs the European Union, as the maximum that is tolerated under unified EU fiscal policies.

Bush's advisers, led by Richard Darman, needed to reach a budget compromise with a Congress controlled by Democrats to reconcile conflicting fiscal priorities. The Democrats insisted that tax increases be part of any package that included spending reductions or entitlement reforms. Bush agreed and received support from Republican leaders. However, he lost the support of Republican voters. In 1990, *The New York Post* ran the headline READ MY LIPS . . . I LIED.

From the perspective of fiscal prudence, Bush 41's actions were justified. The debt-to-GDP ratio first leveled off then began to decline slightly, back toward the critical 60 percent level. His policy may have been sound economics, but it was lousy politics. Bush lost the 1992 election to Bill Clinton partly because of voter dissatisfaction with his breach of the no-tax pledge. Starve-the-beast worked. The United States was back on a path of a reduced debt-to-GDP ratio. Unfortunately for Bush 41, the beast devoured his chances at reelection. The new president, Bill Clinton, would now have to deal with Reagan's starve-the-beast legacy.

Clinton was the first Democratic president in twelve years. The last Democrat before Clinton was Jimmy Carter, a fiscally conservative southern governor and technocrat. Carter's spending options were severely limited by runaway inflation and the dollar's near collapse that occurred on his watch. Before Carter, Republicans held the White House for eight years. The last big-spending liberal Democratic president was Johnson, who left office in 1969. Liberal Democrats had waited a generation, twenty-four years from LBJ to Clinton, for a chance to revive big social-spending programs of the kind they associated with FDR, Harry Truman, and LBJ. Clinton embodied the liberals' hope that big spending would return.

They were soon disappointed. Clinton was faced with the same tough budget realities as Bush 41. The ghost of Reagan's starve-the-beast policies haunted the West Wing. Democrats and Republicans agreed on the need for fiscal prudence to bring the debt ratio back below 60 percent. The only disagreement was on the right mix of taxes, spending cuts, and entitlement reforms to achieve that goal. Clinton's first economic adviser, Bob Rubin, warned Clinton of a new danger—the so-called bond vigilantes. The vigilantes were major bank bond dealers and institutional investors who were hypersensitive to the threat of inflation. The 1990s vigilante heyday was long before the deflation scares of the early 2000s. Large deficits were considered potentially inflationary at the time because it was feared the Fed would monetize the debt as it had in the 1970s. Higher interest rates caused by inflation fears could slow economic growth. Rubin urged Clinton to cut spending and raise taxes to reassure the bond vigilantes that the deficit was not out of control. Clinton's closest political adviser, James Carville, said: "I used to think if there was reincarnation, I wanted to come back as the president or the pope or as a .400 baseball hitter. But now I would like to come back as the bond market. You can intimidate everybody." That remark captured the reality facing Bill Clinton at the start of his first term.

Fortunately for Clinton, the Democrats controlled congress until January 1995, and were able to push his tax increases through in the Deficit Reduction Act of 1993. This raised the top individual tax rate from 31 percent to 39.6 percent, where it remained until the 2017 Trump tax cuts. Clinton was also the beneficiary of the so-called peace dividend, a cut in defense spending. The Reagan-Bush victory in the Cold War was so complete that defense spending could be reduced substantially without jeopardizing national security. The impact of lower defense spending on the debt-to-GDP ratio was no different after the Cold War than after World War II; the debt ratio came down. This combination of higher taxes, lower defense spending, and sound monetary policy by Fed chair Alan Greenspan worked wonders on the debt ratio. It fell steadily during the Clinton years, dropping to 56.4 percent by the end of Clinton's second term, decisively below the 60 percent critical threshold.

Despite political opposition, and impeachment, Clinton's personal popularity remained high. He presided over the longest peacetime economic expansion in U.S. history. At the end of Clinton's presidency, he even produced a small budget surplus for the first time since 1969. There was talk among the bond vigilantes that the U.S. Treasury market might disappear because Clinton's policies could retire the national debt for the first time since Andrew Jackson.

Bush 41 and Bill Clinton both succumbed to the starve-the-beast trap laid by Ronald Reagan. Both raised taxes as a result and paid a political price. Bush lost reelection in 1992 and Clinton lost Congress in 1994. Still, their policies brought the debt ratio back under control. That progress toward a sustainable debt-to-GDP ratio ended abruptly with Bush 43's inauguration in January 2001 and the 9/11 attacks. Less than eight months after George W. Bush was sworn in, America was again at war. This was not a cold war, it was a red-hot shooting war, yet not against a nation-state. Bush waged the War on Terror. Not surprisingly, the U.S. debt-to-GDP ratio began to rise again as in the Revolutionary War, Civil War, World War I, World War II, and the Cold War. The difference was that the increase started from a higher level. The Cold War victory had not been paid for by the time the War on Terror emerged.

Bush 43 promptly pivoted from Clinton's and Bush 41's starve-the-beast policy to a new version of Reagan's original feed-the-beast approach. Bush pushed through two major tax cuts in 2001 and 2003 and drastically ramped up defense and intelligence spending. By 2003, Bush was fighting three wars at once, in Afghanistan, Iraq, and against global terror. Most Americans did not initially question these wars and the increased spending that went with them because of the trauma of the 9/11 attacks and the perceived need to defend U.S. interests in the Middle East. Most Americans also welcomed the Bush tax cuts as relief from the 2000–2001 recession, the dot-com market crash, and the high taxes of the Clinton years.

Nevertheless, the impact on the debt ratio was swift and predictable. The ratio rose from 56.4 percent when Bush took office to 82.4 percent by the end of his two terms in office, the highest since the Truman administration and the aftermath of the Second World War, and well beyond the 60 percent critical threshold that Clinton salvaged. Yet this debt ratio increase fit the historical pattern of increased debt during wartime, albeit from a higher level. By the end of Bush's term, the war in Iraq was over, and the war in Afghanistan and War on Terror turned into long-term struggles that were costly but did not involve big spending increases of the kind seen from 2002 to 2007. Bush 43 was ready to repeat the Reagan playbook. He governed on a feed-the-beast approach, but now wanted to serve a starve-the-beast menu to his successor, Barack Obama. Bush would tie Obama's hands by leaving him no choice but to reduce spending to get the debt ratio back under control. Bush 43 intended to do to Obama what Reagan did to Bush 41 and Clinton.

Fate intervened. In the final months of Bush 43's term, the United States was struck with the worst financial crisis since the Great Depression. This gave Obama the perfect rationale to increase spending to offset the financial crisis, rather than to reduce spending. Instead of starve-the-beast, Obama doubled down with more feed-the-beast. In 2009, under Obama's leadership, the United States took a decisive turn toward complete financial ruin.

Obama's massive first-term deficits (2009–13), should be understood not only in the context of Bush 43's starve-the-beast gambit, but also in the long sweep of progressive Democratic presidents and their vision for America. Neither Bill Clinton nor Jimmy Carter lived up to the expectations of progressive Democrats for expanded spending and entitlement programs. Carter was a fiscal conservative constrained by hyperinflation. Clinton was a moderate constrained by bond vigilantes and a Republican Congress after 1994.

Progressives had to look back to LBJ's Great Society (1965), and before that to FDR's first one hundred days (1933) to find the kind of government activism they wanted. The landmark Social Security and Medicare programs were passed by FDR and LBJ. There was no social legislation of comparable magnitude for over forty years by the time Obama was sworn in. Progressives were hungry for social spending. Obama seemed the progressive leader they had been waiting for.

Obama had ready-made cover to do exactly what progressives wanted without having to nod in their direction. The 2008 global financial crisis sent the economy crashing and unemployment skyrocketing. The White House economic team of Christina Romer, Larry Summers, Austan Goolsbee, and Steve Rattner were not radical progressives; they were conventional neo-Keynesians. Their solution was predictable—massive deficit spending to stimulate the economy. Stimulus would come from a mystical Keynesian multiplier. Each $1.00 of deficit spending would produce more than $1.50 of growth, according to Christina Romer's estimates.

It was left to Obama and his closest political adviser, Valerie Jarrett, to blend the progressive wish list with neo-Keynesian stimulus into what became known as the American Recovery and Reinvestment Act of 2009. This was an $831 billion deficit-spending package piled on top of both preapproved baseline spending and automatic stabilizer spending for unemployment insurance and food stamps, which rise in recessions.

The 2009 stimulus act was touted as facilitating shovel-ready infrastructure. This was a Larry Summers fraud. Only a small portion was directed at critical infrastructure or productive capacity. The money went mostly to support liberal interest groups such as teachers, municipal workers, health-care workers, community organizers, and others who might have been laid off in the recession. The 2009 stimulus was the greatest progressive spending spree in U.S. history.

For seventy years, from 1946 to 2016, the average annual budget deficit was 2.11 percent of GDP. In contrast, deficits as a percentage of GDP for the early Obama years were 9.8 percent in 2009, 8.7 percent in 2010, 8.5 percent in 2011, and 6.8 percent in 2012. Not until 2014 did budget deficits move closer to the historical norm. The Obama years, 2009 to 2017, saw the national debt more than double, from $9 trillion to almost

$20 trillion. The debt-to-GDP ratio soared above 100 percent, the opposite of what George W. Bush expected from his attempt to impose a starve-the-beast policy.

Obama produced the worst possible combination of massive deficits, a skyrocketing debt-to-GDP ratio, and substantial tax increases. This might have been acceptable if the economy had yielded the robust growth expected by the neo-Keynesians. Obama's advisers believed that if debt increased by $11 trillion, then $15 trillion would be added to growth, mitigating the impact of the debt on the debt-to-GDP ratio. This never happened. Instead, the economy grew at a 2.05 percent average annual rate from the beginning of the Obama recovery in June 2009 until the end of 2016, the weakest recovery in U.S. history. Growth was far below the 3.19 percent annual average for post-1980 economic expansions, and the 5 percent average annual growth in the early years of the Reagan expansion (1983–86).

Ominously, the dismal Obama economic performance was produced in peacetime, not in a time of war. There was no peace dividend, as there had been for Bill Clinton. There was no deferred consumption, labor-market slack, or investment catchup as there was in the aftermath of past wars. Far from deferring consumption and investment, Obama's deficits brought growth forward, leaving a permanent output gap and little prospect for strong growth in the next administration.

Donald Trump was sworn in as the forty-fifth president on January 20, 2017, amid great expectations from the U.S. stock market and global investors. Trump's declared policies of tax cuts, reduced regulation, and larger deficit spending on defense and critical infrastructure were ripped from Ronald Reagan's playbook. Indeed, some of Trump's closest economic advisers, including David Malpass, Steve Moore, Larry Kudlow, Art Laffer, Steve Forbes, and Judy Shelton, were veterans of the 1980s Reagan Revolution. Trump was ready to feed the beast again with tax cuts and larger deficits. But the beast had already been fed $14.4 trillion by Bush 43 and Obama through war debt and progressive party payoffs. Trump's cupboard was bare.

Trump's advisers urged him to run the Reagan playbook, yet the conditions that prevailed in 1981 were absent in 2017. Reagan's debt-to-GDP ratio of 35 percent was a distant memory. Trump inherited a 105 percent debt-to-GDP ratio. His administration had no space for fiscal stimulus, and there is considerable doubt that so-called stimulus would work given the high debt burdens already in place.

The looming loss of confidence in U.S. credit was no impediment to reckless fiscal policy by the White House and a Republican Congress in the first two years of the Trump administration. In late 2017, Congress passed the Trump tax cuts, which added $2.3 trillion of debt over ten years, after quietly abandoning a requirement that tax cuts be revenue neutral. In place of revenue-neutral tax costs, Congress and the White House relied on the Laffer Curve, which, as we've seen, says that tax rate cuts stimulate enough growth so that added taxes on the growth mitigate lost revenue from the cuts. There is no empirical support for the Laffer Curve in the real world, except at extremely high starting tax rates. The Laffer Curve is largely a fiction, as was the neo-Keynesian multiplier on which Obama relied.

In January 2018, just a few weeks after passing the tax cuts, Congress removed spending caps on defense and discretionary domestic spending. Republicans wanted to increase defense spending and Democrats wanted to increase domestic spending; they compromised by doing both. Removal of these spending caps added over $300 billion to the deficit over two years. (These spending increases do not include approximately $140 billion of unbudgeted disaster relief in fiscal year 2017 for Hurricanes Harvey, Irma, and Maria, and the California wildfires). This combination of tax cuts and increased spending signaled the return of trillion-dollar annual deficits that will soon push the U.S. debt-to-GDP ratio from 105 percent to 115 percent. Foreign investors sense the coming debt crack-up and are reducing their exposure to U.S. Treasury securities. Net buying of U.S. Treasury securities by foreign investors began to decline after 2010, when the Obama deficits emerged. Buying shrank steadily until 2016, when net buying turned to net selling. A slow stampede out of U.S. government debt in anticipation of a debt crisis has started and will gain momentum.

Another tax-cut supporter claim is that the Trump tax bill changed the rules on U.S. taxation of global corporate offshore earnings. These changes allowed multitrillion-dollar bundles of offshore earnings to be brought back to the books of U.S. parent companies at highly favorable rates. Repatriated earnings would create a cash wave washing on U.S. shores, to be used for investment in plant and equipment and job creation to stimulate U.S. growth. This is nonsense. Almost all the cash from "offshore" earnings of U.S. global companies was already invested in U.S. markets and always had been. There was no rush to bring home the money; it was already here. The offshore money was held on the books of Irish and Cayman Islands' subsidiaries for accounting purposes, yet was mostly invested in U.S. bond and money markets. The Trump tax law allowed that money to be recorded on the books of the head office, and allowed the reversal of deferred tax expense. This is an accounting entry, not a tsunami of cash washing ashore. The repatriation story was always a myth designed to induce the media, Congress, and everyday citizens to go along with what was really a huge accounting windfall for corporate donors to the Republican Party. It is true that the offshore cash previously invested in Treasury notes, corporate bonds, and bank deposits could be invested in plant and equipment. Still, that's another myth, because the cash is mostly *not* being redeployed to new plant and equipment, it's being used for dividends and stock buybacks, another windfall for shareholders that does little to support long-term growth and job creation. Global companies that wanted to invest in plant and equipment in the United States for the past ten years could have done so easily by taking a 2 percent bank loan secured by the offshore cash. As far as the Trump tax law is concerned, the growth and investment story is smoke and mirrors.

The Trump corporate tax effects are even worse than the missing re-patriation stimulus. One unintended consequence of the new tax law is that it creates incentives for U.S. corporations to move new investment *offshore* instead of onshore. This is because in exchange for a one-time reduced tax rate on the repatriation of offshore profits, U.S. companies got what they have wanted for fifty years—an exemption from all future taxa-tion of offshore earnings.

Until the Trump tax bill, the U.S. taxed global companies on their global profits, either immediately or upon repatriation, or as a deemed repatriation under certain highly technical rules. Now the United States taxes only domestic profits; offshore profits are exempt. Tax-bill support-ers point to the U.S. corporate tax reduction from 35 percent to 22 percent as a reason for companies to invest at home. Still, 22 percent is higher than zero. As long as companies can find tax haven jurisdictions with zero tax rates, they prefer to invest there rather than in the United States. The United States now has no way to tax those profits currently or on a de-ferred basis. The profits, and associated jobs, stay offshore forever.

Trump advisers insist they can avoid a debt crisis through higher than average growth. This is mathematically possible yet extremely unlikely. The debt-to-GDP ratio is a product of two parts—a numerator consisting of nominal debt and a denominator consisting of nominal GDP. Mathe-matically it's true that if the denominator grows faster than the numerator, the debt ratio declines. The Trump team hopes for annual nominal deficits of 3 percent of GDP and nominal GDP growth of 6 percent, consisting of 4 percent real growth and 2 percent inflation. If that happens, the debt-to-GDP ratio will decline and a crisis will be averted.

This forecast invites incredulity. Deficits are already approaching 5 percent of GDP according to Congressional Budget Office forecasts and are projected to go higher in the years ahead. These CBO estimates are almost certainly optimistic, because they project no recessions for the next twenty years. That projection is practically impossible considering that the current expansion is already the second longest since the Second

World War. Economic expansions don't die of old age, but they do die. If a recession were to begin in the next three years—a likely scenario—additional hundreds of billions of dollars would be added to the deficit due both to the automatic stabilizers and reduced tax collections from slower economic growth. A new recession will decimate growth and inflate deficits at the same time. Even without a recession, official CBO projections expect 2.4 percent real growth and 2.1 percent core inflation in fiscal 2019. That yields 4.5 percent nominal growth, not enough to match the 5 percent deficit projection. The debt-to-GDP ratio will rise even under CBO's rosy scenarios.

The CBO also makes no allowance for substantially higher interest rates. With $22 trillion in debt, most of it short term, a 2 percent increase in interest rates quickly adds $440 billion per year to the deficit in the form of increased interest expense in addition to currently projected spending. The United States is past the demographic sweet spot that Obama used to his budget advantage from 2012 to 2016. From now on, retiring baby boomers will make demands on Social Security, Medicare, Medicaid, disability payments, veterans' benefits, and other programs that drive deficits higher.

Finally, the CBO fails to consider groundbreaking research by Kenneth Rogoff and Carmen Reinhart on the impact of debt on growth. A 60-percent debt-to-GDP ratio is considered by economists a red line beyond which debt levels may become nonsustainable. The Reinhart-Rogoff research shows there is an even more dangerous threshold of 90 percent debt-to-GDP, where the debt itself causes reduced confidence in growth prospects partly due to fear of higher taxes or inflation, which results in a material decline in growth relative to long-term trends. This is where the debt death spiral begins. The United States is well past the 90 percent death spiral trigger level and the situation grows worse by the year.

These headwinds insure Trump's growth projections are unrealistic. With higher than expected deficits, and lower than projected real growth, there is one and only one way for the Trump administration to reduce the debt ratio before a crisis of confidence emerges—inflation. If inflation increases to 4 percent, and Federal Reserve financial repression can keep a cap on interest rates at around 2.5 percent, and if there is no recession, then it is barely possible to achieve 6 percent nominal growth with 5 percent deficits—just enough to keep the debt ratio under control and even reduce it slightly. Still, this scenario is unlikely. The Fed failed to generate more than 2 percent inflation for seven years. It's not clear how it could create 4 percent inflation in the near term. Five percent deficit projections are also unrealistic because of the tax cut, sequester relief, student loan defaults, and other adverse factors. A U.S. debt death spiral is now likely.

Conspiracy of Looters

Recent vacillation between prudence and neglect on debt is nonpartisan. Administrations that greatly increased the debt-to-GDP ratio in the past forty years included three Republicans—Ronald Reagan, George W. Bush, and Donald Trump—and one Democrat, Barack Obama. Presidents who held the line and either maintained or reduced the debt-to-GDP ratio included one Republican, George H. W. Bush, and one Democrat, Bill Clinton. Neither party bears exclusive blame for out-of-control debt. Both parties bear some blame, while both parties have held the line at different times.

The control variable on deficit spending is not the party in the White House, it's the mood of Congress regardless of party control. Congress was supportive of Reagan's tax cuts in response to 1981's severe recession. Congress was also supportive of greatly increased defense spending under Reagan because defense had been neglected by Jimmy Carter, and because of the threat posed by the Soviet Union, which Reagan identified as the "evil empire." Similarly, Congress cooperated in a bipartisan way to raise taxes and reduce spending in 1990 during the Bush 41 administration. By then, the Berlin Wall had fallen, the Soviet Union was disintegrating, and the United States was the sole hegemonic power. Conservative Republicans wanted to get spending under control, while Democrats insisted on tax increases as the price of their support for spending cuts. In 1990, Congress did both. Bill Clinton also raised taxes in 1993, but wanted more spending to go along with the new tax revenue. After losing control of the House of Representatives to Newt Gingrich and the Republicans in the 1994 midterm elections, Clinton too had to go along with spending cuts. The result not only reduced the deficit, it ultimately produced budget surpluses in Clinton's final years in office. Deficits are not so much a product of White House wish lists as of shared priorities between the White House and Congress.

The increase in defense spending included in the February 2018 bipartisan budget deal that eliminated sequester caps on all discretionary spending is just a down payment. Defense spending cycles can run ten years or more, followed by equally long spending droughts as reaction sets in. As the military purchases existing weapons systems, develops new ones, upgrades capabilities, and replenishes depleted cruise missile stocks, that expanded capacity requires costly maintenance, training, and deployment. As long as Democrats insist on near dollar-for-dollar domestic spending as the price of military spending, the $300 billion deficit impact for 2018 is expected to grow to $400 billion per year or higher in 2019 and stretch for years beyond.

Republicans are mostly to blame for the Trump tax-bill fiasco. Democrats are mostly to blame for the domestic spending pig-out. The White House went along with all of it. The two major political parties are in this debt debacle together at the expense of everyday citizens who suffer the consequences of slower growth and higher interest rates. America's solvency is now threatened.

In addition to tax cuts, budget cap riddance, and other drivers of increased debt, one must consider an 800-pound gorilla in the room no one in Washington, D.C., wants to acknowledge—student loan debt. Total student loans outstanding in 2019 are over $1.6 trillion. To put that in perspective, the total amount of subprime and other high-risk mortgages outstanding in 2007 at the start of the mortgage meltdown was $1 trillion. The student loan debt pile is more than 50 percent larger than the junk mortgage pile in the last financial crisis. The $1.6 trillion figure is not a static amount. It will grow to $1.7 trillion by 2020 and continue growing after that. Student loans are a greater financial threat than mortgages, because default rates are higher. At the height of the 2007–2008 mortgage crisis, default rates on all mortgages were just over 5 percent. That's historically high for mortgages, yet manageable. Student loan default rates are in excess of 15 percent and growing rapidly.

Reasons for this high default rate are diverse. Student loans are given out to part-time and full-time students in qualified schools regardless of income, assets, or credit history. Many borrowers lack basic financial literacy. Borrowers don't realize how much debt they are taking on relative to their earnings prospects. Students graduate from school a hundred thousand dollars in debt only to discover they can't get jobs paying more than minimum wage. They move back into their parents' homes and hope for the best. Within months the student borrowers are in arrears on debt payments. Interest and penalties accrue, and soon the outstanding debt has grown by 50 percent because of the compounding effects.

Student-loan defaults impact the budget deficit because approximately 90 percent of all student loans are guaranteed by the U.S. Treasury. These guaranteed loans are originated by banks and serviced by banks or specialist loan-servicing companies. Treasury guarantees are off the books from a federal budget perspective as long as the loans are performing. When the loans first go into arrears, lenders and servicers work with borrowers to resolve the case. Grace periods on late payments are allowed. Certain types of public service can result in loan-payment deferrals or forgiveness. In some cases, consolidation refinancings can be used to stretch out maturities and lower monthly payments. As long as these workout processes are ongoing, the bad debt does not hit the Treasury's books. This extend-and-pretend charade has been going on for years. Increasingly banks are hitting the end of the line with borrowers and demanding payment from the Treasury. At a certain point, the Treasury pays off the bank lender and assumes ownership of the loan file sitting with the servicer.

Arrears were exacerbated by 2016 presidential election rhetoric. Candidates Hillary Clinton and Bernie Sanders understood that younger voters were distressed about their student loan debt loads. Both proposed various forms of relief, including loan forgiveness and free tuition for new students. Millennials heard the campaign promises and some simply stopped paying their loans in anticipation of a Clinton victory and a debt jubilee. The Clinton victory never came; a wave of debt defaults did. This campaign promise bait and switch will be more pronounced in the 2020 presidential election cycle as Democratic candidates polish their debt relief proposals. Another spike in defaults based on false hopes is coming.

The student loan fiasco has negative economic effects that go beyond the deficit. When young adults go into arrears on their student loans, their credit ratings take a hit. A poor credit rating makes it more difficult to get a job, rent an apartment, qualify for a mortgage, or get a car loan. Student loan arrears and bad credit ratings are standing in the way of household formation and consumption that comes with it from purchases of furniture, appliances, linens, and the like. The student loan headwind hits the denominator of the debt-to-GDP ratio through slower growth and hits the numerator through higher deficits; it's a double whammy in terms of U.S. capacity to sustain its national debt. A microburst of student loan losses is about to hit the U.S. Treasury. Losses will be $200 billion per year or higher based on current default rates. This default wave is not properly accounted for in official budget deficit estimates, yet defaults will increase the deficit by additional hundreds of billions of dollars in 2019 and beyond. Failure to address this issue intelligently with financial counseling and better loan underwriting is another example of bipartisan neglect.

The Point of No Return

A venerable dictum in economics is that if something can't go on forever it won't. The U.S. debt-to-GDP ratio is approaching the point at which it cannot expand much further without inducing a crisis of confidence. The United States will never default on its debt because the Fed can print the money to pay it off. Inflation is an all-purpose remedy for excess debt. The issue is how the inflation is catalyzed, since central banks seem incapable. Major U.S. creditors such as foreign central banks, sovereign wealth funds, and large institutions won't wait for the other shoe to drop. They'll look at trends, see that inflation is the only way out from under the debt, and shift assets from dollars in anticipation. This dollar dumping will depress the dollar's exchange value, increase Treasury borrowing costs, and catalyze a debt death spiral. It is this shift in investor perceptions, a psychological phenomenon, that triggers inflation more than central bank policies. The difficulty for policymakers and bankers is that the shift can happen almost overnight. Inflation can emerge seemingly from nowhere.

Critics of this debt-bomb scenario have a simple rebuttal. Unlike Greece or Argentina, U.S. debt is denominated in a currency the United States can print. No matter how high the debt is or how high interest rates go, the Treasury can simply sell the debt to the Fed directly or indirectly through bank primary dealers. The Fed prints the money to pay for the debt and stows the debt away on the Fed's balance sheet until maturity. The flaw in this reasoning is the assumption of unlimited confidence in the dollar's value. In this view, no amount of money printing or borrowing can shake confidence in the dollar, in part because of legal tender laws, and in part the necessity of citizens to acquire and hold dollars to pay their taxes. Yet this view ignores history, psychology, and common sense. Confidence in money is fragile, easily lost, and impossible to regain.

Even if dollars can be created in unlimited quantities (they can), and required in payment of taxes (they are), this does not mean that citizens can be forced to hold dollars beyond what is needed for tax payments. Citizens can allocate after-tax funds to other assets such as land, natural resources, fine art, or private equity. Citizens can also dump their dollars for food on the shelf, gas in the car, new clothes, other necessities, and even luxuries, vacations, and costly gifts. As citizens race to dump dollars for readily available alternatives, the result is a higher velocity of money on top of a bloated money supply. The quantity theory of money shows that expansion in money supply *and* an increase in money velocity together in excess of the economy's potential growth rate must result in inflation.

Central banks have failed to achieve desired inflation levels in the past ten years, not for want of trying. The Fed expanded the money supply with ease while assuming velocity would follow. It hasn't. Velocity plunged for the past twenty years. The Fed does not grasp that velocity is a behavioral variable rather than a constant or linear function. Psychologically driven behavior can change instantaneously once a critical threshold is exceeded. Physicists call this a phase transition. Mathematicians call it hypersynchronicity. Wall Street analysts call it a black swan without necessarily understanding the dynamics behind it.

Whatever the name, the result is the same—an instantaneous loss of confidence in the dollar and a sustained desire to dump dollars in favor of other currencies, hard assets, or goods and services. Higher inflation, even hyperinflation, is the inevitable result.

Investment Secret #2: Prepare for slow growth and periodic recessions for decades to come.

Even the most generous forecasts, including those of the Congressional Budget Office, show a steady increase in the U.S. debt-to-GDP ratio over the next five years and an exponential increase beyond that as baby boomers retire in increasing numbers and the prime-age workforce shrinks. These forecasts most likely overestimate growth and revenues due to persistent model error. More realistic models show the U.S. debt-to-GDP ratio will surpass 115 percent by 2023.

The research is also compelling that debt-to-GDP ratios in excess of 90 percent are an independent cause of slower real growth due to consumer and investor expectations of higher inflation, higher taxes, or disruptive debt defaults. In effect, consumers save more and businesses invest less, both on a precautionary basis. Governments cannot borrow their way out of a debt problem.

Taking the economic forecasts and economic research together reveals the United States is in for a prolonged period of slow economic growth punctuated by occasional technical recessions. The United States is Japan. The Japanese suffered the infamous "lost decade" from 1990 to 2000, and have suffered almost two additional lost decades since. The United States had its first lost decade from 2007 to 2017, and is now well into its second lost decade. This low-growth pattern will persist absent an inflationary breakout, which the Fed seems powerless to ignite in the short run; a war; or severe depression perhaps caused by a new financial crisis.

Given a baseline scenario of prolonged slow growth, there are three specific strategies investors can pursue both to profit and preserve wealth. The first strategy is to reduce exposure to high-valuation, high-growth stocks in technology, media, and advertising, especially the FAANG basket (Facebook, Apple, Amazon, Netflix, and Google). These stocks may continue to gain in the short run but are overdue for a fall as the reality of another lost decade sinks in. Avoiding these stocks avoids large losses when the inevitable correction commences.

The second strategy is to allocate part of one's portfolio to sectors that perform well in low-growth and deflationary environments, including utilities, ten-year U.S. Treasury notes, and high-quality municipal bonds. These investments provide steady yields while offering capital gains potential as disinflationary tendencies persist.

The third strategy is to increase your allocation to cash. A cash allocation reduces the overall volatility of your portfolio and offers deflation protection, since the real value of cash goes up in deflation. Importantly, cash offers optionality and an ability to pivot rapidly into other asset classes should war or inflation intrude unexpectedly. Cash also offers the holder the ability to go bargain hunting should another financial panic occur that drives asset values down 50 percent or more, as happened in 2008.

This slow-growth portfolio provides steady yields, hedges deflation, avoids losses on highfliers, and offers a chance to bottom fish in the next recession or crash. The United States took fifty years to dig itself into a nonsustainable den of debt, and will not escape the room quickly. Patient investors can wait out the debt denouement and avoid pitfalls that will ensnare others.

CHAPTER THREE
FIND THE COST OF FREEDOM

It is much easier, as well as far more enjoyable, to identify and label the mistakes of others than to recognize our own.

—Daniel Kahneman, *Thinking, Fast and Slow* (2011)

Beep, Beep, Beep

I lived for a decade on a 150-acre estate on the Long Island Sound in Connecticut. I didn't own it; I rented a perfectly nice yet modest house on the estate, with a water view amid more important structures, including a Mediterranean-style mansion, carriage house, and stables from a bygone age. My landlords were descendants of a family who owned the estate for over 120 years, heirs to fortunes in baking powder and tobacco. Some of the buildings are vacant now, although the stables are still active with Thoroughbreds handled by trainers with access to the facilities. I often imagined the Gatsbyesque parties that took place there in the 1920s. Today it is mostly empty and quiet; a great place to write.

The estate has a network of private roads suitable for horse-drawn carriages in the 1890s, yet too narrow for two cars to pass today. There's little traffic. Still, the few residents and visitors who do drive are courteous when the time comes to yield to another vehicle passing by.

One quirk of living on a large estate is that my house was a half mile from the nearest public road. The few mailboxes on the property are situated on a small roundabout not far from the public road, more accessible to the postal service. This made collecting my mail slightly more effortful than just stepping outside. Typically, I stopped by the mailbox in my car on my way to and from town.

Then the battle began.

If I arrived at night, I aimed my car at the mailboxes, using my headlights for visibility in the dark; left the engine running; and hopped out.

Beeeeeeeeeeeeeeeep.

My car, an Audi A5, would make the most obnoxious high-pitched continuous beeping sound. I don't exactly know why. It could be because I left the key in the car. It could be because I left the door open with the engine running and the lights on. It could be because my seat belt was unbuckled with the engine running while I was out of the car. It could be all of the above. The noise was unfortunate, because the estate is usually still and silent unless the wind's up off the Sound, in which case the crashing waves and salt air scent make it even more delightful. The beep ruined the peace.

I would hop back in the car, throw the mail on the front seat, and continue the drive to my house. At this point, I was just a thousand yards from home on private roads with no traffic. I often did not refasten my seat belt for this stretch. There was no objective danger except for leaping deer. After ten years I knew them by name; I'd take my chances. Some German engineer had other ideas.

Ding, ding, ding, ding.

My car was telling me my seat belt was unfastened. I already knew that. I quickly calculated that the seat belt ding alert stops after four dings and does not alert me again for thirty seconds. If I sped up a bit and there were no leaping deer I could make it home before the next round of dings. This strategy usually failed. The ding, ding, ding returned before I made it past the dressage ring.

Now I'd be in front of my house. It's night, the house is locked, the lights are off. Again, I'd use my car as a 2-ton flashlight pointed at my front door in the dark. I'd hop out of the car with my house keys.

Beeeeeeeeeeeeeeeep.

Eventually I'd unload the car, not forgetting the mail, move the car to its parking place, make it inside, and settle in for some peace and quiet. Maybe I'd do some writing in my studio. No more beeps and dings.

Wrong.

Once I turned my computer on, the horrific host of prompts, reminders, dings, and alerts start up again. At least I know how to disable or mute most of those. I dread that if I ever tried to reprogram the German-engineered prompts on my A5, the result would be disastrous, possibly including arrest by some car safety SWAT team of whose existence I was unaware.

For one who's thinking I could easily make these annoyances disappear by turning off my car engine at the mailbox, fastening my seat belt in the final stretch, and closing the car door behind me in the driveway, my answer is, "Yes, you're right, I can make the prompts go away. All I have to do is obey."

Life isn't more quotidian than picking up the mail and opening my front door. That's the point. If one can't get through the most routine tasks without a constant stream of audible, digital, visual beeps, dings, and bells, consider the sensory cognitive bombardment one undergoes in making fateful decisions regarding a 401(k), life insurance, health-care plans, and credit cards. Your employer's 401(k) election form is designed to make it more likely you will join the plan than other less manipulative designs. Insurance applications are designed to steer you into long-term plans with savings features rather than toward simpler, less expensive coverage.

Credit card applications are adorned with scenes of exotic getaways and expensive meals without highlighting 20 percent interest rates on unpaid balances and thirty-five-dollar "late fees" that apply within days of the bill being issued. These prompts go beyond mere advertising into a dark corner of behavioral psychology called "choice architecture," where financial forms are engineered by scientists who look out for the best interests of plan sponsors, not you.

It wasn't always this way. People have made important decisions on health, safety and income security for over a century, since the passing of a more self-reliant age. But they weren't always bullied about it. That's relatively new.

We know exactly whom to thank for this constant compulsion in our lives—Richard H. Thaler and Cass R. Sunstein, two intellectuals who find the temptation to tell others what to do simply irresistible. Thaler and Sunstein are the best-known, but far from only, practitioners of a branch of social science called behavioral economics. Their most influential contribution to the field is their book *Nudge* (2008), a handbook by big brains who want to push you around. Their full pedigrees are more pernicious.

Richard H. Thaler is professor of Behavioral Science and Economics at the University of Chicago, former president of the American Economic Association, and recipient of the 2017 Nobel Prize in Economics. He is the author of numerous books in his field and a prominent public intellectual.

Thaler's interest in the economics of behavior and personal choices was present from the start of his career, as shown in his Ph.D. thesis, "The Value of Saving a Life: Evidence from the Labor Market," published as an article by the National Bureau of Economic Research in 1976. In this thesis, Thaler creates a model of what a worker's life is worth to the worker and the employer by using pay differentials in various risky occupations, such as fishing and mining. I'm not sure how many deep-sea fishermen Thaler ever met; I've met quite a few. They assume the risks of fishing without regard to pay differentials for a love of the sea, camaraderie aboard their vessel, and fresh seafood from the ship's cook while under way.

When it comes to risky occupations, high-altitude mountain guides may take the prize. I've met many mountaineers. Guides work in one of the most deadly and least well-paid occupations. I've had the opportunity to discuss their professional motivations while on expedition. We all know the risks of death. Money is the least important consideration in climbing. Mountain guides do what they do because they love the view. Thaler's first model leaves little room for spectacular vistas.

Cass R. Sunstein is a Harvard professor and director of the Program on Behavioral Economics and Public Policy at Harvard Law School. He is a prolific writer—author, coauthor, or editor of almost fifty books and hundreds of articles in both academic and popular publications. His most important role outside of academia was administrator of the White House Office of Information and Regulatory Affairs (OIRA) during the first term of the Obama administration. The White House website describes the role of the OIRA as "the United States Government's central authority for the review of Executive Branch regulations [and] approval of Government information collections." If your goal is to control the behavior of others using behavioral psychology and unseen influence, there is no more powerful seat in government than head of OIRA. Obama and Sunstein were well acquainted from their days together teaching at the University of Chicago Law School in the mid- to late 1990s.

Thaler and Sunstein's book *Nudge* is by far their most influential and well-known effort at social control. It was a *New York Times* bestseller with over 750,000 copies in print in many languages. Most of the book is a straightforward account of insights on human behavior gained over the past fifty years from the work of behavioral psychologists. These insights begin with Stanley Milgram's seminal work on powerful yet controversial experiments on obedience in the 1960s.

Milgram's most famous experiment involved a subject (who didn't know he was the subject), under the direction of the experimenter, who was asked to assist in a program on learning and memory. Another participant, supposedly the learner, but really a collaborator in the experiment, is seen strapped to a chair. The real subject's role is to administer electric shocks to the learner under the experimenter's supervision. Soon the learner appears to suffer acute pain from the shocks and demands to be released from the chair. The experimenter insists that the method is safe and the subject should continue to administer shocks to the learner. In repeated experiments, the subject most frequently continues to administer electric shocks to the learner up to the highest settings on the apparatus.

Milgram's work was influenced by his desire to understand the behavior of Nazis and their collaborators in the Holocaust. His electric shock experiments were devised and conducted in the aftermath of the 1961 trial of Adolf Eichmann, the SS-*Obersturmbannfüher* responsible for logistics and operations in the murder of 6 million Jews. Eichmann never denied his role; his defense relied on the claim that he was just following orders.

Milgram's conclusion from his experiments is that at some point the subject relinquished his independence or agency to the experimenter based on a mélange of beliefs that the experiment was for the good of science and the experimenter was a benign figure. Once the subject surrenders agency to the experimenter, he is just following orders. With Milgram's work as a foundation, behaviorists went on to explore diverse aspects of human behavior at odds with common assumptions about rationality and good intentions.

Behavioral psychology made its greatest strides, including those most closely associated with economics, in the 1970s, through the experimental work of Daniel Kahneman and Amos Tversky. These landmark experiments were described and analyzed in two books, *Judgment Under Uncertainty: Heuristics and Biases* (1982) by Kahneman, Tversky, and their collaborator, Paul Slovic; and *Choices, Values, and Frames* (2000) by Kahneman and Tversky. These books laid the foundation for what is called prospect theory in contrast to the longstanding economic paradigm of utility theory.

In brief, utility theory claims that humans are rational decision makers with a clear view of the future and a strong sense of those choices that maximize happiness expressed as material well-being. When aggregated across a society and expressed through markets for the exchange of goods and services, utility theory forms the basis for a classical liberal, free-market economy that produces the greatest good for the greatest number, as espoused by nineteenth-century utilitarian philosopher Jeremy Bentham.

Prospect theory claims the opposite. Humans are riddled with cognitive biases that lead them to decisions not at all rational from a wealth-maximizing perspective. Not only are these biases irrational on their own terms, they contradict each other in ways that make behavior difficult to predict in individual situations and volatile in the aggregate.

In one famous experimental setup, subjects are offered a choice between $4.00 with an 80 percent certainty of receiving the reward, and $3.00 with 100 percent certainty of receiving it. A simple bit of math shows that the first choice has a higher expected return. An 80 percent probability of receiving $4.00 has an expected return of $3.20 (0.80 x $4.00 = $3.20). The second choice has an expected return of $3.00 (1.00 x $3.00 = $3.00). As $3.20 is greater than $3.00, a rational wealth-maximizing individual would take the first choice. From the mid-nineteenth to the late twentieth century, a facile belief that individuals would make the rational choice was the basis of free-market economics. Since 1947, the same belief forms the bedrock of modern finance.

Kahneman and Tversky demolished these and like assumptions about rational behavior through ingeniously designed experiments involving real humans. The experiments show that in the choice between an expectation of $3.20 versus $3.00, subjects overwhelmingly chose $3.00. The reason is that they value the certainty of some reward independently of the mathematical expected value. Individuals are highly averse to coming away empty-handed. If subjects chose the $4.00 offer, there's a 20 percent chance of getting nothing. Simple fear of losing outweighs the chance of making more in the minds of the subjects, despite the math.

This particular bias is called risk aversion. Based on experimental results, one might conclude humans shy away from risk in almost all life encounters. Yet that's not true. Other experiments show that humans underestimate risk and inflate their chances of success in diverse situations. This bias is called the overconfidence effect. The contrast between risk aversion and overconfidence shows individuals both avoid risk and embrace it depending on specific circumstances.

In uncertain situations, people overestimate their capacity to perform tasks and rank their competence more highly than others, even in the face of objective evidence to the contrary. This bias manifests itself both in excessive optimism while confronting adversity and wishful thinking in the face of a looming reversal of fortune. Overconfidence can be dangerous when applied to critical tasks in law, finance, or engineering. As Kahneman wrote, "In general, . . . you should not take assertive and confident people at their own evaluation unless you have independent reason to believe that they know what they are talking about. Unfortunately, this advice is difficult to follow: overconfident professionals sincerely believe they have expertise, act as experts and look like experts. You will have to struggle to remind yourself that they may be in the grip of an illusion."

So, are humans risk averse slugs or overconfident pretenders? The answer is both, depending on past circumstances and current conditions at a point of decision. This behavioral contradiction, one of many, illustrates why it is so difficult to make sense of human behavior in markets.

Other contradictions in the cognitive bias litany include anchoring (the tendency to make judgments based on past events rooted in the subject's mind), and recency bias (the tendency to make judgments based on the most recent experience or information received). So, is human judgment influenced by the distant past or the latest news? Again, the answer is both, depending on the setting.

Experiments in behavioral psychology have identified over 180 specific cognitive biases. New biases are added to the taxonomy all the time, based on new experiments. These biases present contradictions of the kind just noted and make the practice of behavioral psychology highly demanding. The science is compelling, yet application is complex.

Although Kahneman is a behavioral psychologist, he was awarded the Nobel Prize in Economics in 2002 for his insights into how cognitive biases affect market behavior. His collaborator, Amos Tversky, died in 1996 and did not receive the Nobel Prize because it is not awarded posthumously. Had he lived, Tversky would no doubt have been a corecipient that year.

Kahneman is commendably candid on the limits of behavioral psychology. While his insights have revolutionized thinking in social psychology and economics, those same insights instill modesty about what can realistically be known of outcomes in complex conditions. The blending of biases in billions of individuals where the biases are both contradictory in real time and adaptable over time makes the art of composite predictive analytics harrowing. It's one thing to know that a herd can turn and run; it's another to know where or when the herd will do so.

These limitations have not stopped Thaler and Sunstein from molding social behavior to their liking. They have enlisted behavioral psychology in pursuit of what they call libertarian paternalism. There's nothing libertarian about it. This is revealed in their book when they write: "Many of the most important applications of libertarian paternalism are for government." How the augmentation of state power is libertarian remains a riddle. The word "paternalism" sufficiently describes their aim. The channel of choice for their paternal agenda is choice architecture.

Choice Architecture

The new social and economic science of choice architecture proceeds from the necessity of design. Thaler and Sunstein point out that human-made systems inevitably have a design. Autos can have three-point seat belts, lap-style seat belts, or no seat belts. Cafeteria lines can start with candy or carrots. Ballots can list Democratic candidates first or Republicans. Every system includes design elements that involve choices made by the designer about placement, ease of use, color, vocabulary, and other factors.

At the same time, the human user facing a designed system with embedded choices has choices of her own. As a consumer moves through a cafeteria line, she asks herself, "Do I want the cheesecake today? Should I have more carrots to help cure a vitamin deficiency?" Consumer choice meets design choice in everyday settings.

By presenting design choices in a certain way, you can predictably affect consumer choices by preying on biases unveiled by behavioral psychology. This interface between design choice and consumer choice is the domain of choice architecture. In Thaler and Sunstein's words:

> Decision makers do not make choices in a vacuum. They make them in an environment where many features, noticed and unnoticed, can influence their decisions. The person who creates that environment is, in our terminology, a choice architect. . . . Our goal is to show how choice architecture can be used to help nudge people to make better choices (as judged by themselves) without forcing certain outcomes upon anyone, a philosophy we call libertarian paternalism. The tools we highlight are: defaults, . . . feedback, structuring complex choices, and creating incentives.

This manifesto makes clear that Thaler and Sunstein's agenda goes beyond science. Behavioral psychology is supported by an enormous body of empirical data derived from well-designed experiments on real human subjects. It is sound science, not mere conjecture or ideology masquerading as science. Yet the application of science is another matter. Nuclear physics is sound science; nuclear weapons are a matter for debate. Thaler and Sunstein have weaponized behavioral psychology.

Some examples illuminate how Thaler and Sunstein proceed in practice. The authors consider charitable giving, in which typical solicitations might include a range of suggested contributions in the form of $50, $150, $250, $500, and so on. Research shows that the larger the suggested amount, the greater the contribution given. Thaler and Sunstein would recommend the charity increase its suggested gift levels to $100, $300, $500, and $1,000. That simple change in choice architecture results in higher contributions. This suggestion makes use of the anchoring bias. The target of the solicitation anchors her behavior in the higher amounts used in the second example, and makes a larger gift as a result. This interaction of design choice and consumer choice is predictable and can be used to increase charitable giving.

Another example involves the overconfidence bias. Data shows that the five-year failure rate for new businesses is over 50 percent. Yet when entrepreneurs are asked in a survey about the chance of success of their business, the typical answer is 90 percent; some say 100 percent. Obviously entrepreneurs on the whole are overconfident with respect to the potential for the success of their businesses. Thaler and Sunstein have a remedy for overconfidence. They write, "If people are running risks because of unrealistic optimism, they might be able to benefit from a nudge. In fact, we have already mentioned one possibility: if people are reminded of a bad event, they may not continue to be so optimistic."

So, with simple design choices as suggested by Thaler and Sunstein, consumers can be influenced to give more to charity and entrepreneurs can be cautioned to avoid excess risk. Sounds wonderful, but is it? If Thaler and Sunstein's outcome is superior, why is the manipulation needed? Put differently, why do the academics maintain an a priori assumption that the uncovered bias is undesirable? Even if the list of suggested charitable contributions used the smaller dollar amounts, there's nothing to stop a contributor from donating a larger amount. Are all charities automatically desirable? There's nothing stopping an entrepreneur from taking a hard look at her business model and concluding that success is a longshot without being reminded that bad things happen to good businesses. Those possibilities aren't good enough for Thaler and Sunstein because they don't trust the judgment of typical donors or entrepreneurs. They feel compelled to give what they call a "nudge" to achieve a supposedly superior outcome.

With reference to their book title, Thaler and Sunstein state, "A nudge, as we will use the term, is any aspect of choice architecture *that alters people's behavior in a predictable way* without forbidding any options or significantly changing their economic incentives" (emphasis added). Nudge is a euphemism; hard shove is a better descriptor given what we know about the power of behavioral science. Euphemism is the refuge of the authoritarian. The rationale for Thaler and Sunstein's regimentation is that they're smarter than you and me.

The twin social engineers are explicit about their superior smarts. They subscribe to a process described as "taking steps to help the least sophisticated people while imposing minimal harm on everyone else." This is not that difficult to do because "humans are not exactly lemmings, but they are easily influenced." With reference to framing, a kind of behavioral manipulation, Thaler and Sunstein write, "Framing works because people tend to be somewhat mindless. . . ." They acknowledge that deception is sometimes needed to put their smart ideas over on the less sophisticated. Even good is not good enough for Thaler and Sunstein. They advise, "If you want to nudge people into socially desirable behavior, do not, by any means, let them know that their current actions are better than the social norm." The authors claim that "individuals make pretty bad decisions—decisions they would not have made if they had paid full attention and possessed complete information, unlimited cognitive abilities, and complete self-control." Since Thaler and Sunstein are in the nudge business, presumably they are the ones with unlimited cognitive abilities, not you.

The field of choice architecture and nudges is shot through with arrogance, unexamined premises, and adverse consequences. Take the example of the charitable solicitation where more is more; higher suggested contributions result in higher actual contributions. What is the basis for the implicit assumption that institutionalized charity is good? Random acts of kindness are certainly good, and don't need nudges. Consider the mass-marketing apparatus behind the kinds of solicitations that Thaler and Sunstein want to nudge. If you support gun control, do you favor Thaler and Sunstein's technique to help the NRA Foundation increase tax-deductible donations used to promote assault rifles? If you are pro-life, do you favor the Thaler and Sunstein nudge to increase contributions to Planned Parenthood Federation, the nation's largest abortionist? Thaler and Sunstein promote a pro-charity nudge as an uncontested good without examining what charities do with the money.

The pair's suggestion that entrepreneurs should be reminded of failure to discourage overconfidence in the face of a 50 percent flop rate is equally misguided. It is true that most new businesses fail within a few years. It is also true that entrepreneurs consistently overestimate their chance of success on average. So what? Thaler and Sunstein are compelled to apply their big brains to warn off entrepreneurs from their endeavors. Yet this ignores the asymmetry in the results of success and failure. An early entrepreneurial failure typically involves relatively few lost jobs and little lost capital because the business did not get that far out of the gate. Start-up business failures happen fast due to poor execution, poor quality, or simple lack of demand for, say, the original one-size-fits-all, waterproof, stain-resistant ice-cream glove. The opportunity costs of these efforts are low and the unsuccessful entrepreneur is on to her next enterprise in no time. In contrast, the few entrepreneurial successes can be huge. They can create thousands of jobs, generate large investments in plant and equipment, and produce prodigious profits for investors to support consumption or re-invest in new enterprises. Indeed, this pattern of many small failures offset by a few large successes is the bedrock assumption of the venture capital business. Who are Thaler and Sunstein to discourage entrepreneurs by reminding them of a "bad event"? Society should encourage entrepreneurship every step of the way. Thaler and Sunstein also ignore the fact that the entrepreneurial dream itself has value independent of ultimate financial success. We need dreamers, not academic Debbie Downers.

Thaler and Sunstein claim their work is designed solely to protect people from their own mistakes. Since the mistakes are predictable due to innate biases, why not structure choices in ways intended to lead the consumer-citizen to good choices instead of bad ones? Thaler and Sunstein place great weight on the absence of coercion. While they admit to using choice architecture to increase the likelihood of certain outcomes, they emphasize that the consumer still has a choice; nothing is forced. This is what they mean by their grandiose claim of libertarian paternalism. Libertarian in the sense that the consumer has a choice, yet paternal in the sense that economists are looking out for you and protecting you from your own childlike impulses.

Thaler and Sunstein claim that design choices are inevitable; no system works without some design, conscious or random. Not making a design choice is a choice. You are left with whatever design the originator chose, including the results of her biases. This produces a likely result based on that particular design. Why not be proactive? Why not identify desirable outcomes, design the form or interface to encourage that result, and reap the benefits of better choices at little or no cost? It seems the closest economics has to offer to the proverbial free lunch. Significant gains in welfare are achieved with no more effort than rearranging a few boxes on an application.

The best-known operation of the Thaler-Sunstein approach is to revise application forms from opt-in to opt-out elections. For example, a company's new employee information questionnaire might offer the new employee a chance to join a company benefit program. The form has a box for that choice. If you check the box, you're in the program. If you do not check the box, you're not. Checking the box is called opting in to the program. Behavioral research shows that people don't like filling out forms and are averse to checking boxes, independent of the substance or benefits of the choice. Many new employees leave the box blank and skip the program because of this bias. What if the benefit program is a 401(k) plan that offers tax deferral on current income, tax deferred compounding of plan earnings, and employer matching funds? The choice architects reason that those features are desirable, so they redesign the form. The new questionnaire informs you that you are automatically enrolled in the benefit program *unless* you check the box. If you do nothing, you're in the program. If you check the box, you're not. The result is that far more people enroll in the program because of the human bias against checking boxes. With this simple change in the form design, Thaler and Sunstein can greatly increase plan participation. That's their nudge. Welfare is improved because more employees are making the "right" choice, as defined by Thaler and Sunstein. No one is forced to make a particular choice. Everyone has full information about the consequences of the choice. Coercion is nonexistent and the costs of changing the form are low. (The biggest cost is probably the consulting fees that choice architects earn to make these recommendations, yet when spread over thousands or millions of applications even that cost is trivial.)

What's wrong with this enlightened, low-cost, noncoercive approach to human behavior? Almost everything.

The first problem is that the Thaler-Sunstein method seeks to displace an older solution to behavioral bias, called learning. Humans have enormous capacity to learn based on imitation, imagination, and the harder technique of learning from your mistakes. As a young driver in the late 1960s, I once hopped out of my car, shut the door behind me, and left my lights on. When I returned to my car the battery was dead because of the drain from the lights. I had no money and no membership in AAA. What followed was an ordeal. I walked to a pay phone to call my father—no mobile phones in those days. He arrived eventually with a set of jumper cables. We opened the hoods of the two cars, his and mine, connected the cables, and jump-started my battery. Then we were both on our way. The point is, I never accidentally left my lights on again. On separate occasions

I have locked my keys in the car. That's a more challenging situation than a dead battery, because you have to call the police or a locksmith to open the car door, using the same tools and techniques as a professional car thief. Again, I learned a lesson. Today, I don't need a beeping sound to remind me of what to do when I get out of my car. Importantly, the dead-battery and locked-door lessons have carried over to other endeavors. In time, I learned to stop and think before making sudden moves.

A slight pause before an unthinking action is invaluable. While mountain climbing on fixed ropes there are situations where one rope ends and another begins, with both ropes anchored to the mountain using ice screws or other fixed points. The climber is attached to the first rope through a system of slings, carabiners, and a climbing harness. In passing from one rope to another, the technique is to clip on to the second rope using a second carabiner before unclipping from the first. It's just as easy to reverse the technique by unclipping from the rope before clipping onto the next rope, with one important difference. When you unclip first you are momentarily unattached to either rope before you clip on to the second. If you slip or get hit with a wind gust in that moment and lose balance, the result can be fatal. Seasoned climbers learn to move slowly and think clearly in these situations. Fortunately, Thaler and Sunstein have not yet pursued choice architecture for mountaineers at twenty thousand feet. In life, a few mistakes go a long way. Once you've been impulsive at some cost, you learn to be less impulsive in future. That's how hominids survived 3 million years of evolution to become university professors. Thaler and Sunstein's efforts to replace hard learning with soft nudges moves us backward. They prefer automatons to autonomy. Experience is a better teacher.

The second deficiency in the Thaler-Sunstein approach is that effects of nudges are not lasting. The two professors ignore another aspect of human nature—adaptive behavior, and the ability of people to ignore their nudge after a few interactions.

This is the case with my Audi. There might have been a time shortly after I bought the car in 2008 when I took a minute to figure out what the beeps were telling me. If so, I pushed that out of my brain immediately. The beep begins. Seat belts? Lights? Engine running? Door open with the engine running? Keys left in the car? I have no idea. I am numb to nudges. I only know the beeps are annoying; I'm relieved when they finally go away.

Frequent flyers are familiar with this phenomenon. Air travelers are barraged with audio and video nudges from the time they're dropped off at the terminal until the time they land at their destination.

"Take your laptop out of your bag."

"Remove your belt and shoes."

"If you see something, say something."

"Empty your pockets."

Once they're on the plane, the cannonade continues. Does anyone really watch those cutesy video safety presentations? (They're cutesy because travelers long ago tired of the by-the-book versions.) A flyer's reaction to the in-flight seat belt sign is optional, a decided "If I feel like it" response. The only nudge flyers pay attention to is the final "ding" at the gate that signals it's okay to get out of your seat. That's more of an antinudge, because passengers are already primed to pop out of their seats and would do so even sooner but for the ding.

The screener's and airline's shouts, orders, and prods might have served some purpose at some time, but are long lost on frequent flyers. It's not clear why a silent video demonstration near security checkpoints would not serve just as well for first-time flyers. But flyers' response to the cattle punching has quickly gone from grudging acceptance to cold compliance to complete insensitivity. Adaptive behavior trumps the nudge effect over time.

A third flaw in the Thaler-Sunstein conceit is that the costs of nudging are low. They're not. The cost of changing a choice on a single application may be trivial. The marginal manufacturing cost of making my car beep at me is practically zero. Yet even trivial costs add up when replicated in thousands of applications imposed on busy humans. A practical accounting should consider the weight of imposing thousands of nudges per week on busy individuals just trying to get through their day.

An alarm clock is more than a nudge; it's like a bucket of cold water in the face, but it's how we start our days. You make coffee. The coffee machine beeps when the coffee's done, as if you didn't know from the aroma. You log on to your computer. An uninvited pop-up nudge asks if you want to update your apps. The nudge won't take no for an answer; that's not one of the choices. You can say yes, in which case you have to restart the computer you just started, or you can say "Remind me later today," or "Remind me tomorrow." You can check one or the other, but they're both lies, because you really don't want to be reminded at all; you just want to be left alone to scan the news or email.

The nudges are just getting warmed up. At the commuter train station you are admonished to "Step back from the platform," "Mind the gap," and "Watch out for the sliding doors." If you drive instead of taking the train, you'll encounter a roadside laser-guided speed indicator that flashes your speed in red and displays "SLOW DOWN" if you're one mile per hour over the speed limit, but turns green and offers a warm "THANK YOU" if you slow down.

There is more to the proliferation of nudges than mere annoyance. In one hospital, the digital prescription system sent so many nudges designed to reduce medication errors that the staff learned to ignore them. This resulted in more incorrect dosages than when the staff relied on their own training and judgment. In one case described by Dr. Bob Wachter of the University of California, San Francisco, a doctor entered certain incorrect information about a teenage patient into a medication robot. The robot issued a warning, "but the doctor clicked out of it because unnecessary warnings popped up on the screen all the time." The robot then dispensed 38.5 times the intended dosage, which was handed to a nurse. A bar-coded backup system next issued a prompt to the nurse, telling her that she was administering the pills to the correct patient despite her misgivings about the dosage. The patient nearly died.

Choice architecture is rapidly approaching the point of totalitarian overreach. In July 2018, Argentina enacted a law making all 44 million citizens of the country involuntary organ donors. As Thaler would no doubt commend, there is an opt-out provision, but it requires an affirmative act. Who knows if the government bureaucrat who receives the opt-out notice records it properly or if that record is readily available when needed? Declarations of death are often not as cut and dried as most imagine. The temptation to take viable organs in borderline cases is strong. Thanks to choice architecture, state power can now literally rip your lungs out without your consent. That's quite the nudge.

The nudges never stop coming. Online or in real life, the audio-video-digital cavalcade of nanny-nudges inundates us like a never-ending word to the wise. We learn to ignore it, but the cost in cognitive dissonance is high; not quite the free lunch Thaler and Sunstein suppose.

Transcending these singular objections is choice architecture's quintessential weakness—the idea that Thaler and Sunstein are smarter than you and have correctly identified the right choice in every design. Thaler, Sunstein, and their ilk base this belief on their higher IQ scores, educational attainment, and academic credentials. This presumed intellectual superiority empowers behavioral economists to prescribe various "correct" courses of conduct for the rest of us, and to implement those prescriptions with nudges embraced by institutions that interface with the public.

The evidence for this presumption is entirely absent. On binary outcomes, economists have worse forecasting records than random guesses produced by monkeys, due to deficient models, herding behavior, and fear of losing one's professional standing with an out-of-consensus forecast (an incorrect yet in-consensus forecast is always acceptable because "everyone thought the same thing").

There's more to economists' dismal analytical ability than herding and self-interest. Prevailing economic models bear no relationship to the real dynamics of capital markets or economic systems. Examples of this discordance include the Phillips Curve, the presumed inverse relationship between employment and inflation, which has no empirical support. As noted, the period from 1960 to 1965 exhibited low unemployment and low inflation. The period from 1965 to 1968 exhibited low unemployment and high inflation. The period from 1977 to 1981 exhibited high unemployment and high inflation. The period from 2008 to 2013 exhibited high unemployment and low inflation. In sum, there is no causal relationship between employment and inflation. Still, economists insist on using the Phillips Curve to guide monetary policy with grotesque results, including a 120:1 leverage ratio on the Federal Reserve's balance sheet. Another myth maintained by economists is value at risk, or VaR. This is the primary risk-management model used by banks and regulators. It assumes that the degree distribution of risk events is normal (the bell curve), that there is a risk-free rate (short-term Treasuries), that markets are efficient, and that prices move continuously in response to news. None of these assumptions is true. The degree distribution of risk events is a power curve, not a bell curve. Treasuries are not risk-free, as recent U.S. government credit downgrades and debt-ceiling debates reveal. Markets behave irrationally, and prices gap violently up and down with no opportunity to buy or sell as the market reacts to shocks. VaR is junk science, yet it rules the roost of risk. The most egregious example of junk science in economics is the widespread use of dynamic stochastic general equilibrium models, DSGE, for economic forecasting and policymaking. The name gives it away. Capital markets are not "equilibrium" systems; they are complex systems. This explains why professional economic forecasters are not only frequently wrong, they are directionally wrong, persistently wrong, and wrong by orders of magnitude. With this modeling record as a calling card, why should everyday citizens accept the choice architecture of economists?

For their part, the economists are unabashed. As noted, the most highly proclaimed success of choice architects like Thaler and Sunstein is their ability to manipulate employees into signing up for 401(k) tax-deferred savings plans. This is done by switching new employee choices from opt in to opt out.

Prior to choice architecture, a typical new employee document would include a question in the following form:

Our company offers a 401(k) savings plan. (Please see separate disclosure document for details.)

Please check here if you would like to participate: _____

This is an example of an opt-in clause, because the employee has to take an affirmative act to join the plan. Choice architects redesigned the form to read as follows:

Our company offers a 401(k) savings plan. (Please see separate disclosure document for details.) You have automatically been enrolled in this plan.

Please check here if you would not like to participate: _____

This is an example of an opt-out clause, because the employee has to take an affirmative act not to join the plan.

The changed wording is subtle yet powerful. In *Nudge*, Thaler and Sunstein give examples of employee savings plans where initial participation by employees increased from 20 percent to 90 percent once the switch from opt in to opt out was made. Thaler and Sunstein pride themselves on the fact that nudges still leave individuals free to choose. This is disingenuous because aggregate results are highly predictable even if individual cases technically allow choice. Thaler and Sunstein are preying upon personal biases to produce a result to their liking. They cannot easily evade responsibility for the outcome by hiding behind choice.

A real-world example shows why economists' choices should not necessarily be trusted. Assume that two employees, Sue and Joe, both aged fifty-three, go to work for two companies with adjacent headquarters in a midsized city. Their salaries are identical at two hundred thousand dollars per year. Both are married and file joint tax returns with their spouses. Sue's company and Joe's company both offer 401(k) plans. Sue and Joe were each hired on the last business day of December 1999, and completed their new employee paperwork that day. Sue's company uses an opt-in enrollment form; Joe's company uses the opt-out form. Sue does not opt in and is not in her company's plan; Joes does not opt out and is in his company's plan. This is a predictable result according to behavioral psychologists, and a desirable result according to choice architects.

Sue and Joe both receive a discretionary $10,000 performance bonus on the first business day of each year; $10,000 is the maximum employee contribution that Joe can make to his plan. Each year Sue receives her $10,000 on the first business day of the year, pays her taxes on that amount at a 21 percent effective tax rate, and invests the $7,900 after-tax remainder. Joe also receives $10,000 on the first business day of the year, all of which goes into his tax-deferred 401(k) plan. No taxes are due for Joe until he withdraws the money upon termination or retirement. For portfolio selection, Sue invests her after-tax bonus in physical gold bullion, which she keeps in safe non-bank storage. Joe invests in an equity index fund tied to the performance of the Dow Jones Industrial Average. In addition to normal market fluctuations, Joe's stock portfolio pays 2 percent in dividends, which were reinvested and compounded tax deferred.

On the last business day of December 2017, Sue and Joe both retire from their jobs at age seventy-one, after eighteen years of service. Sue has no plan distribution since she never joined a plan. She sells her gold and pays a 28 percent capital gains tax at the special rate applied by the IRS to collectibles. Joe takes a lump-sum distribution from his plan, and pays his taxes at ordinary rates on the previously deferred income. With cash in hand, Sue and Joe look forward to their retirement years with one important difference. Sue has more money.

In this example, Sue's cash balance at the end of 2017 is $265,725 and Joe's cash balance is $265,713. It's a small difference, but Sue wins.

In certain cases, more extreme than the one described here, Thaler and Sunstein describe a decision not to join a company savings plan as "foolish beyond a doubt," and ask with regard to a more typical case, "How can we nudge these people to join more quickly?" What they do not ask is whether choice architecture produces better real-world outcomes.

There's a lot to parse in this example. The dollar price of gold was near twenty-five year lows in 1999, which gave Sue an attractive entry point and a head start on Joe. Still, gold suffered its worst bear market in history from 2011 to 2015, in which 50 percent of the gains from 1999 to 2011 were lost. Sue invested after-tax dollars while Joe invested more pre-tax. Joe had a 2 percent tax-deferred dividend on his portfolio, while Sue's gold had no yield. And Joe enjoyed one of the longest stock bull markets in history from 2009 to 2017, including blockbuster years 2013 with a 26.50 percent gain, and 2017 with a 25.08 percent gain. On the whole, Sue faced enormous headwinds, one reason Thaler and Sunstein nudge employees into 401(k)s.

Still, Sue won the race.

Some of the difference between Sue and Joe is due to taxes. Prior to sale, Sue's gold was worth $313,762, while Joe's 401(k) had a predistribution balance of $408,957. Yet distributions are mandatory for Joe and taxes are inevitable. Joe did not have to take a lump-sum distribution; he could have taken smaller annual distributions over time. That's true, but Sue did not have to sell her gold either. She could have held it indefinitely and paid no taxes, while Joe faced mandatory distributions and tax bills every year. The comparison is also artificially constrained by putting Sue 100 percent in gold and Joe 100 percent in stocks. If Sue had invested 50 percent in gold and 50 percent in stocks, her returns would have far surpassed Joe's even without the benefit of 401(k) tax deferral. In a fifty-fifty portfolio, Sue could have created her own tax deferral simply by not selling her stocks until the end of 2017 and paying the lower capital gains tax rate, versus Joe's ordinary income tax rate. Likewise, if Joe had invested 60 percent in stocks and 40 percent in a money market fund, his returns would have been greatly diminished, and Sue would have dominated the contest again.

There is an infinitely large set of Sue versus Joe examples that could be devised with variations in start dates, end dates, tax rates, and rates of return. Sue wins in some, Joe wins in others. That's not the point. The point is that the choice architect's a priori assumption that 401(k)s produce superior results and that employees should be pushed in the direction of joining a plan is false. Thaler and Sunstein would never even have constructed an example along the lines just described because their training and mind-set do not admit the consideration of gold as an investible asset. Yet Sue is not "foolish beyond a doubt," as the *Nudge* authors would have it, even if Thaler and Sunstein appear to be arrogant in the same measure.

Apart from these obvious deficiencies of choice architecture (a bias against learning, dissipating impact, hidden costs of excessive nudging, adverse adaptive behavior in response to nudging, and false assumptions about superior choices), the nudge project contains a huge hidden irony. Thaler and Sunstein begin their book by mocking the model of humans making efficient decisions guided by rational expectations, so-called *homo economicus*. They go through a litany of behavioral biases confirmed by experimentation, including risk aversion, confirmation bias, and recency bias, that show human decision making is "irrational." Then they present the field of choice architecture, which creates traps devised to push behavior toward efficient decisions guided by rational expectations, exactly what they mocked. The Thaler-Sunstein affection for *homo economicus* is palpable. If *homo economicus* does not exist in the real world, they will nudge him into existence like latter-day Frankensteins. They come not to bury *homo economicus*, but to raise him from the dead.

What Thaler and Sunstein don't comprehend is that what they deem irrational behavior is a highly evolved adaptation well suited to survival in stressful circumstances. As in the classic experimental model noted earlier, in which a subject is offered the choice of $3.00 with a 100 percent probability of receiving it (expected value $3.00), or $4.00 with an 80 percent probability of receiving it (expected value $3.20), subjects overwhelmingly take the $3.00 even though the expected value is less than the $4.00 option. This is considered irrational by the behaviorists. Yet it's completely rational. In an Ice-Age survival situation (where some of these biases evolved), the cost of not receiving a "payout" could be death by starvation or hyperthermia. Taking the lower expected value with certainty was a small price to pay to avoid an uncertain outcome that could be deadly. The difference between the higher and lower expected values is, in effect, an insurance premium the subject pays to avoid a catastrophic outcome. *Homo economicus* does not exist, but neither do bundles of bias in need of the ministrations of choice architects. People know what's best for them without nudges. Addictions and bad behavior will always exist, no matter how many forms Thaler and Sunstein design. The keys to improved outcomes are better education and more information, not manipulation and behavioral modification.

The difficulty is that Thaler and Sunstein bring their own biases and irrational beliefs to the table. They are biased in favor of employer savings plans despite high taxes on distributions. They are biased in favor of stock portfolios despite regular market collapses of 30 percent or more. They are biased against gold despite centuries of wealth-preservation performance. They are biased against tobacco despite musical geniuses, ballet dancers, and painters who smoked two packs a day and created lasting beauty in their art. They are biased in their belief that the future will resemble the recent past. They believe that deep-seated survival skills are anachronistic despite evidence of civilizational collapse from the Bronze Age and ancient Rome to Watts and Katrina. Their greatest bias is they think they're smarter than you, me, and everyone else. They're not. Choice architects should confine themselves to academia and leave the rest of us in peace.

Bad Ragaz

Switzerland appears on a map as an irregular rectangle, the horizontal longer than the vertical. In the lower left-hand corner is Geneva, the portal to France. In the lower right-hand corner is Lugano, the pathway to Italy. In the upper left-hand corner is Zurich, a window on Germany. In the upper right-hand corner is—nothing, except the high peaks of the Swiss Alps and villages snug among them. It's here you'll find Davos, home of the uber-elite World Economic Forum. Not far away is St. Moritz, the classic and still exclusive ski resort. Least known, and farthest from big cities and elite venues, is the quintessential alpine town of Bad Ragaz in the Swiss canton of St. Gallen.

"Bad" means *spring* or *bath* in German, a reference to the natural thermal springs that have made Bad Ragaz a destination for centuries. Bad Ragaz is tiny, six thousand souls in a mere ten square miles, nestled among the high peaks of the Graubünden Alps, just three miles from the border with Liechtenstein.

I was in Bad Ragaz on March 10, 2016, as a panelist at a private investment conclave for a small group of the largest asset managers in the world. The two-day conclave took place at the ultraluxurious Grand Resort, which offers a private thermal spring, a wellness spa, and a shuttle to nearby skiing for those inclined to the outdoors. The conference theme was "How Will the Euro End?" This conference took place in the wake of the 2010–2015 European sovereign debt crisis, when elite opinion was certain the euro was heading for a crack-up. Greece, Spain, Ireland, and Portugal were urged to quit the euro or be kicked out. Italy was not far behind. My remarks to the assembled money mavens said that the euro

was not breaking up, it was strong and getting stronger, and that new nations would be added to the euro while none would exit. That was the same
analysis I had been presenting since 2010, mostly to elite ridicule. Yet my
analysis proved valid in 2010, 2016, and is still true today.

One of the perks of public speaking is hopping from one exclusive
venue to the next. The Bad Ragaz Grand Resort held up its end in that regard. Another perk is the chance to spend time with the other keynote
speakers. Downtime at meals or offstage offers the chance to chat informally with renowned experts in diverse fields. While at Bad Ragaz I spoke
privately with Dan Ariely, the leading behavioral psychologist in the world
after Nobelist Daniel Kahneman. Our encounter was an opportunity for
me to explore aspects of the Thaler-Sunstein art of behavioral manipulation that had troubled me since I first encountered them.

Ariely is an American by birth, who moved with his family to Israel
when he was three years old. He lived in Ramat Hasharon on Israel's central coast just north of Tel Aviv. Ariely attended Tel Aviv University and
received his B.A. in psychology, with a concentration in physics and mathematics. He later gained a Ph.D. in cognitive psychology from Duke University, and another doctorate in business administration from Duke. The
second Ph.D. was pursued at the urging of Ariely's mentor, Daniel Kahneman, because it would facilitate the application of Ariely's behavioral
insights in the realms of economics and business.

As a high school student, Ariely was preparing canisters for an illumi-
nation ritual conducted by his youth group, Hanoar Haoved, when a mix
of gunpowder and other chemicals exploded in his hands. He suffered
third-degree burns over 70 percent of his body. Ariely spent three years in
and out of Israeli hospitals, undergoing treatments to prevent infections,
skin grafts, and rehabilitation. He was left partly disfigured and disabled.
The accident was thirty-six years ago, yet Ariely lives in pain to this day.

His horrific burns and subsequent treatment were the inspiration for
some of the most insightful experiments in behavioral psychology ever
conducted. Ariely was intrigued by the method used by hospital nurses to

remove the bandages of burn victims. Most people who have removed Band-Aids from minor cuts or burns are familiar with the dilemma even in far less painful circumstances than those confronting Ariely. If a bandage is removed quickly, the pain is intense, yet over quickly. If a bandage is removed slowly, the pain is reduced but lasts longer because removal takes longer. Removing a bandage involves a trade-off between the intensity and duration of the pain involved for the patient.

Ariely noticed that standard practice for bandage removal was to proceed quickly, increasing the intensity of pain, but getting it over quickly. Ariely understood the nurses' dilemma; as a burn victim he lived with it for years. Yet he wondered if nurses were making a rational choice or were succumbing to a bias. In a series of studies in the late 1990s and early 2000s, Ariely and his collaborators, including Kahneman, demonstrated that the slower, less painful approach is usually better for the patient. The matter is complicated by numerous factors, including repetition, sequencing with other procedures, and the patient's control or lack of control of his circumstances. Still, on balance, the slower, less painful approach is better despite the fact that the pain is prolonged. It turns out that the quick, intense approach was practiced by nurses because it reduced their discomfiture with the bandage removal. It was the nurses who wanted to "get it over with," not the patients. Ariely's insights have led to changed medical procedures for burn victims around the world.

Ariely's ethical approach to behavioral psychology differs from the Thaler-Sunstein method. He is more interested in pure discovery; he's simply inquisitive about how humans make decisions. Thaler and Sunstein are more driven by the need to manipulate human behavior in pursuit of what they define as enlightened ends. That said, Ariely does do extensive work in the field of choice architecture as a hired gun for corporations and political parties, as do many of his peers. It was the political work I wanted to discuss with Ariely.

Given the power of choice architecture to affect outcomes, there's obvious scope for politicians to use the techniques of behavioral psychology to sway voters to support their program or reject that of a rival. Instead of tricking new employees into signing up for a 401(k), the choice architects can trick voters into voting one way, not another, or staying home on Election Day, which can mean lost votes for an opposition candidate and victory for the candidate using behavioral tricks.

The choice architects were not initially troubled by this because the early adopters of behavioral manipulation were campaigns such as the 2012 Obama reelection effort. Since academics, including Ariely, Thaler, and Sunstein, generally favor liberal causes, they were cheered to see Obama adviser David Plouffe leapfrog old-school Republican door-to-door methods. Plouffe managed Obama's 2008 campaign and oversaw his 2012 reelection from the White House as a senior adviser. Plouffe's savvy use of social media, text messaging, data mining, and choice architecture left Republican adviser Karl Rove's canvassing techniques in the dust. In 2017, Plouffe joined Facebook founder Mark Zuckerberg's social advocacy organization to facilitate a wide range of typically liberal initiatives.

By 2016, Republicans not only caught up to Democrats but leapfrogged them, as Plouffe had earlier done to Rove. This was due to advanced data mining and social media technology offered to the Trump campaign by Robert Mercer, Cambridge Analytica, and Brad Parscale, who was tapped to lead Trump's 2020 reelection bid. Trump's own media savvy on Twitter and TV was an enormous asset to a team focused on a digital campaign. In a reversal of the 2012 election, it was the Democrat, Hillary Clinton, who stuck to old-school television appearances and wonky policy papers, while Trump ran under the mainstream-media radar screen and effectively campaigned at low cost on Facebook and Twitter.

This new alignment of political forces was amplified by highly sophisticated digital Russian intervention in the 2016 campaign. Whether Russian intervention was explicitly to help Trump or designed to sow chaos and dissension in American political discourse is unclear. What is clear is that the Russian effort was pervasive and effective. This should come as no surprise, since Russians have been master propagandists for over a century, first under Communist direction (1917–91), then more recently under the direction of former KGB spy, now president, Vladimir Putin. Behavioral psychology and digital media were mere force multipliers for Russia's well-practiced arts of deception.

By 2018, the use of choice architecture on digital platforms by neofascists was widespread. China implemented a "social credit score" program applicable to its 1.4 billion citizens, backed up by a planned 600 million surveillance cameras, digital facial and gait recognition software, and near complete control of internet message traffic. Chinese citizens are assigned a social credit score based on good or bad behavior in a myriad of categories, including smoking in public, tweets, cheating on taxes, community service, or buying locally made goods instead of imports. Citizens with low social credit scores are denied access to government services such as transportation, school admissions, and government jobs. A typical case was that of Chinese citizen Liu Hu, as reported by CBS News:

> When Liu Hu recently tried to book a flight, he was told he was banned from flying because he was on the list of untrustworthy people. Liu is a journalist who was ordered by a court to apologize for a series of tweets he wrote and was then told his apology was insincere. "I can't buy property, my child can't go to a private school," he said. "You feel you're being controlled by the list all the time."

China has rolled out the ultimate Thaler-Sunstein voluntary nudge. You're still free to smoke in China; just don't expect to fly anywhere or see your kids go to school.

This was my question to Ariely when we met. I asked, "Your techniques are powerful. You're bombarded with requests from clients to apply your techniques all the time. How do you decide who the good guys and bad guys are? What's to stop you from applying behavioral modification techniques for the next Hitler?"

Ariely paused and said, "That's a question I ask myself all the time. My students and associates ask me that also. Here's the answer. When I'm offered a fee to work for a client I ask myself if I would do this work for free. If you remove money from the equation, would I work for this client based on his values being in sync with my own? Only if the answer is yes will I take the assignment."

Ariely deserves credit for at least trying to devise a filter for the use of the powerful tools of choice architecture. Yet as with the Thaler-Sunstein assumption of superior judgment, there are many flaws in Ariely's values-based filtering method. The first flaw is his assumption that his "values" are universal and invariably correct. That's extremely unlikely. What is more likely in today's political environment is that half the people agree with him and half disagree on important public-policy issues. This means whenever Ariely takes up a project he's "screwing" half the population, in his phrase. Democracy is an imperfect mechanism for achieving consensus among divergent views. Choice architecture based on the proclivities of academics doesn't come close.

The larger problem is that whatever Ariely's leanings, not all experts in behavioral psychology are as scrupulous as he. Some choice architects are mercenaries—guns for hire—who work for Big Tobacco or big banks in ways detrimental to the physical or financial health of everyday citizens. Other experts are pure ideologues, out to prevail for a particular cause without regard to money, ethics, or other constraints. There's nothing new in this. Joseph Goebbels and Leni Riefenstahl used radio and film to make Hitler appear charismatic on the one hand, and a warm friend to children and pets on the other. What is new is the project's global reach and the relatively low distribution costs compared with traditional media. When manipulative content is combined with data mining, micro-targeting, and digital platform distribution, the effect on behavior is forceful and pervasive.

Choice architecture and other behavioral modification techniques will no doubt become subject to self-regulation by academics and social media firms in the near future. That won't be enough to prevent abuse because of the inherent biases of those purporting to self-regulate. Some voices will be heard, others squashed, on a nondemocratic basis. Government regulation will follow, which is at least partly democratic yet hardly efficient. In the end, users of social media and citizens trying to navigate the maze of beeps, buzzers, and contrived choices will have to rely on their own education and common sense to avoid the not always benign corporate and media puppeteers.

This brings the debate full circle to the definition of "irrational." Society can readily agree that behavior that is demonstrably and materially harmful to others, directly or indirectly through environmental channels, or harmful to oneself can be regarded as irrational in some sense. When it comes to choices that are not obviously harmful, but simply suboptimal according to consensus rankings or a programmatic approach, more thought is needed before separating the allegedly rational from the irrational.

Most of the approximately two hundred biases that behavioral psychologists have identified represent a kind of intuitive or instinctive response to uncertainty. Kahneman and Tversky called these responses heuristics—a shortcut for decision making in the absence of more time or data to make a more reasoned response. Yet these heuristics do not come from the ether. They are the product of millions of years of evolution from hominids to modern humans. Some heuristics may be destructive and fade over time through natural selection. Still, evolutionary science suggests that most of the biases serve some purpose in the cause of human survival. Paleoanthropologists and biologists continually marvel at how humans have survived without claws, fangs, massive bodies, or exceptional speed in a world of predators. The answer, of course, is the human brain. And the brain, as we now know, is a bundle of biases.

Consider the unexamined assumptions behind the Thaler-Sunstein approach. They assume the future resembles the past. They assume that markets will remain open and liquid. They assume that governments will not resort to confiscatory policies to support state power. They assume tax rules will not retroactively change. They assume the smooth functioning of critical digital and financial infrastructure. They assume continuation of the rule of law.

Every one of these assumptions is false. History is filled with dislocations and dark ages. The New York Stock Exchange has been closed for months at a time. Market liquidity is deteriorating and has vanished completely during certain flash crash episodes. Governments confiscate wealth all the time; just ask U.S. gold owners in 1933, Chinese in 1949, or Venezuelans today. Tax rates in the United States have been as high as 90 percent on occasion. Wall Street came close to complete collapse in 1998 and 2008. Puerto Rico was without adequate electric power a full year after Hurricane Maria in 2017. The rule of law broke down in the United States during the Civil War, the First World War, and in riots since then. This is a small sample of how Thaler-Sunstein complacency is misplaced. On balance, sustained periods of social stability are the exception, not the rule. Efforts by Thaler and Sunstein to overcome a "bias" against joining 401(k)s enshrines their own bias that a society looks tomorrow as it does today. That's the most dangerous bias of all.

The difficulty with behavioral psychology is not the science, it's the application. The pure science exemplified by Kahneman, Tversky, and Ariely has been misapplied by economists such as Thaler and bureaucrats like Sunstein. The Thaler-Sunstein approach assumes not only that the future resembles the past, but that people frankly are stupid and need their highly educated help, another debatable proposition.

A better approach to applied behavioral psychology has been offered by Samuel Bowles, director of the Behavioral Sciences Program at the Santa Fe Institute, a leading center of complexity theory. The title of his 2016 book, *The Moral Economy: Why Good Incentives Are No Substitute for Good Citizens*, candidly displays his own bias in this debate. While

Bowles is completely familiar with the work of Thaler, Sunstein, and other choice architects and agrees it has its place in social governance, he argues for greater latitude for true choice rather than contrived choice.

Bowles cites the case of a group of child day-care centers that had difficulty with late pickups by parents. To encourage on-time behavior by parents, the centers imposed a fine for late pickups, a classic nudge. The fine failed. Late pickups doubled under the new system of fines. The reason for the failure goes to the dichotomy between altruistic and selfish motives. Without the fine, the parents operated on a kind of honor system when it came to being on time. They did their best out of respect for the day-care center staff and their own sense of duty, despite some lateness. Once the fines were imposed, parental action become purely contractual. The costs of a nudge displaced the sense of duty. Parents coolly calculated the value of their own time and chose to pay the fine in exchange for more flexibility in their schedules. There was no sense of shame at being late; the fine meant being late was all business, just another rational economic choice.

A better approach by the day-care center would have been to build on the sense of duty with "on-time" reminders in the form of posted signs and brochures. Incentives in the form of "parent of the month" recognition for the most on-time pickups might have created a friendly competition and improved performance without coercion and manipulation. Behavioral applications that involve information are not nudges; they are educational. These nonhidden incentives play to our best instincts, not our worst.

Behavioral psychology has a broad and beneficial role to play in economic science. Illuminating biases can help individuals make decisions in their best interests. The way to achieve this is education. When education slides into indoctrination through "nudges" contrived by condescending scholars who supposedly know better (but don't really), we are well down the path to despotism wrapped with a bow.

Investment Secret #3: Beware the hidden hand of behavioral manipulation. Watch out for nudges.

Investors need to improve their situational awareness of manipulation by choice architects. Only when you see through the social engineering behind the financial choices presented to you will you be able to counter the engineer's biases and act in your own best interests.

Before you can counter the biased manipulation of choice architects, you must understand your own biases. In general, people do not like to fill out forms or check boxes regardless of the content of the form or the question being asked. Choice architects use this bias to create a path of least resistance on applications that leads individuals to a result preferred by the choice architect and her corporate sponsor. Investors must mobilize patience as the antidote to the choice architect's assumption that you don't have any. As you read questions on forms, pause, take a minute, and ask yourself if there's a hidden agenda. Is a financial choice already made for you (with a separate opt-out box)? Ask yourself if that design is intentional, to get you to go along the plan sponsor's preferred path. Ask if the more difficult path (checking the opt-out box) is better for you by allowing more choices and degrees of freedom in the construction of a portfolio that preserves wealth. It's important to understand that the 401(k) and other similar provisions of the U.S. tax law were not benignly bestowed by Congress, but were heavily lobbied for by Wall Street as a way to boost assets under management and inflate stock prices. Before you sign up to Wall Street's wish list, think of your own.

Individuals also need to consider the biases of choice architects. These masters of manipulation are either following orders from corporations that hired them or are implementing their own view of how markets and economies function. A long series of market extremes beginning in 1987 (22 percent one-day market crash), including 1994 (Mexico), 1997 (Asia), 1998 (Russia and LTCM), 2000 (dot-coms), 2007 (mortgages), and 2008

(Lehman and AIG), give lie to the notion of rational, efficient markets. Efforts by choice architects to nudge people toward so-called rational choices are a trap for the uninformed. Rational markets don't exist.

There's nothing safe in investing. Stocks, bonds, currencies, and commodities all crash with some frequency. When markets crash, Wall Street still wins with wrap fees, commissions, and spreads. The losers are the clients. You can level the playing field by reducing your allocations to products promoted by the financial industry (and their choice architects) and increasing allocations to less traditional alternatives. Investments in income-producing real estate, natural resources, museum quality collectibles, and other asset classes not usually available in 401(k)s are an excellent way to preserve wealth, diversify risk, and escape the designs of hired-gun social engineers. If you take a buy-and-hold approach, tax deferral happens automatically, even without the much-touted tax shelter of the 401(k).

Another trap laid by the choice architects is an all-or-none view when it comes to 401(k) elections. The choice architects are so certain their preferences are the right ones for you they engineer sign-up forms to steer investors toward maximum participation. That's not necessarily the best choice. If a 401(k) plan has optional participation rates of 5 percent, 10 percent, and 15 percent of gross income (subject to a ceiling), you do not have to elect 15 percent. You could opt for a smaller amount (say, 10 percent), which leaves some discretionary income for investment outside the 401(k) bubble of Wall Street–sponsored funds. In a future crisis of the kind described in this book, these alternative investment paths disdained by choice architects may prove the best wealth preservation strategies.

CHAPTER FOUR
THE ALPHA TRAP

— — — — — — — — —

If we were all passive investors, there would be no mechanism to adequately value companies in the market based on their business, and therefore, it would be virtually impossible to trust the values for anything.

—Gerry Frigon, "What Would Happen If We
Were All Passive Investors?" *Forbes* (2018)

Alpha, Beta, ... Omega

Investors are told time and again, "You can't beat the market." This dissuasion is both a pillar of modern financial theory and the go-to marketing pitch for the index fund industry. Of course, the proposition is wrong; investors beat the market all the time. And those who beat the market aren't just lucky, as the professors would have it; they know exactly what they're doing.

There are two ways to beat the market other than sheer luck—inside information and market timing. This was shown by Harvard professor Robert C. Merton and a collaborator in two seminal papers published in 1981 by the University of Chicago. Merton shared the Nobel Prize in Economics in 1997 for his contributions to the Black-Scholes options pricing formula. It would have been more fitting if Merton had won the prize for his market timing papers. There are serious deficiencies in Black-Scholes, not least of which is the idea of a risk-free asset. In contrast, Merton's ideas on how to beat the market are nearly flawless and have stood the test of time.

The claim that investors can't beat the market is a colloquial form of the more formal efficient market hypothesis, or EMH, a theory most closely associated with economist Eugene Fama. This hypothesis, like most tenets of modern financial theory, is only loosely related to reality, yet holds a powerful sway over academic economists and their Wall Street brethren. EMH says that markets are highly efficient at incorporating new information into prices. If a company announces disappointing earnings, the market instantaneously marks down that company's stock price to reflect the new earnings outlook. If an energy company makes a large, unexpected discovery of oil and natural gas, the market immediately boosts the price of that company's shares. It's simply the case that a single investor can't benefit from the news in ways that beat other investors. For better or worse, all investors are in the market together and receive the same information at the same time. An investor can win or lose; she can't outperform.

Objections to EMH are too numerous to detail in depth here; an overview will suffice. If markets were efficient at incorporating new information as the thesis requires, there would be no flash crashes, panics, manias, or bubbles. Yet those events happen all the time. In 1987, the Dow Jones Industrial Average fell 22 percent in one trading day for no apparent reason. Liquidity crises occurred in 1994 (Mexico) and 1998 (emerging markets) based on fundamental trends that were on full display months before each crisis. Market participants ignored them. Bubbles occurred in 1999 (dot-com stocks), 2007 (subprime mortgages), and 2017 (bitcoin) based on greed and wishful thinking; there was nothing efficient about market pricing of those instruments. Behavioral psychologists have catalogued over 188 cognitive biases from the availability heuristic to the zero-sum effect, which induce irrational behavior relative to the robotic wealth-maximizing android required by EMH. Empirically, EMH lies in shreds even as academics and analysts continue to use it as a bedrock belief for forecasting.

Yet long before the rise of behavioral economics in the 1990s, and the run of crises from 1987 to 2017, Merton had blown a hole in the EMH edifice. His key was the use of inside information; knowing what the market does not. With insights provided by inside information, an investor could buy ahead of price spikes or sell ahead of drawdowns—an exercise in market timing—and easily outperform benchmarks. Inside information and market timing are two sides of the same coin. Used together these twin tools leave EMH in the dust.

The term "inside information" raises objections about legality and whether individual trading on inside information is not somehow cheating. The suggestion is that EMH is valid so long as rational actors don't break the law. The truth is that almost all inside information is perfectly legal. Inside information is defined as material nonpublic information. It's information important enough to affect prices, yet not known to the market as a whole. For inside information to be illegal, the information must be obtained in breach of some duty; it's a two-part test.

If you are on a corporate board of directors and are informed of a pending takeover of your firm, it's illegal to trade your company's stock based on that. As a director, you have a duty to keep the takeover information confidential. If you use that inside information to advantage in personal trading, it's as if you stole a valuable corporate asset, no different than stealing a company-owned car. Of course, such trading happens all the time. Still, it's illegal and some insiders go to jail. This trading meets the two-part test—purchase or sale of a security based on material nonpublic information obtained in breach of a duty.

Yet most material nonpublic information is *not* obtained wrongfully. The information is generated through research and belongs to the party who created the information. Hedge funds use private satellite companies to obtain images of store parking lots taken from space. By comparing those images over time, analysts can ascertain if store traffic is up or down (assuming there's little pedestrian traffic). If the hedge fund has information on average purchases by customer, average shoppers per car, and vendor margins, it's even possible to estimate a store's net income using the satellite photos in advance of any public announcement by the owner. Such information is material and nonpublic, but was not stolen or obtained in breach of a duty. The information was obtained through diligent research by the party who hired the satellite, and that party is free to trade on the information and usually does. It's perfectly legal.

The satellite story and many more like it are examples of investors using inside information. Buying the affected security just prior to an earnings announcement, when other public information has been fully incorporated into prices, is an example of market timing. Inside information and market timing used together can beat the market—one more example of how EMH fails; exactly what Merton pointed to in his 1981 academic papers.

EMH exists in so-called weak, semistrong, and strong forms. The weak form tests your ability to beat the market using historical prices and returns only. Few analysts confine themselves to so little information; research just outside these narrow bounds should produce superior returns. The semistrong form takes into account historical prices and returns plus all other public information. That sets a high bar for investors who try to outperform. The strong form includes all information, historical, public, and private, including the satellite imagery noted above. EMH proponents call it the strong form because outperformance is almost impossible. Yet no single investor could possibly have all the private information; that's what makes it private. It's like saying EMH does not work in real-world conditions, but works fine in conditions that don't exist. As a rule of thumb, whenever a grand theory is broken into subtheories (weak, semi-strong, and strong) that's a good indication something's amiss with the grand theory. It's safe to discard EMH as a guide to market behavior.

Just because it's possible to beat the market does not mean that most investors do so—they don't. There is ample research that demonstrates that not only do active portfolio managers not beat benchmarks, they do worse. This research is the calling card of the index fund industry. Why give your money to active managers, pay higher fees, and underperform popular benchmarks when you can invest in a low-fee index fund, earn the market return, and not sweat the details? Since stocks go up over long periods of time, your portfolio should perform well, especially if you begin to invest thirty years before your planned retirement. You can ride out the market drawdowns, capture big gains on the bouncebacks, and retire on that sailboat or vineyard you've always dreamed about.

Before deciding that index investing is superior, it's important to understand *why* the data shows passive investing outperforms active investing. If you don't know why, then your index fund idea is just a leap in the dark. The index fund industry will trot out EMH as an explanation, yet we've already seen that's nonsense. Markets are not at all efficient; the reason lies elsewhere.

Next, the passive-investing industry claims that their outperformance is due to lower fees and expenses. Index funds do have lower fees than active funds. If you're just going to allocate investor money across the components of a popular benchmark like the S&P 500 Index, you don't need armies of analysts making trips to the headquarters of issuing companies. All you need is a computer and an automated order entry system. Still, lower fees account for a relatively small portion of passive investing outperformance. Another factor must be at work.

Begin with definitions of two key terms: alpha and beta. Alpha is a measure of return over or under a given index. If your index is the S&P 500, and it returns 10 percent while your investment returns 15 percent, the alpha on that investment is +5. If your investment returns 5 percent, the alpha is -5. Positive alpha indicates the investment outperformed the index on a risk-adjusted basis; it produced excess returns.

Beta measures the volatility of an investment relative to an index. If an investment produces twice the return of an index, it has a beta of +2. If an investment return moves in the opposite direction of an index, beta is negative. An investment that falls twice as fast as the index rises has beta of -2.

Alpha and beta are used together to assess portfolio performance relative to the risk taken to produce that performance. A gambler playing roulette with your portfolio can easily double your money by betting on red; if the ball falls on red you win the bet. Of course, if the ball falls on black or green you lose all your money. Some players win at roulette, but most lose. Roulette has negative alpha; returns do not compensate for the risks.

A passive- or index-investment strategy seeks a beta of 1 (return matches the index performance) and an alpha of 0 (return is consistent with risk). The Holy Grail of investing is to have positive alpha and a beta of 1. That means you are taking market risk, yet getting an above-market return. Index managers who accomplish this attract more assets under management on which to charge management fees. Hedge fund managers with positive alpha charge performance fees that give them a piece of the action for superior performance.

One huge analytic problem with alpha and beta (and portfolio risk management in general) is the proper selection of benchmarks and the concept of the risk-free rate. If you have a large and highly diversified portfolio of U.S. stocks, then the S&P 500 may well be a suitable benchmark. If a portfolio is sector specific, say, in technology stocks or mining companies, using the S&P 500 will produce meaningless measures of alpha and beta. Likewise, the calculation of alpha requires the use of a risk-free rate of return so that the excess return attributable to manager skill is isolated. The yield on one-year Treasury bills is often used as the risk-free rate. Yet risk-free is a misnomer. Treasury bills' rates reflect inflation risk and a term premium for risk of default or nonpayment. Those risks are small, but growing. In theory, the true risk-free rate would be zero if a risk-free asset could be identified. Gold comes to mind.

This brings the analysis full circle. Active investing can outperform passive investing using inside information and market timing as described by Merton. Markets are not efficient and offer ample opportunities for risk-adjusted outperformance measured by alpha. Yet with the exception of a few legends like Bruce Kovner and Dave "Davos" Nolan, active managers do not outperform. The reason has nothing to do with EMH or fees, the two reasons often cited by the passive-investment industry to sell their wares. The two reasons for active-management underperformance are behavioral psychology and a statistical concept called skew.

A Bend in the River

Ironically, the same phenomenon that causes markets to be inefficient—behavioral bias—causes active managers to underperform benchmarks. Active managers are people too. In particular, active managers are subject to confirmation bias—the tendency to emphasize information that supports an investment thesis, and to discard information that contradicts it. A related bias is anchoring—the tendency to stay attached to an investment thesis that is primed in memory or experience, and to resist change. Anchoring creates inertia that makes it difficult for an active manager to detect changes in prevailing market dynamics or the macro policy environment, and to adapt an investment strategy accordingly.

There are myriad examples of highly intelligent active fund managers succumbing to behavioral biases, often due to a lack of cognitive diversity in decision making. Partners at Long-Term Capital Management, including two Nobel Prize winners and legendary fixed-income trader John Meriwether, tripled investor funds from 1994 to 1997, paid out most of the profits in a $3 billion all-cash distribution, then lost 92 percent of the re-

mainder in a few weeks in August and September 1998. The LTCM partners failed to detect a gathering global liquidity shortage and deleveraging
at competing firms. These failings were examples of anchoring in a previously successful investment process, and confirmation bias in discarding
evidence of market stress coming from Asia. The billionaire hedge-fund
manager Bill Ackman is another illustration. Ackman and his partners
produced above-average returns throughout the 1990s and early 2000s.
Then between 2013 and 2018, Ackman's firm, Pershing Square, lost over
$4 billion in one disastrous investment in Valeant Pharmaceuticals and
$1 billion more on a short position in nutrition company Herbalife. Ack-
man's fund lost 20.5 percent in 2015, 13.5 percent in 2016, and 4 percent
in 2017 as these losing bets were unwound. A host of cognitive biases, including those labeled postpurchase rationalization and selective perception, played a role. None of the geniuses at LTCM or Pershing Square
suddenly became dumb. Still, they did succumb to behavioral biases; indeed, the strength of their bias was amplified by prior success, a kind of
"I can do no wrong" bias.

Active managers who do produce alpha over long periods of time are
those who do a better job of neutralizing behavioral biases. In my decades
of experience in hedge funds, the best manager I ever encountered in
terms of taming behavioral bias was Bruce Kovner, the fabled founder of
Caxton Associates. Today, Kovner ranks 108 on the Forbes 400 list with a
net worth of over $5 billion, and 372 on a separate Forbes list of global bil-
lionaires. From 1983 through 2012, Kovner ran Caxton Associates. Caxton averaged 21 percent per year net returns during his time there. At its
peak, Caxton managed $14 billion, but Kovner had a practice of periodic
multibillion-dollar distributions to investors to reduce Caxton's size. This
was done to maximize returns on a finite set of winning trades. Hedge
funds charge management fees based solely on fund size, and performance
fees based on alpha. In numerous funds, this dual-fee structure sets up a
conflict of interest, where managers earn fortunes on a huge pool of assets

even with mediocre or losing performance. Kovner did not believe in size for its own sake.

I worked for Caxton in the early 2000s after my roller-coaster ride at LTCM in the late 1990s, and had many interactions with Kovner. Despite a congenial demeanor, he was ice cold when it came to risk management; he excluded cognitive bias from investment decision making better than anyone in the business. Interestingly, Kovner's academic background includes studies at the Juilliard School of Music; he's an accomplished harpsichordist. He finds a resonance in markets not rooted in the artificial mathematical constructs of the quants.

Kovner's method was old school; not difficult to understand but extremely difficult to practice, because cognitive bias pulls in the opposite direction. Trade ideas began with fundamental and technical research and development of a thesis on the likely performance of the trade. Diverse perspectives were pulled into the discussion to make sure no critical factors were missed. If the trade passed muster, the trader would execute, using futures markets whenever possible to gain leverage and conserve cash. The cash conserved is invested separately to improve alpha on the trade.

The key to Kovner's success was tight stop-loss limits, one of the oldest yet most effective risk-management tools. If your trade lost money, you had to close it out, take the loss, and move on to the next idea. Loss limits varied by market. They might be as little as 1 percent in currency markets or 3 percent in stock and bond markets. For Kovner, a loss was nature's way of telling you that you had missed something in your analysis. If the trade made money, you had a trailing stop, which meant the stop-loss limit moved with the market to make sure you did not give up all your profits if things went in reverse. For example, if you bought a stock at $40 per share, your initial stop loss might be $39 per share, down 2.5 percent. If the stock went to $50, the stop loss might be adjusted to $47, down 6 percent, but still a nice profit on the $40 purchase price. There were no preset limits on how much a trade could make, unless the opportunity cost of tying up cash was an issue. Yet exit strategies were always considered. This style of trading is summed up in the old Chicago rule, "Let your profits run and cut your losses short." Kovner didn't invent this system; stop-loss limits have been around as long as liquid tradable markets have existed. Others have used limits successfully, including the Commodities Corporation where Kovner got his start as a trader.

The challenge with this risk-management style was that it cuts against the grain of almost every known cognitive bias. Risk aversion tells a trader to sell a winning trade early for fear of losing her gains. Anchoring causes traders to stick with a losing trade based on belief in the original thesis, even after losses pile up. Confirmation bias causes traders to ignore incoming information that calls a thesis into question. A range of cognitive biases lumped under the heading of denial, including the ostrich effect, postpurchase rationalization, and selective perception, cause traders to ignore losses with the comment, "Don't worry, the market will come back."

Other biases cause traders to buy securities after price run-ups have already occurred. These come under the headings of availability heuristic and attention bias; the trader is attracted to a security because it receives ample attention in the media due to recent outperformance. This often leads to a poor entry point for the trader. Kovner was categorical on the topic of entry and exit points. He said a proper investment thesis was only half of what was required to make money. The other half was getting the entry point right. The combination of chasing momentum on the entry point and rationalizing losses on the downdrafts leads most investors to a buy-high, sell-low dynamic guaranteed to lose money.

Kovner had a simple solution for these and other behavioral quirks. You either followed his rules or you were fired. Kovner kept written trading authorizations in his own name on file with all of Caxton's brokers. A trader might have authority to buy and sell securities with the broker, but as soon as the rules were broken Kovner could override his traders and close out the trade directly with the broker. By the time the trader found out, he might already be on his way out the door.

Some traders lost money, followed the rules, and obeyed the stop-loss limits, yet remained convinced their trading thesis was a winner. These traders could appeal to Kovner for another chance to reenter the trade. Kovner insisted that the trader take a time-out, compose a written thesis on why the trade was a potential winner, and then meet personally with him to discuss the potential for reentry. In practice, a good night's sleep after exiting a losing trade was usually enough to convince the trader he should move on to a new idea.

Kovner and his ilk are rare exceptions. Most traders cannot overcome cognitive biases and do fall victim to the buy-high, sell-low trap of the momentum trader or the early-sale trap of the risk averse. Kovner beat the market for decades with skill, not luck. He is living proof it's possible. Still, most traders are not Bruce Kovner. On the whole, active investors do not outperform passive investors, hence the allure of indexing. Cognitive bias is part of the reason, yet an even bigger part is skew.

In this context, skew refers to the fact that a large percentage of total returns in broad-based stock indices are attributable to a small percentage of the stocks in the index. For passive managers who buy the index, skewness does not matter. They own the handful of big winners along with numerous small winners and losers and will exactly match the index return; that's the whole idea of indexing.

For active managers, skewness can be fatal. If you happen to pick the winners, good for you; you'll show outperformance. Still, active managers constructing portfolios based on subsets of the index components will miss big winners more often than not, because the winners are so few. The handful of big winners that drive index returns are like a needle in a haystack. If fifty active managers each grab a handful from the haystack, only one has the needle; the rest just have hay.

It's not impossible for all of the active managers to find the needle in the haystack; it's just extremely unlikely because the needle—the winning stock—often soars based on some unexpected news or exogenous shock that no amount of fundamental research will reveal. This harks back to Merton's emphasis on inside information.

A recent research paper succinctly describes the impact of skew:

> To illustrate the idea, consider an index of five securities, four of which . . . will return 10% over the relevant period and one of which will return 50%. Suppose that active managers choose portfolios of one or two securities and that they equally weight each investment. There are 15 possible one or two security "portfolios." Of these 15, 10 will earn returns of 10%, because they will include only the 10% securities. Just 5 of the 15 portfolios will include the 50% winner, earning 30% if part of a two-security portfolio and 50% if it is the single security in a one-security portfolio. The mean average return for all possible actively managed portfolios will be 18%, while the median portfolio of all possible one- and two-stock portfolios will earn 10%. The equally weighted index of all 5 securities will earn 18%. Thus, in this example, the average active-management return will be the same as the index . . . *but two-thirds of the actively managed portfolios will underperform the index because they will omit the 50% winner* (emphasis added).

There is no better illustration of the skewness effect than the FAANG stock mania of 2016 to 2018. FAANG is an acronym for Facebook, Apple, Amazon, Netflix, and Google. From January 1, 2016, to March 1, 2018, the FAANG stocks outperformed the S&P 500 by over 50 percent. The FAANG stocks accounted for more than 30 percent of the S&P 500's total gains over the same period. An active manager who owned 495 of the 500 stocks in the S&P 500, or a representative subset, but did not own the five FAANG stocks, would have underperformed a passive index manager using the S&P 500 benchmark by 30 percent.

The evidence is that active managers can beat the market, yet few do so because of behavioral bias and skewness. Those few active managers who can beat the market, such as Bruce Kovner, tend to have high fees or closed funds, or retire early to manage private portfolios as family offices. This leaves everyday investors with few options other than to join the crowd in index funds. Still and all, the zombielike march of investors into passive indexing has created an entirely new set of dangers that are little understood and will prove to be far more destructive to wealth than active-manager underperformance. In the move to indexing, one kind of risk has been traded for another, and the new risk—hypersynchronicity—is the most dangerous of all.

The Everything Bubble

The demise of active investing and rise of indexing have created a positive feedback loop that insures the next stock market crash will be the greatest ever. Professionals understand this, but don't care; they make good money in the meantime on commissions or wealth management wrap fees, and invest their own money in ways quite different from those they advise clients. I have yet to meet a hedge-fund billionaire, and I've met many, who does not have a large personal allocation to physical gold. They are ready for what's coming. Their clients are not.

The positive feedback loop dynamic is straightforward. Index managers are desperate to match their benchmark index and may lose their jobs, or at least assets under management, if they fail. At some point in a bull market, a small set of stocks or a particular sector may begin to outperform the index as a whole. The FAANG stocks are a good example, but not the only one. The Nifty Fifty stocks of the late 1960s, and the dot-com stocks of the late 1990s are other examples. The reasons for the initial outperformance are irrelevant for purposes of studying the dynamic. Reasons could be fundamental, based on growth prospects. They could be technical, based on chart patterns. More likely there is no discernable reason. That's typical of an emergent property in a complex dynamic system; events just happen.

Once the dynamic outperformance begins, investors have to buy more of those stocks in order to rebalance portfolios and keep up with the index. The added buying tends to drive up the price and leads to further outperformance. This leads to further buying and further price increases. The dynamic continues like a cat chasing its tail, with more buying, higher prices, more buying to keep up with the index, and higher prices still.

Eventually the positive feedback loop turns negative. This happened with the Nifty Fifty in the 1973–1974 stock market crash, a 45 percent decline measured on the Dow Jones Industrial Average, and with the dot-com crash in 2000–2002, a 78 percent decline measured on the NASDAQ Composite, both popular index benchmarks. It happened with the FAANG stocks in late 2018. A bull market feedback loop can operate for years before its phase transition to a bear market feedback loop. The changed direction in the feedback loop emerges suddenly, unexpectedly, and often for no evident reason, although there is never a shortage of just-so stories to ostensibly explain what occurred.

The emergence of an outperforming stock sector in recent years and the rise of asset valuations generally are products of former Fed chair Ben Bernanke's seven-year experiment with zero interest rates and quantitative easing, continued for a time by his successor, Janet Yellen, from 2008 to 2015. Bernanke relied on what he called the portfolio channel effect. The idea is that if the Fed holds short-term rates at zero, and depresses long-term interest rates by buying Treasury notes, investors are forced to look elsewhere for higher yields. In doing so, investors will bid up the prices of stocks, corporate bonds, real estate, emerging markets, and other assets. The resulting gains in asset prices will provide collateral for loans to corporations and boost consumer confidence as the gains show up in 401(k) statements. This newfound wealth and confidence would gin up spending and more lending. The combination of corporate borrowing, investment, and consumer spending would soon set the U.S. economy back on the path of self-sustaining trend growth.

Bernanke's experiment failed. Investment and consumption did not return to trend. Average growth in the U.S. economy in the nine years after the end of the recession in June 2009 was 2.2 percent, far below long-term trend growth, and the weakest recovery in U.S. history. The Fed's balance sheet was leveraged over 120:1 and stuffed with $4.5 trillion of bonds that left it ill-prepared to deal with a new recession, should one arrive.

Like various failed experiments, there were noxious by-products. Debt issuance by governments and corporations exploded on the back of low rates. Consumers took on $1.6 trillion of student loans. Skyrocketing default rates on student loans damaged credit ratings of graduates and parent cosigners, which impeded hiring and household formation and healthy consumption patterns that go with each. The most poisonous side effect was the inflation of asset values into what observers call the "everything bubble."

Evidence for an everything bubble is abundant. Robert Shiller, winner of the Nobel Prize in economics in 2013, made this observation in a 2015 interview:

> I define a bubble as a social epidemic that involves extravagant expectations for the future. Today, there is certainly a social and psychological phenomenon of people observing past price increases and thinking that they might keep going. So there is a bubble element to what we see. But I'm not sure that the current situation is a classic bubble. . . . In fact, the current environment may be driven more by fear than by a sense of a new era. . . . This time around, bonds and, increasingly, real estate also look overvalued. This is different from other overvaluation periods such as 1929, when the stock market was very overvalued, but the bond and housing markets for the most part weren't. It's an interesting phenomenon.

Shiller's surmise is that bubble dynamics are emerging not because of pie-in-the-sky hopes of stock investors, but for fear of missing out on gains that might be available on any risky asset class in a world of zero interest on safe assets. This fear is driven by a desperate attempt to rebuild lost savings destroyed in the 2008 global financial crisis. Bubble dynamics appear in stocks, bonds, real estate, auto loans, student loans, emerging markets, cryptocurrencies, and beyond. This result would come as no surprise to an Austrian School economist. The everything bubble is classic malinvestment—the misallocation of savings—that accompanies easy money.

Between 2010 and 2016, the S&P Case-Shiller Home Price Index for San Francisco rose 68 percent, from 139 to 234. The comparable index for Sydney showed a 69 percent increase, from 98.9 to 167.6. The Canada Real Residential Housing Price Index was comparably bubbly, rising from 100.0 in January 2010 to 143.1 in September 2017, a gain of over 43 percent. Similar gains were seen in housing markets all over the world, from Melbourne to Miami and from London to Los Angeles. Some of this was indigenous demand from Silicon Valley billionaires, but diverse gains were driven by flight capital as Russian oligarchs, Chinese princelings, and Venezuelan elites fled unstable and capricious jurisdictions for safer climes.

The stock market had its frothy fables as well. As of August 2017, Tesla had a market capitalization of over $750,000 per vehicle sold, compared to $16,000 for Toyota and $5,500 for General Motors. The auto sector as a whole was kept afloat on a sea of loans. Between 2010 and 2017, U.S. auto loans outstanding surged from $650 billion to $1.1 trillion, of which $280 billion were rated subprime. In the same period, delinquent auto loans increased by $23 billion. Corporate credit was in no better condition than consumer credit. As of August 2017, U.S. corporate debt outstanding stood at $5.9 trillion, a 54 percent increase from 2010. American dollar-denominated debt issued by emerging-markets companies exceeded $9 trillion by 2017, according to the Bank for International Settlements, or BIS.

These equity and credit bubbles were visible from bank and corporate balance sheets. Behind those was a wall of invisible liabilities in the form of derivatives. The five largest U.S. banks held $157 trillion of derivatives measured by gross notional value at the end of 2017, a 12 percent increase from the comparable amount of derivatives immediately before the 2008 global financial crisis. That increase may seem modest, yet it is contrary to repeated claims by regulators that the financial system is safer and less leveraged; it's not. Even the 12 percent increase in derivatives exposure since the last crisis is not a complete picture. That figure includes only what banks hold in off-balance-sheet positions. Trillions of dollars of derivatives have been moved out of banks to third-party clearinghouses. These clearinghouses are intended to be another safety valve, because they allow simultaneous netting of multiple derivatives exposures from multiple banks instead of the simple bilateral netting that occurs when banks resort to self-help against failing counterparts in a crisis. That's helpful when one bank is failing and remaining solvent banks want to liquidate positions quickly. Yet when multiple banks are in danger of failure, as was the case in 1998 and 2008, a clearinghouse is more like a game of musical chairs with no chairs. Like dominoes in a row, as each bank fails the liquidity burden falls on fewer strong hands, until those banks fail also. In that case, the clearinghouse itself is in jeopardy and no longer able to fulfill its functions. Member banks do not record this contingent liability for clearinghouse risk on their balance sheets. Clearinghouses do not eliminate risk, they merely move risk around in ways that make it more difficult to discern. Where derivatives are concerned, the financial system is not smaller, not safer, and not more sound.

While these bubbles grew, a surge in passive investing acted like a force multiplier to malinvestment. Markets have reached the point where indexing itself is a bubble that feeds these individual asset bubbles.

Wall Street never saw a bubble it didn't like if there was money to be made by inflating it. The index bubble is no exception. Index fund sponsors and passive managers began to crank out easy-to-trade bespoke products that required no active stock selection by investors. The most popular of these were exchange-traded funds, or ETFs, and their close cousins, exchange-traded notes, ETNs. The ETFs and ETNs are technically securities, are registered with the SEC, and trade as listed products on the New York Stock Exchange, NASDAQ, and other exchanges. Each ETF and ETN trades like a single share of stock, producing a simple buy or sell decision for an investor, yet is constructed to have an underlying basket of stocks or notes. For example, an emerging-markets ETF might include equities from companies in Turkey, Brazil, Indonesia, Malaysia, and other developing economies. A retail ETF might include equities from companies in brick-and-mortar store sales such as Walmart, Home Depot, Starbucks, and other similar firms. The possibilities don't stop with the variety of investment sectors. ETFs can be leveraged so that an investor receives three times the return (or three times the losses) of the underlying basket. For example, a two-times health-care ETF returns twice the gains of an underlying basket of health-care-related stocks such as UnitedHealth Group, Medtronic, and Aetna. The assets under management in the leveraged equity ETF sector have grown from $5 billion in late 2007, when the product was invented, to over $30 billion by early 2018. Finally, ETF returns can be inverse to the underlying stocks, so if the selected group goes up, the ETF goes down. Such ETFs leave the purchaser in the position of a put option seller without standard safeguards. To sell put options in a brokerage account requires special account forms, added due diligence by the broker, risk disclosures, and stringent margin requirements. None of that is required with inverse ETFs; you just buy them and take your chances. Leaving no stone unturned, Wall Street naturally offers inverse-leveraged ETFs.

The real danger in ETFs, especially those structured with leveraged and inverse performance, is relative illiquidity. When an investor sells a share of an individual stock such as IBM, they are selling into a relatively deep pool of potential IBM buyers. When investors sell a technology-oriented ETF that may happen to include IBM along with other less-liquid technology stocks, the pool of buyers for that ETF may be quite small, especially in a steep market drawdown, let alone a panic. The ETF could fall faster than some of its components, placing selling pressure on all of the components, as authorized dealers buy the ETF and short the underlying stocks as an arbitrage. Any ban on short selling, as happened in 2008, eliminates the arbitrage and leaves the ETF in free fall. These positive feedback loops ("positive" in the sense of self-reinforcing, not in the sense of desirable) are possible to model theoretically as hypersynchronous events, yet cannot easily be predicted as real-world events. The feedback loops are unforeseen emergent properties of complex dynamic systems; what some call black swans, and they are everywhere.

ETFs and ETNs are not the most exotic creatures in the passive-investing menagerie. Another more vicious creature goes by the name risk parity. A risk parity strategy is an asset allocation plan that aims to maximize returns for a given level of volatility. These asset allocations are supposedly an improvement on simpler asset allocation plans such as 60/40, a mixture of 60 percent equities and 40 percent bonds. In the case of individual 401(k) plans, the traditional 60/40 allocation was typically adjusted to increase bond exposure and reduce equity exposure as an individual grew older, in order to account for risk aversion; bonds have lower volatility and older investors have less time to recoup losses, so reducing portfolio risk made sense.

With risk parity, portfolio composition is optimized by risk-adjusted returns rather than fixed percentages of stocks and bonds. Risk parity strategies allocate investor funds among stocks, bonds, commodities, and other asset classes based on the risk weight in each asset class, rather than dollar weightings such as 60/40. Since stocks are far riskier than bonds, a risk-parity portfolio might begin with a smaller allocation to stocks than a traditional portfolio. In a simple case, the dollar weighting of stocks in a risk-parity portfolio might be 33 percent rather than 60 percent, because 33 percent in stocks represents close to 60 percent of the total risk in the portfolio.

When risk parity strategy was introduced by hedge fund giant Bridgewater Associates in 1996, it performed exceptionally well. In the panic of 2008, risk parity strategies outperformed other strategies because they had proportionally smaller stock allocations and therefore had smaller losses, since 2008 losses were heavily concentrated in stocks.

Still, there are fatal flaws in risk parity that have now come to the fore. The first flaw is that metrics used to optimize allocations in a risk parity portfolio implicitly rely on the efficient market hypothesis, which as we have seen is junk science. Portfolios that are based on EMH perform as expected most of the time because the overlap in the degree distribution of risk between the bell curve (used in EMH) and the power curve (used in complex dynamic systems) is large. This fools the observer into believing EMH is a good representation of reality. When events occur outside the bell curve distribution (but consistent with a power curve distribution), the results are catastrophic to portfolios modeled on EMH, including risk parity.

The other flaw is the positive feedback loop between volatility and asset allocation. If equities enter a period of low volatility, as they did in 2017, computers and robo-advisers detect that equities are less risky and therefore deserve a larger dollar allocation under risk parity. The larger dollar allocation results in more buying, higher equity prices, and lower observed volatility, as equity prices seem never to fall. This feedback loop among lower volatility, higher equity allocations, and higher equity prices has been amplified by a simple buy-the-dips strategy, in which every small equity drawdown is immediately met with a surge of buying, on the theory that low volatility and ever higher equity prices are a semipermanent state space supported by central bank interventions.

Risk parity strategies also rely on a presumed inverse correlation between movements in equity and bond prices. In a simple model, a slowing economy produces lower equity prices and lower interest rates, which means higher bond prices. The gains on bonds offset the losses on stocks and helps reduce the overall volatility of the portfolio. This inverse relationship contributed to the success of risk parity strategies in 2008, as plunging stock prices also mean plunging interest rates and huge gains in bonds.

Yet from February 2–8, 2018, markets were shocked when stocks and bonds became highly positively correlated, with stocks falling 11 percent in one week and bonds falling in tandem on fears of inflation and higher interest rates. With higher U.S. deficits producing debt death-spiral fears and higher rates, this correlation between lower stock prices and lower bond prices persists along with higher volatility overall. The falsity of the assumptions behind risk parity are being exposed. Now there is nowhere for investors to hide.

Another vogue in this passive-investing procession is smart beta. This strategy involves indexing, yet the index is rule based rather than an off-the-shelf index such as the S&P 500. Wall Street loves smart beta because the strategy is so ill-defined almost any confection that links loosely to a market factor rule passes muster. Smart beta indices can be based on book values, cash flows, or more exotic factors, including demographic trends and natural resources. This gives banks and brokers unlimited leeway to concoct new products.

Smart beta is similar to risk parity in the sense that rules used to construct an index pay more attention to volatility than traditional factors such as market capitalization. This means smart beta suffers from the same flaws as risk parity, specifically a fatal fixed point attractor or map sink in which higher allocations produce lower volatility, which produces higher allocations, and still lower volatility, and so on until the system can no longer evolve and nears collapse.

The mother of all passive strategies is VaR, or value at risk. VaR was originally a risk-management strategy developed in 1989 by JPMorgan as a proprietary tool, then later spun off as a separate company called Risk-Metrics. The VaR tool was made freely available to the marketplace and was widely adopted.

In its simplest form (there are sophisticated variations), VaR looks at historic time series of prices of each security or position in a portfolio. It then computes the covariance of components, or the extent to which two positions tend to move together, in opposite directions, or exhibit no correlation at all. This identifies positions in a portfolio that might constitute natural hedges producing lower risk than either position taken in isolation. Finally, the aggregate portfolio risk based on historic prices and covariance is calculated in terms of standard deviation, or the likelihood that certain extreme loss events might occur. This entire process is usually summed up in expressions such as, "Our $1 billion portfolio has a less than 1% chance of losing more than $100 million in any three-month period."

Like the other passive strategies, VaR is haunted by the specter of scientism. The historical time series of prices used to compute risk are typically too short. Quants use 20, 30, or 50 year time series, when they should look at 100 or 500 year time series (using proxy prices as needed) to get a better grasp of the possible. Even if a given time series were adequate, the assumption of a normal distribution (bell curve) of risk behind the concept of a standard deviation is contrary to empirical evidence from markets. The fact that VaR is a grossly deficient methodology is doubly disconcerting, since VaR-like methods underlie other indexing strategies such as risk parity.

These passive-indexing strategies—ETFs, ETNs, risk parity, buy-the-dips, smart beta, VaR, and more—are made more dangerous by the rise of robo-advisers and machine trading. Since these strategies are data driven, it makes sense that computers can be used to aggregate the data on historic prices and do the processing on covariance, risk weightings, and standard deviations. Yet the machines have now gone beyond data aggregation and processing into the realms of machine learning and artificial intelligence. Machine learning involves the ability of machines to make predictions based on hidden correlations that are difficult for humans to discern, or new correlations machines discover on their own after working with training data. Artificial intelligence refers to actionable recommendations made by a machine, which can either be relayed to a human for action or executed by the machine itself.

Machine trading, now widely embraced by wealth managers, hedge funds, and banks, removes the last shred of human intuition or reserve from the investment process. Investment managers and traders who rely on passive-indexing strategies will seek to squeeze alpha from the index by being the first to adjust their quantitative allocations based on changed risk measures or factor weights. Active managers are even more eager than others to execute ahead of the crowd since their returns live or die based on inside information, market timing, and diminution of the market impact of their moves. Artificial intelligence pleases both camps, with speed and stealth. The portfolio is on autopilot. The fact that the plane is flying through a thick fog of false assumptions about historic prices and degree distributions seems not to perturb passengers in the least.

No Bid

On Monday, October 19, 1987, I sat at my desk in a small office overlooking Greenwich Harbor in Connecticut. I was chief credit officer of one of the world's largest dealers in U.S. government securities. That day, I witnessed the greatest crash of U.S. stocks in one trading session in history. The Dow Jones Industrial Average fell 22.6 percent, 508 points at the time, equivalent to 5,600 Dow points from today's levels. In percentage terms, the 1987 crash was almost double the October 28, 1929, crash that is generally cited as the start of the Great Depression.

Yet the October 1987 crash did not presage a depression, it did not even signal a recession; the long expansion that started in November 1982 continued for almost three more years, until the next recession began in July 1990. The 1987 crash told us nothing about economic fundamentals. Yet it told us volumes about the operation of complex system dynamics in capital markets. It was a warning that the new age of the flash crash was upon us. That warning was little understood at the time and has since been consistently ignored.

There was no shortage of after-the-fact explanations for why stocks crashed. By 1987, economic growth had slowed from the torrid pace of 1983–1986. A weakening U.S. dollar threatened U.S. growth despite Treasury secretary James Baker's efforts to halt the dollar's slide through the Louvre Accord, signed on February 22, 1987. The Treasury bond market crashed in the spring of 1987, six months before the stock market crash. Oil prices dropped 50 percent in the first half of 1986, as OPEC discipline evaporated. The "tanker war" in the Persian Gulf, which began with the sinking of the U.S. frigate *Stark* by an Iraqi missile in May 1987, had escalated in the days immediately before the stock market crash. Iranian missiles hit two U.S.-flagged oil tankers on October 15 and 16. On October 19, the day of the crash, the United States attacked Iranian oil wells in the Gulf as retaliation for the tanker attacks.

Economic historians can reenact *Murder on the Orient Express* by profiling the sundry suspects—a falling dollar, sinking bonds, collapsing oil prices, slowing growth, a hot war in the Middle East—and accusing one as the market murderer. There is no definitive answer, and in a way it doesn't matter. The market was already primed to fall the same way a snowpack is set to become an avalanche. One catalyst, one snowflake, does as well as another. What matters is what comes after the catalyst, a chaotic cascade in desperate search of a bottom.

Once the stock selling began in New York that Monday, an early species of passive trading called portfolio insurance was set in motion. In its fundamental form, portfolio insurance required institutional investors to sell stock index futures as stock markets declined. The short futures positions insure against declines in the stock portfolio itself. The more stocks declined, the more futures are sold to protect the portfolio, an early example of risk parity.

This analytically arrested approach suffered from what Keynes called a fallacy of composition. What may work in a single case does not work in the aggregate; the whole is different from the sum of its parts. As portfolio managers sold stock index futures, other market participants on the Chicago futures exchanges had to buy them. This gave Chicago futures brokers and locals a long index position, which they hedged by selling stocks! The risk of a declining stock market had not been hedged at all in the aggregate; it had merely been recycled from New York to Chicago and back again. This feedback loop was amplified by the fact that Chicago stock index futures were under such pressure that they traded below their equivalent value in New York Stock Exchange stocks. This triggered arbitrage activity consisting of buying "cheap" futures and selling "expensive" stocks to capture the spread. The arbitrage selling added to the already fierce downward price pressure on stocks. The only force that stopped the bloodbath was the clang of the closing bell.

The October 19, 1987, flash crash in stocks displayed the dynamics of every flash crash since and, ominously, those to come. The term "flash crash" is common parlance today, but is a relatively new phenomena. Of course, markets have crashed periodically as long as markets have existed. The United States experienced notable market crashes, usually yet not always accompanied by recessions or depressions, in 1825, 1837, 1873, 1893, and 1907, among others. Older examples from Europe include the bursting of Netherlands's Tulip Mania Bubble in 1637, France's Mississippi Bubble in 1720, and the U.K.'s South Sea Bubble, also in 1720.

All of these crashes followed similar and predictable patterns. The status of a particular asset such as land, railroads, royal favor, bitcoin, and bizarrely, tulip bulbs, is singled out for attention. Promoters point to unique properties of the privileged asset. The media bring scrutiny to the sudden price increases. Leverage is applied to amplify gains. Suddenly small investors are sucked into the whirlwind as the prospect of money for nothing is impossible to resist. Then the price peaks, the spell is broken, reality intrudes, and a crash begins with frantic selling by those hoping to capture gains with no bidders in sight. Most investors are ruined, yet some walk away with fantastic gains if they sold before the top. Depending on how much leverage was used and the health of lenders, crashes may or may not spread to the real economy and cause a downturn due to contagion.

Boom-and-bust patterns still occur today—bitcoin comes to mind—but a contemporary flash crash is different in at least one respect. A flash crash may include traditional elements like euphoria and leverage; fear and greed never go out of style. Yet these elements are not required. Flash crashes emerge literally from nowhere with no clear catalyst. The main difference between today's flash crashes and past market crashes is automation. The ubiquity of automated trading, the similarity of algorithms across platforms, and the speed of execution mean that markets crash instantaneously, without waiting for ripples to spread from trader to trader. Computers never sleep in, take a vacation, or drop the kids at school like human traders. There is no latency.

The infamous flash crash in 10-year Treasury note yields on October 15, 2014, is a case in point. Yields plunged beginning at 9:33 A.M. that day, and just as quickly rallied back at 9:39 A.M., covering a 37-basis-point range in twelve minutes. Volatility of greater magnitude had occurred only three times from 1998 to 2014, and in each instance it was the result of a surprise policy announcement. There was no surprise on October 15, 2014. An extensive review of that flash crash conducted by the Treasury, Fed, and other financial regulators, published on July 13, 2015, nine months after the crash, found no reason for it. In fact, there *was* no reason for it except that certain algorithms began buying Treasury notes, which triggered more buying by other algorithms until the price surge and yield crash spun out of control in a hypersynchronous event. Eventually computer buying triggered computer selling in the form of limit orders deep in the back of the book, at which point the buying momentum turned on a dime. Matt Levine, a writer for Bloomberg, offers a good summary:

> There is an obvious dumbness to this: The algorithms stopped their orgy of buying not because they got some new economic data,

or because a new buyer spotted value and jumped into the market, but just because they saw their shadow and got spooked. . . . We—and the regulators—don't know what set the algorithms off on their buying spree, but a reasonable guess would be that, whatever it was, it was dumb. . . .

But what I like about the Treasury flash crash is just how convincingly the algorithms mimicked human folly. For six minutes one morning in October, some computers built themselves a bubble. They bid up the prices of assets for no particular reason, just because all their algorithm friends were doing it too, and what algorithm would want to sell when everyone else was buying? And then they saw some big sell orders that spooked them and made them realize that they were at the top. So for the next six minutes they busily popped their bubble, selling down to more or less where they started. They did most of the work themselves: *Algorithms bought from algorithms on the way up, and sold to algorithms on the way down* (emphasis added).

This particular flash crash came and went without contagion or collateral market damage. That pattern is not preordained. A different program could have canceled sell orders from the back of the book before the buying spree reached that level, leaving prices to rise and yields to crash with no cushion until serious damage was done to dealers or banks.

Other notable flash crashes in recent years include the U.S. stock market crash on May 6, 2010, a 9 percent plunge that wiped out over $1 trillion of wealth in just over thirty minutes. The market quickly recovered most of that loss. On January 15, 2015, the euro crashed 20 percent against the Swiss franc in thirty minutes. On June 24, 2016, pounds sterling plunged 12 percent against the U.S. dollar over the course of a few hours. The 2010 stock market collapse had no clear catalyst. The 2015 euro crash was due to the Swiss National Bank breaking a currency peg unexpectedly. The 2016 sterling crash was due to the surprise U.K. vote to leave the EU, the so-called Brexit. With or without an identifiable catalyst, the fact remains that these crashes and others were made violent in their speed and amplitude by automated trading.

As a result of these diverse developments, markets now confront a lethal brew of passivity, product proliferation, automation, and hypersynchronous behavioral responses. This accumulation of risk factors is entirely new, and outside the experience of any trader or quant.

By late 2017, $11.9 trillion of stocks were held by entities that passively track an index, such as ETFs, index funds, or institutional index managers. Another $17.4 trillion of stocks were held by active managers, such as hedge funds and mutual funds. Total passive ownership in U.S. equity funds in 2017 was estimated to be 37 percent, nearly double the 19 percent share for passive ownership in 2009. This growth in passive strategies showed no signs of abating. ETFs attracted over $215 billion in new assets during 2017, while active strategies suffered over $125 billion in redemptions.

Passive-investment strategies are best understood as parasites on the bodies of active allocators. The active manager expends substantial time and effort either to identify fundamental value in the manner of Warren Buffett or to create inside information in the sense that Merton used the term. Active investors commit capital and catalyze price discovery by placing bids and offers with no certainty their endeavors will hit or miss.

The best active managers can earn rich returns, yet most fail for reasons we have seen. Passive investors hitch a free ride on the active-investing community. They avoid cognitive bias and adverse skew, while capturing gains created by the insights of the best active investors, including Bruce Kovner. Passive investors contribute nothing to price discovery, yet reap rewards by going along for the ride. Passive parasites may indeed thrive— until they kill the host.

Passive investing rests on another fallacy of composition, although the composition in this case exceeds $1 quadrillion dollars, the sum total of all stocks, bonds, currencies, and derivatives in the world. What works in the individual case does not work in the aggregate. Passive investing began as a hitchhiker on an 18-wheeler, barely noticeable. Today it is more like a clown car of occupants that threaten to overwhelm the vehicle in which they ride.

The risk is that passive investors rely on active investors to buy when passives want to sell. As the scale of passive investing grows, the pool of potential active buyers dries up. The active buyers see this dynamic while passive sellers are blinded by algorithms. Eventually this leads to a market where everyone is a seller and no one is a buyer. The market goes no-bid, which in trading means no bottom in price.

Passive investing and algorithmic trading are not alone in fostering this unstable state of affairs. The Federal Reserve is also to blame for engendering an illusion of safety in the form of the pernicious Fed Put. The Fed Put is jargon for the market's belief that the Federal Reserve will act decisively to truncate disorderly stock market declines. A succession of these puts have been named after the Fed chairs who offered them.

The Greenspan Put, named after Alan Greenspan, was exhibited in September and October 1998 when Greenspan cut interest rates twice in three weeks, including an unscheduled emergency cut, to control the damage from the collapse of hedge fund Long-Term Capital Management.

The Bernanke Put, named after Ben Bernanke, was exhibited on numerous occasions, notably the launch of QE2 in November 2010, after QE1 failed to stimulate the economy, and the September 2013 delay of a taper in the Fed's long-term asset purchases in reaction to an emerging-markets meltdown resulting from mere "taper talk" in May 2013.

The Yellen Put, named after Janet Yellen, was frequently on display. Yellen delayed the first Fed rate hike in nine years from September 2015 to December 2015 to calm markets after a Chinese shock currency devaluation and consequent U.S. market meltdown in August 2015. The Yellen Put was used again starting in March 2016, when the Fed delayed expected rate hikes until December 2016 in reaction to another Chinese currency devaluation and a U.S. market meltdown in January 2016.

In short, there is a long history of the Fed cutting rates, printing money, delaying rate hikes, or using forward guidance to calm nervous markets in order to pump up asset prices in response to disorderly market declines. The new chair, Jerome Powell, installed in February 2018, has given no reason to doubt that a Powell Put will be deployed as needed in accordance with past practice.

The most extreme example of the Fed Put was the 2008 global financial crisis, when Ben Bernanke and other regulators guaranteed every money market fund in America, guaranteed every bank deposit in America regardless of FDIC insurance limits, pushed interest rates to zero, printed money, acquired bad assets, and engineered over $10 trillion of hidden currency swaps with the European Central Bank (ECB) and other central banks. These Fed actions were an extreme example of the "whatever it takes" philosophy of modern central bankers. The idea of free markets finding a level at which markets clear and rotten banks fail is passé.

In ways that Fed governors and staff cannot comprehend, the Fed Put has bled into passive investing and algorithmic trading by training market participants to buy every dip. In effect, savvy investors front-run the Fed by buying on weakness before the put is activated. This results in the smoothing of volatility and an asymmetry of returns, where markets persistently rise and seldom fall. Diminution in volatility causes risk parity strategies to overallocate to formerly risky asset classes. Index strategies blithely tag along. Active managers throw in the towel and become closet indexers. At that point the market is primed for catastrophic collapse.

This brings the analysis full circle. If alpha strategies are likely to fail for all but a few, and beta strategies are fated to follow indices to near extinction, are there investment processes that produce superior returns in most markets yet preserve wealth in market crack-ups? Such processes are possible, but only by utilizing science that accords well with how markets function.

These new alpha models begin with complexity theory, a branch of physics that perfectly describes the dynamics of capital markets. Complexity theory includes concepts such as emergent properties (black swans), phase transitions (the switch from fear to greed), scaling metrics (how large systems produce diminishing marginal returns before collapsing), network effects (contagion), and hypersynchronicity (herd behavior).

The next input in an alpha model that works is behavioral psychology. This is simply a matter of identifying cognitive biases so they can be factored out of AI-based trading systems.

An effective alpha model would use Bayesian updating to test an initial investment hypothesis to increase or decrease the probability of an expected outcome, based on the likelihood that posterior events would or would not occur if the anterior guess were correct. Bayes' rule uses a rigorous statistical method that acknowledges the inexactness of real-world behavior relative to expected outcomes. Bayes' rule teaches that it is better to be approximately right than exactly wrong.

The final element in an effective alpha model is history. This input is not seriously considered by the quants and developers who rule Wall Street modeling because historical narrative is subjective and nonquantitative. That's their loss. Anyone who studied how President Grant broke the gold corner in 1869 would have foreseen the collapse of the Hunt Brothers' silver corner in 1980. Anyone who studied how J. P. Morgan saved the banking system in 1907 would have known how to manage a soft landing for LTCM in 1998. There really is nothing new under the sun.

These elements—complexity, psychology, Bayes' rule, and history—can be combined in neural networks as nodes populated with market data and plain text read with meaning by machines like IBM's Watson using advanced cognitive linguistic techniques. The nodes are linked with weighted recursive functions to produce actionable third-wave AI predictive analytics.

Wall Street and central banks are a long way from adopting these twenty-first century risk-management techniques. In the meantime, the passive index-investing bubble grows. The alpha trap is baited. The odds are close to nil that capital markets will embrace efficacious models before the next financial failure.

Investment Secret #4: Seek diversification away from exchange-traded markets by allocating to cash, gold, and alternatives.

The best strategies for investors in the face of these embedded structural risks are:

Avoid less-liquid ETFs and those with exotic features such as inverse performance or leverage. These products will not find ready buyers in a market crash.

Maintain a 30 percent cash allocation at all times. This reduces the overall volatility of your portfolio and gives you "dry powder" to shop for bargains in the aftermath of a crash.

Maintain a 10 percent physical gold allocation. This performs well in inflation and provides insurance in the event that a futures-market meltdown results in account freezes or exchange closures.

Allocate 10 percent of investible assets to private equity and venture capital by investing in firms where you personally know the founders and operators. These firms will not offer liquidity, yet they may offer huge upside and low correlation to traded markets. Worthwhile sectors to explore are financial technology and natural resources.

CHAPTER FIVE

FREE MONEY

— — — — — — — —

The poor you will always have with you, and whenever you wish
you can do good to them.

—Jesus Christ, Mark 14:7

The Trouble with Debt

In his 1925 poem, "The Hollow Men," T. S. Eliot wrote, "This is the way the
world ends / Not with a bang but a whimper." These lines, which end the
poem, are the most quoted not just in Eliot, but all of twentieth century
English poetry. "The Hollow Men" was Eliot's response both to the horrors
of the First World War and the burdens of the Treaty of Versailles, which
imposed humiliations on Germany and presaged new conflicts. Taken at
first glance, the lines contrast customary notions of the end of the world
as a violent apocalypse on the one hand with a gradual dimming and darkness on the other. The darkness vision, also expounded by the late physicist Stephen Hawking, says processes simply end without much ado.

Yet the "bang" ending was also noted. In a *Saturday Review* interview in 1958, Eliot said he was not really sure how the world will end. He pointed to the paradox of one whose home was bombed. From an external perspective, there was certainly an explosion, but the victim herself never heard it; darkness and death came before the sound reached her ears.

Poetic ambiguity aside, these lines have provided ample ammunition for analysts and writers to create their own metaphors in the past century. Eliot himself borrowed from Joseph Conrad's *Heart of Darkness* in his opening epigraph, "Mistah Kurtz—he dead," a reference to Conrad's Kurtz. Filmmaker Francis Ford Coppola extended the reference in his epic film *Apocalypse Now*, which featured Marlon Brando as Kurtz reading lines from Eliot in the film's final scenes.

Now, it's the economists' turn to extend Eliot's meaning. America, and the world, are inching closer to what Carmen Reinhart and Ken Rogoff refer to as the "bang" point, the unquantifiable yet real point where an ever-increasing debt burden triggers creditor revulsion, forcing a debtor nation into austerity, outright default, or sky-high interest rates. The bang point is when, to paraphrase Eliot, the debtor's world ends not with a whimper, but a bang.

The bang point is described by others using different names, including fiscal limit, but the phenomena is the same. A country begins with a manageable debt-to-GDP ratio commonly defined as less than 60 percent. In a search for economic growth, perhaps to emerge from a recession or simply to buy votes, policymakers start down a path of increased borrowing and deficit spending. Initially, results can be positive. Some Keynesian multiplier may apply, especially if the economy has underutilized industrial and labor-force capacity and assuming the borrowed money is used wisely, in ways that have positive payoffs.

Over time, the debt-to-GDP ratio pushes into a range of 70 to 80 percent. Political constituencies develop around increased spending. The spending itself becomes less productive; more is spent on current consumption in the form of entitlements, benefits, and less productive investments in amenities, community organizations, and public-employee unions. The law of diminishing marginal returns starts to bind. The Keynesian multiplier shrinks to less than zero.

By now, the public's appetite for deficit spending and public goods is insatiable. Politicians lack the will and foresight to reduce spending, balance budgets, and restore a sustainable debt-to-equity ratio. The public is indifferent and fails to appreciate the dynamic now under way. The debt-to-GDP ratio eventually pushes past 90 percent.

Next comes the endgame. Reinhart and Rogoff's research reveals that a 90 percent debt-to-GDP ratio is not just more of the same, but what physicists call a critical threshold at which a phase transition commences. The debt-creation process and effect of more debt is transformed the way water turns to gas when heat is applied. The first effect is that the Keynesian multiplier, already at zero, turns negative. No growth is created by added debt, while interest on the debt increases the debt-to-GDP ratio on its own. Creditors grow anxious while continuing to buy more debt in a vain hope that policymakers reverse course or growth spontaneously emerges to lower the ratio. This doesn't happen. Society is addicted to debt and the addiction consumes the addict.

The United States is a particularly difficult case to discern under Eliot's bang and whimper dichotomy. The United States is the best credit in the world; for that reason alone, it can pursue a nonsustainable debt dynamic longer than other nations. The United States also borrows in a currency it prints. This sets the United States apart from countries like Argentina, which print pesos but borrow in dollars. In that case, a default is easier to forecast, because the decline in hard currency reserves is observable; the local printing press plays no role. The only major economy like the United States in these respects is Japan, which is also highly creditworthy and borrows in a currency it prints—the yen. The Japanese debt-to-equity ratio at year end 2017 was 253 percent, more than double the U.S. ratio. If Japan is the canary in the coal mine of developed economy insolvency, this suggests the United States is far from a bang point.

Those considering endgame scenarios agree the bang point may not be imminent. This does not mean all is well. The salience of the Reinhart-Rogoff research is not the bang point but the whimper of structural head-winds to growth. Of particular importance to the United States and Japan is their paper "Debt and Growth Revisited" (2010). This study focused on developed economies, in contrast to their other work, which included both developed and developing economies. Their main conclusion is that for debt-to-GDP ratios above 90 percent, "median growth rates fall by 1%, and average growth falls considerably more." Importantly, Reinhart and Rogoff emphasize "the importance of nonlinearities in the debt-growth link." For debt-to-equity ratios below 90 percent, "there is no systematic relationship between debt and growth." Put differently, the relationship between debt and growth is not strong at lower ratios; other factors in-cluding tax, monetary, and trade policies all guide growth. Once the 90 percent threshold is crossed, debt is the dominant factor. Reinhart and Rogoff are not complexity theorists, yet the emergent nonlinear property they identified through empirical and historical studies is immediately recognizable to a student of complexity. Above 90 percent debt-to-GDP, an economy goes through the looking glass into a new world of negative marginal returns on debt, slow growth, and eventual default through nonpayment, inflation, or renegotiation. This bang point is sure to arrive, yet it may be preceded by a long period of weak growth, stagnant wages, rising income inequality, and social discord—the whimper phase where dissatisfaction is widespread yet no dénouement occurs.

Research in support of the bang point hypothesis is extensive and convincing. In September 2011, the Bank for International Settlements, sometimes called the "central banker's central bank," published research that agreed with the Reinhart-Rogoff thesis that 90 percent debt-to-GDP is a critical threshold beyond which negative effects on growth overwhelm stimulus effects (the report suggests 85 percent). Titled "The Real Effects of Debt," the BIS study states, "Used wisely and in moderation, [debt] clearly improves welfare. But, when [debt] is used imprudently and in excess, the result can be disaster. For individual households and firms, overborrowing leads to bankruptcy and financial ruin. For a country, too much debt impairs the government's ability to deliver essential services to its citizens."

Another study published by the European Central Bank in 2010, titled "The Impact of High and Growing Government Debt on Economic Growth," reports the same result. That ECB report concludes, "a higher public debt-to-GDP ratio is associated, on average, with lower long-term growth rates at debt levels above the range of 90–100% of GDP."

These BIS and ECB studies on the impact of government debt on growth are sponsored by central banks. This is not research from the fringe of economics; it comes from the heart of the international monetary system. Other respected research reaches the same conclusion. Reinhart and Rogoff may have led the way in this field, but they are not out on a limb. Evidence is accumulating that developed economies, in particular the United States, are on dangerous ground and possibly past a point of no return.

Neo-Keynesian critics Brad DeLong and Anatole Kaletsky are apoplectic about the Reinhart-Rogoff results. They cling tenaciously to a belief that debt is always and everywhere good policy to stimulate aggregate demand when the private sector is not spending enough. In particular, neo-Keynesians are bitter about government-dictated austerity policies applied in Europe in the wake of the global financial crisis. While G20 leaders agreed in November 2008 that fiscal policy could play a role in helping global recovery, dissent emerged almost immediately. Angela Merkel, chancellor of Germany, saw debt-to-GDP ratios for the Eurozone as a whole rising past the 60 percent level specified in the Maastricht Treaty that created the euro. In some cases, especially Italy and Greece, those ratios were far higher. Beginning in 2011, Merkel slammed the brakes and insisted on cuts in government spending, sales of public assets, and increased tax collections as the price of German and EU help in refinancing existing sovereign debt.

Mainstream economists, prominently Nobel Prize–winners Paul

Krugman, formerly of Princeton University and now at the City University of New York, and Joseph Stiglitz of Columbia University, were scathing in their attacks on Reinhart and Rogoff. They claimed the failure to use more fiscal stimulus, really deficit spending, would not only hurt growth in the short term, but would lead to long-term losses as temporary unemployment segued into structural unemployment due to lost skills and lost connections to the workplace.

Other views emerged. Economist and Keynes biographer Robert Skidelsky neatly summed up the main lines of thought following the financial crisis:

> After the immediate threat of a depression was averted, economists vigorously debated the merits of withdrawing stimulus so early in the recovery. Their arguments, which can be broken down into four identifiable positions, open a window onto the role that macroeconomic theory played in the crisis. Those in the first camp claimed that fiscal austerity—that is, deficit reduction—would accelerate the recovery *in the short run*. Those in the second camp countered that austerity would have short-run *costs*, but argued that it would be worth the long-run benefits. A third camp, comprising Keynesians, argued unambiguously against austerity. And the fourth camp maintained that, regardless of whether austerity was right, it was unavoidable, given the situation many countries had created for themselves.

The first view suggests austerity produces short-run benefits through a confidence boost—if private citizens saw governments acting prudently on fiscal policy, they would have greater confidence in the future and begin to invest, borrow, and spend more. While appealing, there was little empirical evidence to support this view. Certainly, the experience in Europe, where fiscal stimulus was reduced and economic contraction resumed not long after the crisis, tended to negate this hypothesis. In any case, this view was quickly abandoned by all but a few scholars.

The second view is the one espoused by Reinhart and Rogoff. They do not reject the idea that efforts to rein in runaway spending might slightly reduce growth in the short term. Their point is that failure to reduce deficits is almost certain to create a wealth gap—the difference between actual and potential growth—that will grow in a nonlinear fashion and leave society substantially poorer over time. In extreme cases, hyperinflation, outright debt defaults, currency collapses, and social disorder are in the cards.

The third view is the neo-Keynesian dogma of Krugman, Stiglitz, Brad DeLong of UC Berkeley, and most mainstream economists. This view says if growth is below potential because of lack of aggregate demand, it is the duty of government to fill the demand gap with government spending. Resulting growth relative to austerity will have multiplier effects and eventually return a country to trend growth. Resulting government debt will be manageable because increased growth expands the denominator of the debt-to-GDP ratio. It's not that debt will go down, it's that growth will be sufficiently robust to make added debt sustainable.

The fourth view is more conclusory than analytic. It looks to markets rather than economic theory. If the market will not refinance your maturing debts, then austerity, either voluntary or involuntary, is the only possible outcome. On this view, it is better for countries to manage an austerity process on a voluntary basis than have austerity imposed in a disorderly way by creditors. This view certainly applies to individual cases where the borrower has no access to further credit. Yet where the IMF, EU, or a central bank printing press are on call to bail out an insolvent nation, forced austerity by creditors can be averted with or without voluntary austerity by the debtor. Policy choices and outcomes then become more political than economic. As Skidelsky frames it, the policy debate really does come down to Krugman-Stiglitz versus Reinhart-Rogoff, with their respective supporters and peers cheering them on.

In an open letter to Paul Krugman dated May 25, 2013, Reinhart and Rogoff took on their toughest critic with a nuanced reply to Krugman's prior ad hominem attacks. The Reinhart-Rogoff open letter begins with an observation that the global debt situation today is *unprecedented in history*. It's true the United States had debt-to-GDP ratios at the end of the Second World War slightly higher than today's level. Yet the rest of the world was not nearly as indebted; in fact, the destruction wrought by the Second World War and the elimination of debt owed by vanquished powers such as Nazi Germany and Imperial Japan created ample scope for productive investment and high growth in defeated countries.

In addition, the U.S. had bonded debt, but did not have the enormous contingent liabilities we have today for Medicare, Medicaid, student loans, Social Security, veterans' benefits, farm credit, housing credit, and the myriad programs the United States funds outside the formal government budget. The United States has an astounding $37 trillion of unfunded pension liabilities coming due over the next few decades. If these and other contingent liabilities were added to bonded debt, the U.S. debt-to-GDP ratio would be over 1,000 percent, not the 120 percent recorded at the end of the Second World War.

Reinhart and Rogoff make the point that almost all debt owed by the United States at the end of the Second World War was owed to its own citizens and banks. Today, over 15 percent of U.S. debt is owed to foreign countries including China, Taiwan, and Japan. These foreign holders are likely to be more aggressive than U.S. citizens and banks at diversifying out of U.S. debt and not rolling over maturing debt if they have doubts about U.S. willingness to pay or the prospects for inflation. In short, U.S. and global debt has never been greater and the debt structure never more unstable.

The debate between the Krugman-Stiglitz view and the Reinhart-Rogoff view will rage on for years inside academia. Meanwhile, in the real world, the effects of excessive debt are impossible to ignore. Reinhart and Rogoff point to two possible outcomes of the current unsustainable debt situation. These two outcomes correspond to T. S. Eliot's bang and whimper paths.

The bang point is a rapid collapse of confidence in U.S. debt and the U.S. dollar. At best, this means higher interest rates in order to attract investor dollars to continue financing the deficits. Of course, higher interest rates mean larger deficits, which makes the debt situation worse.

The whimper path consists of another twenty years of slow growth, austerity, financial repression (where interest rates are held below the rate of inflation to gradually extinguish the real value of debt), and an ever-expanding wealth gap. In effect, the next two decades of U.S. growth would look like the last two decades in Japan. Not a collapse, just a slow, prolonged stagnation.

Eliot was candid when he told the *Saturday Review* he did not know how the world would end. Yet his larger point was that it didn't matter. Both bang and whimper were tragic.

Modern Monetary Follies

The oldest joke in academia is that faculty debates are so bitter because the stakes are so small. That punch line sums up the raging crossfire now under way between three schools of economic thought—the neo-Keynesians (NKs), the post-Keynesians (PKs), and the modern monetary theorists (MMTs). If you picture the faculty lounge equivalent of a *West Side Story* gang fight involving the Jets, Sharks, and NYPD, you're on the right track.

The NKs hold the high ground. This is the school that clings most closely to John Maynard Keynes's original concepts of aggregate demand, sticky wages, and the importance of government deficits to boost demand when consumers are in a liquidity trap, hoarding cash and refusing to spend. The NKs emerged immediately after Keynes's death in 1947 under the leadership of Paul Samuelson at MIT and John Hicks at the London School of Economics. In recent decades, the NKs have updated Keynes to incorporate monetarism as developed over the twentieth-century first by Irving Fisher then later by Milton Friedman of the University of Chicago. This blending of neo-Keynesian and monetarist ideas is called the neo-Keynesian consensus, (sometimes the "new neoclassical synthesis"). This new synthesis of Keynesians and monetarists agrees that market failure is real, yet disagree on whether the remedy of government intervention makes matters worse. The NK's most important political victory in recent years was the $831 billion stimulus spending program of "shovel-ready" projects pushed through Congress in February 2009 in response to the global financial crisis. It turned out to be the latest in a long line of stimulus failures. In addition to Paul Krugman, prominent NKs today include Larry Summers and Brad DeLong. When pundits and politicians refer to mainstream economics, they're referring to NKs.

The main rival gang to the NKs are the PKs. Post-Keynesians also built on a foundation laid by John Maynard Keynes, with important differences, and a rejection of some Keynesian tenets. The PKs branched off from the NKs in the mid-1970s, around the same time Keynesians joined forces with monetarists. PKs agree with NKs on aggregate demand and the need for government spending, yet PKs are more progressive and focused on income inequality and worker-friendly policies. They reject the idea that the economy is an equilibrium system that tends toward full employment and that sticky wages are the main impediment to full employment. Instead they call for an aggressive use of monetary policy, especially low interest rates to finance more government spending, as a solution to unemployment, low wages, and weak demand. Prominent PKs include Joan Robinson, Paul Davidson, and Michal Kalecki.

The newest and smallest economic cadre are the MMTs. Modern monetary theorists offer a curious blend of progressivism consistent with PK views, but resurrect a pre-Keynesian concept called chartalism, which Keynes himself endorsed. MMTs are a small but ascendant clique. They are gaining attention from mainstream economists, politicians, and the media. The reason for this increased attention is not hard to discern. MMTs offer the world what the world wants most—free money.

MMTs and PKs are alike in their progressive outlook and emphasis on job creation. They also agree on their point of divergence from the NKs, which is heightened attention to money-creation channels. MMTs and PKs point to the ease with which social problems might be addressed through fiat money alone rather than the fiscal channels favored by the NKs. Yet PKs pay some attention to political and statutory constraints on central bank operations; MMTs do not. As far as MMTs are concerned, the central bank printing press is there for the taking. Any social issue that can be addressed with money should be addressed, because money creation imposes no constraint on government spending.

PKs recognize the U.S. Treasury has a borrowing and spending function and the Federal Reserve creates money and targets interest rates. The two institutions were created separately and have difference governance. The Treasury and Fed work together in myriad ways. The Treasury has an account at the Fed, the Fed buys Treasury debt with printed money, and the Fed remits profits to the Treasury. The Fed acts as fiscal agent of the Treasury in foreign exchange market operations. Still, the institutions have boundaries to be respected by economists and policymakers. The Treasury does not create money and Treasury spending will be constrained if Congress does not authorize it or if the Fed does not accommodate it with low rates and asset purchases.

MMTs throw these constraints aside. In effect, MMTs treat the Treasury and Fed as if they were a single entity. The legal distinctions pointed to by PKs (and NKs, when they think about it) are just welds in a complicated plumbing system that flows continuously from end to end. In the modern monetary theory model, the Treasury creates money by spending. When the Treasury spends money it reduces its bank account at the Fed, but increases private sector bank accounts of citizens or companies who are recipients of their spending. In this sense, private sector wealth is increased by Treasury spending. The more the Treasury spends, the richer the private sector becomes.

Inside the financial plumbing, certain accounting entries are made, but these have no impact on the basic premise that Treasury spending equals money creation and increased private welfare. Treasury spending creates so-called high-powered money, or HPM, by substituting Treasury notes (a form of low-powered credit money) on the Fed's balance sheet for the HPM formerly deposited in the Treasury's bank account. The Treasury's HPM is now deposited in the private bank accounts of the recipients of Treasury spending, such as contractors, consultants, and policy beneficiaries. By combining the Treasury and the Fed, a deus ex machina is created, in which spending is conducted at will and monetized seamlessly. The MMT crew asks rhetorically, "Where would money come from in the first place if the Treasury didn't spend it?"

The appeal of this approach is obvious to progressives and politicians alike. MMT devotees are not coy in their claims. One of the leading treatments on the subject is *Free Money: Plan for Prosperity* (2005) by Rodger Malcolm Mitchell. The brightest advocate of MMT is Professor Stephanie Kelton, née Bell, of Stony Brook University. In 2015, Kelton was chief economist for the U.S. Senate Budget Committee minority staff, led by ranking member Bernie Sanders, Socialist from Vermont. Kelton became an economic adviser to the Sanders presidential campaign in 2016. As Sanders gears up his 2020 presidential campaign, Kelton is expected to play a prominent role in shaping his spending and economic platform.

In the Kelton-Sanders version of MMT, crumbling infrastructure can be fixed immediately by spending money on improvements. The $1.6 trillion mountain of student loan debt impeding household formation and turning the millennials into debt slaves is remedied with debt forgiveness. Unemployment and underemployment can be cured with a guaranteed basic income, in the form of a monthly check sent to every American, with no work requirements or other strings attached. These and other government programs can be funded by Treasury expenditures and debt monetization. Private welfare will be enhanced dollar for dollar, or even more as the benefits of government spending spread to the private sector.

Kelton is also a portal to the dark side of MMT—the government's monopoly on violence and willingness to use it against citizens who demur from the fiat dollar fandango. MMT purports to be a new twenty-first-century approach to the problems of government finance and economic growth. In fact, it is old wine in new bottles. MMT advocates admit this by embracing the tenets of chartalism. Georg Friedrich Knapp is considered the father of chartalism, based on his work *The State Theory of Money*, published in 1924. Yet Kelton and other scholars have traced the idea back even further, to Adam Smith's *The Wealth of Nations* (1776), and even Plato. Old wine indeed. There is no better guide to the definition of chartalism than Professor Kelton herself.

In a pellucid piece, "The Role of the State and the Hierarchy of Money" (2001), Professor Kelton offers a concise history of chartalism and an overview of its application by economists as diverse as Adam Smith, John Maynard Keynes, and Hyman Minsky. Chartalism states that a form of money has value if the state proclaims that money acceptable as payment for taxes. Since taxes are mandatory, enforced by fines and imprisonment for nonpayment, any form of money accepted by the state as taxes must be obtained by individuals so they can pay their taxes. It is this status as acceptable for taxes, not legal tender laws or intrinsic value, that makes a form of money valuable. In Kelton's words, money is a "creature of the state." Kelton writes:

> What makes a currency valid as money is a *proclamation* by the state that it will be accepted at its pay offices; what makes it acceptable to its citizenry is its usefulness in settling these liabilities. . . . [Georg] Knapp explained the process by which a "ticket" or "token" becomes Chartal money:

> When we give up our coats in the cloak-room of a theatre, we
> receive a tin disc of a given size bearing a sign, perhaps a num-
> ber. There is nothing more on it, but this ticket or mark has
> legal significance; it is a proof that I am entitled to demand the
> return of my coat. When we send letters, we affix a stamp or
> ticket which proves that we have by payment of postage ob-
> tained the right to get the letter carried. (Knapp 1924, p. 31).

The defining characteristic of a Chartal means of payment,
"whether coins or warrants," is that "they are pay-tokens, or tickets
used as a means of payment." . . . The cloak-room token and the
stamp, like the money of the state, gain their validity by virtue of
proclamation.

According to Kelton, your money is like the coat-check ticket because
the state says so.

From this reasoning, Kelton and her ilk expand in all directions. If
money is what the state says it is, then anything can be money, including
gold. Prior to the late twentieth-century, most state money was gold. Kelton claims gold was money not because of scarcity or utility, but because
the state proclaimed it money as a matter of custom more than necessity.
Once paper became the object of the proclamation, paper became money
and gold fell by the wayside. Today, the proclamation covers digital dollars,
which serve just as well as paper or gold.

Kelton also explains the double-entry accounting behind chartal money.
Such money is always an asset and a liability at the same time. A dollar is
a liability of the central bank that creates it and an asset of the citizen who
holds it. Once a tax obligation arises, that is a liability of the citizen and an
asset of the state. The citizen tenders his asset (the dollar) to extinguish his
liability (the tax bill). From the state's perspective, both the liability and
the asset are extinguished together when the taxes are paid. As Kelton
explains, "the state actually accepts only its own liabilities in payment to

itself." This may conjure up an image of a snake swallowing its tail, but it's really a simple accounting exercise.

Kelton makes two other points in laying the foundation for MMT. The first is that debt and credit are the same viewed from different perspectives. If the state issues dollars as transfers to citizens, the state is the debtor because dollars are central bank liabilities, and citizens are creditors because they accept and hold the debt. For MMT, money is debt. This is not true if the state proclaims gold to be money, because gold has commodity value independent of the state, but Kelton glosses over this since gold is not proclaimed to be money today.

This conceptual money-equals-debt identity allows Kelton to create what she calls the "hierarchy of money." This is an ontology of money-debt ranked in descending order of acceptability based on liquidity and convertibility of one form to another. At the top of the pyramid are central bank dollars and Treasury bonds, because these are issued by the state. Next come bank deposits, because these are practically indistinguishable from central bank dollars due to the banks' license to create credits to citizen accounts. At the bottom of the pyramid come corporate debt and household debt. While these debts are denominated in dollars, they are not equivalent to bank liabilities due to credit risk and illiquidity. The importance of this ontology is that it demonstrates, at least to the satisfaction of the MMT gang, that the concept of money is highly elastic. Literally anyone can create money in some form by issuing an IOU. It's as if the Federal Reserve expanded its definitions of money supply from M0, M1, and M2, to include M4, M5, M6, and so on. It's all money, all credit, and all debt at the same time.

Kelton is honest about the state coercion needed to make this system work. She writes, "Only the state, through its power to make and enforce tax laws, can issue promises that its constituents must accept if they are to avoid penalties." She does not explicitly say penalties include property confiscation and imprisonment, yet her meaning is clear. State power is the root of state money.

MMT's conflation of Treasury and central-bank functions leads to the heterodox conclusion that high tax rates can control inflation. The logic is that if money has value because it is accepted as payment for taxes, then higher tax rates make money more valuable because citizens need more of it to avoid prison. When money gains value, the effect on prices is deflationary. Kelton offers the example of the U.S. Civil War, during which the Confederacy had taxes equal to 5 percent of spending with 2,800 percent inflation, while the Union had taxes equal to 21 percent of spending with only 100 percent inflation, the implication being that high tax rates contribute to lower inflation. News from Gettysburg and Vicksburg might have more explanatory power for comparative inflation in the Civil War; Kelton acknowledges counterexamples to the thesis, but her point lingers.

MMT theorizing is not merely abstract; it is a means to an end. Once money is viewed as a double-entry bookkeeping exercise initiated by Treasury spending and backed by state power, there is no limit to the amount of money the state can emit. This means there is no limit to how much the Treasury can spend. If that's true, there is no social problem, from poverty to infrastructure to education, that cannot be solved with more spending. The country does not get poorer when the Treasury borrows and spends, it gets richer, because Treasury spending becomes the wealth of the recipients.

Many MMT tenets are true, notwithstanding its muddled conflation of the Treasury and the Fed, and its dodge of the unseasonable truth that gold is one form of money that is not simultaneously debt. It is true that state power can proclaim the kind of money acceptable as payment of taxes. It is true that citizens may regard the declared form of money as money in order to pay taxes and avoid prison. It is true that a central bank and a treasury can work together, not as MMT describes it, but in a condition that former Fed governor Frederick Mishkin calls "fiscal dominance," to monetize unlimited government debt and support unlimited government spending. Finally, it is true that government spending goes into someone's pocket and enriches that individual or company by that amount of spending at least temporarily. All this is true, even obvious.

MMT analysis relies on the fact that the Federal Reserve balance sheet has no legal limit. From 1934 to 1945, the Fed could expand base money to a level that did not exceed 250 percent of the U.S. gold reserve. That 250 percent ceiling was repealed in stages from 1945 to 1965, in part to facilitate deficit spending by President Truman during the Korean War and President Johnson during the Vietnam War. The last vestige of a U.S. gold standard was abandoned entirely by President Nixon in 1971. In the absence of a gold standard, there is no limit on the amount of government debt the Fed can monetize. The Fed is also not subject to mark-to-market accounting. If the Fed buys government debt and interest rates later rise, the Fed is not required to record the decline in the market value of its bonds on its financial statements. The Fed is not subject to minimum capital requirements, nor is there a prohibition on negative equity on the Fed's balance sheet. In a private conversation with a former member of the Fed board of governors at dinner in Vail, Colorado, I pointed out that the Fed was insolvent. She told me bluntly, "Central banks don't need capital." The Fed really does have unlimited capacity to monetize debt, as MMT proponents claim. This implies that the Treasury has an unlimited capacity to spend.

The problem with chartalism and MMT is not that the theory is wrong as far as it goes; the problem is that it does not go far enough. MMT fails not because of what it says, but because of what it ignores. The issue is not whether there is a legal limit on money creation, but whether there is a psychological limit.

The real source of money status is not state power, it's confidence. If two parties to an exchange have confidence that their medium of exchange is money, and others regard it as such, then that medium is money. In times past and in various places, money consisted of gold, silver, beads, feathers, paper tokens, and diverse badges of confidence. At the height of the Zimbabwe hyperinflation in 2009, prepaid cell-phone minutes were a popular medium of exchange for citizens there. The primary forms of money among inmates in the Federal prison system today include postage stamps (a chartalist medium, as reckoned by Knapp) and vacuum-sealed packets of mackerel, called "macks." At current exchange rates, three macks buys you a large bowl of banana pudding made by inmates with bananas stolen from the prison chow hall. The state does not support the mack/banana exchange rate; confidence does.

The difficulty with confidence is that it's fragile, easily lost, and impossible to regain. The great failing of NKs, PKs, and MMTs is that they take confidence for granted. Reasons for ignoring confidence range from overreliance on quantitative models in the case of NKs, to overreliance on state power in the case of PKs and MMTs. As for the former, ignoring psychology because it does not fit neatly into quantitative equilibrium models is no less than willful ignorance. As for the latter, one need only consider the long history of failed states, the most prominent of which include Venezuela, Somalia, Syria, Yemen, and North Korea. Past prominent examples include Russia (1999), Nazi Germany (1945), victims of Nazi Germany (1939–45), Spain (1936–39), and the United States (1861–65). A comprehensive historical review would yield more failed states than still successful ones. State power is not absolute and it is definitely not permanent. To the extent a form of money in which citizens have confidence coincides with a state's proclamation of that same form of money, the relationship is convenient, not causal.

At what point will everyday citizens lose confidence in the Federal Reserve and, by extension, the U.S. dollar? What is the invisible confidence boundary at which the intellectual failure of MMT becomes plain?

Between 2008 and 2014, the Fed printed $3.5 trillion of new money to deal with the global financial crisis. In the process, the Fed's balance sheet ballooned from $800 billion to over $4.5 trillion. MMT advocates like Kelton claim citizen perceptions don't matter, because citizens are forced to accept dollars to pay their taxes. They further claim politicians will not rein in the Fed because politicians are the ones who voted for the deficits and spending in the first place. History shows otherwise. As long as democracy is functioning, disgruntled citizens can vote for politicians with a credible plan to take control of the Fed and halt debt monetization. This implies an extreme form of austerity, but it may be far preferable to the alternative of complete ruin.

Conversely, if Congress continues running deficits and the Fed continues to monetize them, citizens have historically resorted to self-help by turning to alternative forms of payment such as gold, silver, or barter. Perhaps there is no historical record of an all-barter economy, but examples of dentists and landscapers swapping services are legion. Of course, participants refuse to pay taxes on in-kind transactions, negating the state's capacity to proclaim money.

MMT's other blind spot in addition to confidence is money velocity or the turnover of money. Velocity is scarcely discussed in MMT literature. The omission may be a legacy of Milton Friedman's incorrect assumption that velocity is constant. Only by ignoring velocity could Friedman suppose that maximum real growth was achieved by controlling the quantity of money. Only by ignoring velocity can the MMT crew wish away hyperinflation as confidence in state money erodes. The reaction function to lost confidence in one form of money is to spend it as fast as possible or acquire another form. This behavioral adaptation is the real cause of inflation, not money printing. Confidence and velocity are inversely correlated and together are the Achilles' heel of MMT.

MMT has superficial appeal to the uninformed because it purports to offer a painless way out of the slow-growth, high-debt structural stagnation now afflicting the United States, Japan, and Europe. You won't hear MMT advocates talk much about state power, tax police, or hyperinflation. Instead, MMT voices such as former PIMCO honcho Paul McCulley talk about the benefits to society if the Fed simply swaps its dollar debt for Treasury debt.

One voice that disagrees with MMT is the Fed itself. While the Fed may have no legal constraints on its ability to monetize debt, it recognizes political and psychological constraints. Current Federal Reserve chair Jerome Powell expressed these concerns in his comments during a Federal Open Market Committee meeting on October 23, 2012. At the time, he was a member of the Board of Governors. The minutes of that meeting capture his view of unlimited money printing:

> I have concerns about more purchases. . . . Why stop at $4 trillion? The market in most cases will cheer us for doing more. . . . Second, I think we are actually at a point of encouraging risk-taking, and that should give us pause. Investors really do understand now that we will be there to prevent serious losses. . . . Meanwhile, we look like we are blowing a fixed-income duration bubble right across the credit spectrum that will result in big losses when rates come up down the road. . . . My third concern . . . is the problems of exiting from a near $4 trillion balance sheet. . . . We seem to be way too confident that exit can be managed smoothly. Markets can be much more dynamic than we appear to think.

Powell is correct when he says markets are much more dynamic than economists believe. This recognition by Powell, who will be Fed chairman until at least 2022, suggests the destructive portents of MMT may be well understood by those who matter most in monetary policy. Yet Powell's alarm does not mean all is well. We are still left with the unpalatable choice of Eliot's bang or whimper as explained by Reinhart and Rogoff— either a collapse of confidence in the U.S. dollar or decades of economic stagnation.

This poses a dilemma for investors. If the collapse of confidence comes, it will be expressed in the form of higher inflation as investors dump dollars for hard assets and money velocity skyrockets. On the other hand, if the future holds decades of stagnant growth, this suggests a deflationary period similar to the one Japan has suffered since 1990, following the collapse of stock and property values after a 1980s debt-fueled bubble.

Yet the conjurers of free money have another trick up their sleeves. Even as MMT is disputed, its advocates offer the allure of a guaranteed basic income.

More Free Money

For MMT economists like Kelton, free money is not an end itself; it serves a policy purpose with aims including infrastructure spending, health care, and education. The primary purpose proposed by MMT advocates is eradication of unemployment and underemployment. It is beyond the compass of this volume to describe the full scope of the employment crisis in the United States today, and to offer a comprehensive treatment of the proposals for remediation. This book focuses on the international monetary system, especially the future of the system's dollar-based superstructure. As the dollar goes, so goes the real value of dollar-denominated investments in stocks, bonds, and hard assets. Yet the scope of the U.S. employment crisis is so great, and solutions so radical (radical in the sense of going to root causes, not in the sense of left- or right-wing extremism), an acute impact on U.S. fiscal and monetary policy is inevitable.

Real wages will be the dominant domestic policy issue in the 2020 presidential elections. A host of issues including tax cuts, budget battles, and debt ceiling debates will be seen for what they are—mere battles in a larger war to create higher paying jobs. In an earlier crisis, on the eve of a shooting war in the Middle East in November 1990, U.S. Secretary of State James Baker grew exasperated at the inability of the press to understand U.S. policy. At an ad hoc press briefing he blurted, "To bring it down to the level of the average American citizen, let me say that means jobs. If you want to sum it up in one word, it's jobs." Baker's message is as relevant today in the midst of currency wars and trade wars as it was almost thirty years ago preceding the Gulf War. It's jobs. Investors who do not grasp the importance of this will be blindsided by the solutions offered up by politicians and ultimately embraced by the voters.

The greatest official deception propagated by the U.S. government today is that the economy is at or near full employment. Of course, the U.S. government would deny that and insist on the accuracy of its reporting. The difference in views has to do with definitions. The U.S. Bureau of Labor Statistics' report dated November 2, 2018, showed the official U.S. unemployment rate for October 2018 at 3.7 percent, with a separate unemployment rate of 3.5 percent for adult men and 3.4 percent for adult women. The 3.7 percent unemployment rate is based on a total workforce of 160 million people, of whom 153 million are employed and 6.1 million are unemployed. The 3.7 percent figure is the lowest unemployment rate since 1969. The average rate of unemployment in the United States from 1948 to 2018 is 5.78 percent. By these superficial measures, unemployment is indeed low and the economy is arguably at full employment. Still, these statistics don't tell the whole story. Of the 153 million with jobs, 4.6 million are working part time involuntarily; they would prefer full-time jobs but can't find them or had their hours cut by current employers. Another 1.4 million sidelined workers searched for a job in the prior year but are not included in the labor force because they had not searched in the prior four weeks. If their numbers were counted as unemployed, the unemployment rate would be 5 percent.

Yet the real unemployment rate is far worse. The official unemployment rate is calculated using a narrow definition of the workforce, limited to those with jobs or actively seeking work. But millions of able-bodied men and women between the ages of twenty-five and fifty-four are not included in the workforce. They are not retirees or teenagers, but adults in their prime working years. They are in effect "missing workers." The number of these missing workers not included in official unemployment rolls is measured by the Labor Force Participation Rate, or LFPR. The LFPR measures the total number of workers divided by the total number of potential workers, regardless of whether those potential workers are seeking work or not. The LFPR plunged from 67.3 percent in January 2000 to 62.9 percent in October 2018, a drop of 4.4 percentage points. If those potential workers were added back to the workforce, the unemployment rate would be 10 percent.

Of course, there are limits to labor-force participation. Some potential workers suffer chronic pain or other disabilities, some are retired, some are students, some are at home raising children. Those are reasons why the LFPR has never been much over 67 percent since the data have been recorded. Still, the drop in LFPR to 62.9 percent in the ninth year of an economic expansion is stunning. America has a missing workers problem that accounts in large measure for the slow growth, persistent low inflation, stagnant wages, declining money velocity, and social dissatisfaction that have characterized the U.S. economy since the end of the last recession in June 2009. American labor markets are not tight. America is not even close to full employment. America is in a depression.

What is striking about these depressed labor market conditions is the unanimity of opinion from left and right on how serious the unemployment problem is and what needs to be done. Compare the following description from Nicholas Eberstadt, a scholar with the conservative American Enterprise Institute with that of Pavlina R. Tcherneva, a scholar at the progressive Levy Economics Institute at Bard College. It is telling that Eberstadt and Tcherneva have both adopted the language of disease in describing the unemployment crisis in America. That's appropriate in two respects. The first is the direct health consequences suffered by the unemployed and their families in terms of depression, alcoholism, disability, suicide, opioid use, and other less pernicious yet still serious disorders. The second, explored at length by Tcherneva, is the sense in which unemployment spreads like a contagious disease from town to town and county to county across America.

First, the conservative Eberstadt:

Economically, declining LFPRs and falling work rates have made for slower economic growth, widening gaps in income and wealth, greater budgetary pressures, and higher deficits and national debt. They have likewise increased the risk of poverty in the United States, not least for the children whose fathers are found in our huge army of men without work. . . . Americans may be the hardest working people of any affluent society in the world today, yet no other developed nation simultaneously floats such a large proportion of its prime-age men entirely outside the labor force—neither working, nor looking for work, nor doing much of anything else. . . . Social cohesion is a direct casualty of this development, and social trust could scarcely help but be degraded by it as well.

Now, the progressive Tcherneva:

While the national unemployment rate today has reached its precrisis level . . . this "success" is largely due to a mass exodus of people from the labor market after the Great Recession. After correcting for labor force participation rates before and after the crisis [scholars] estimate that there are approximately 20 million missing jobs today. . . .

The unemployed are sicker and spend more on health-care costs. They suffer from increasing rates of alcoholism, physical illness, depression, and anxiety, make more trips to the doctor and take more medication. . . . These multifaceted health effects create a vicious cycle that prevents the unemployed from reentering the labor market. . . . Furthermore, unemployment has significant, robust, and lasting negative effects on individuals' social participation. . . . The isolation that unemployment causes erodes the social network that a person often needs for reemployment.

If a big-box store or manufacturing plant is shut down, throwing hundreds out of work, it's often the case that those displaced workers commute from adjacent communities. Those unemployed spend less money in their home towns, spreading the effects of unemployment from the shuttered site to surrounding districts like ripples in a pond when a stone is dropped. In time, those affected communities suffer their own unemployment, which spreads the jobless virus even further.

It's a species of analytic malpractice for government officials and Wall Street economists to parrot phrases about full employment and tight labor market conditions when labor market reality looks more like the Great Depression. Still, many scholars are not so blind. If the unity of conservative and progressive scholars in diagnosing the labor crisis is surprising, even more surprising is their unity of opinion on what is to be done. While details differ, there is a consensus of left and right that the time has come for a guaranteed basic income, or GBI, or public service employment, PSE, for all Americans. The GBI/PSE movement is potentially the greatest revolution in public policy since Lyndon Johnson's Great Society (1965) or Franklin Roosevelt's New Deal (1933). The implications of this policy revolution for fiscal and monetary policy, and for investor portfolios, cannot be overstated.

The GBI (also called universal basic income, UBI, or simply basic income) is an old idea offered as a new remedy for an economy that produces too few jobs with decent wages. The idea is strikingly simple. Government will pay every citizen a basic income from public resources. The basic income is sufficient to provide a reasonable, if not luxurious, standard of living. It is paid without any requirement for work, and regardless of any other income. Every citizen in a society receives the basic income unconditionally.

The idea of a GBI has explicit roots in Thomas More's *Utopia* (1516), where it is discussed as a way of obviating theft. Of course, public welfare of various kinds has existed at least since the creation of the grain dole in the Roman Republic in the mid-second century BC. The original grain dole instituted by Tiberius Gracchus and his younger brother, Gaius, consisted of sales of inexpensive wheat to citizens on a first-come, first-served basis. While the dole was originally considered temporary, a later tribune, Claudius, won election by offering free wheat. By the time Julius Caesar became consul of the Roman Republic in 59 BC, he found 320,000 Romans receiving the grain dole. Through most of the Middle Ages, poor relief was provided by the Catholic Church. Public assistance, later known as the Poor Laws, was available in England as early as 1531 in the reign of Henry VIII. Later government efforts to assist the poor included Bismarck's social insurance scheme (1883), and Roosevelt's Social Security Act (1935). More recently economists such as Milton Friedman and politicians including Richard Nixon have endorsed variations of GBI, including the negative income tax and earned income tax credit.

What distinguishes the pure form of GBI from these earlier schemes is the absence of so-called means testing (looking at your income to determine eligibility) and conditionality. You do not have to be poor to receive GBI, and you do not have to work. It is given to every citizen, rich and poor, young and old, by the government as a matter of right.

The fullest explanation of this twenty-first-century vision of GBI, including arguments for and against, is presented by Philippe Van Parijs and Yannick Vanderborght in their book, *Basic Income* (2017). The Van Parijs-Vanderborght proposal is that countries around the world set their GBI payment at 25 percent of per capita GDP. Obviously, richer countries could afford higher GBI payments. Using 2015 data, they estimate the GBI payment at "$1,163 per month in the United States, $1,670 in Switzerland, $910 in the United Kingdom, [and] $180 in Brazil." Using the Van Parijs-Vanderborght data and converting to 2018 dollars, their proposed GBI payment to Americans today amounts to $15,000 per year, per person, no strings attached.

Van Parijs and Vanderborght have one of the more extreme, but also simplified versions of GBI. They would pay GBI individually to every member of a household regardless of household size. Payments would be unconditional, so there would be no reduction in GBI if the recipient got a job or received a raise. Reduction of current government assistance when recipients get a job is one of the main criticisms aimed at social welfare programs today. This creates a welfare trap, where the recipient never gets a job for fear of losing benefits. This problem disappears under GBI because there is no means testing and no conditionality.

While Van Parijs and Vanderborght are European scholars, they bring a globalist perspective to the issue. They argue for GBI mainly on grounds of autonomy and human dignity defined in part as freedom of choice. GBI recipients can choose to work or not. They can also refuse what the authors call "lousy, poorly-paid jobs." The two scholars do not expect such jobs to disappear; they expect wages and working conditions to improve as employers compete with GBI itself for workers.

Human dignity is not the only argument for GBI in their view. They also base their support on "the new wave of automation already on the way and predicted to keep swelling in the coming years: robotization, self-driving vehicles, a massive replacement of human-brain workers by computers. It enables the wealth and earning power of some—those who design, control, and are in the best position to exploit the new technologies—to reach new heights, while that of many more plummets." They explain that minimum-wage laws will not protect the most vulnerable. By raising labor costs, minimum-wage laws simply accelerate the replacement of workers by robots.

Van Parijs and Vanderborght are not alone. At the World Government Summit in Dubai in February 2017, Tesla CEO Elon Musk said, "I think ultimately we will have to have some kind of universal basic income, I don't think we are going to have a choice." The *San Francisco Chronicle* reported on July 19, 2017, "Facebook co-founder Chris Hughes, venture capitalist Marc Andreessen and Y Combinator president Sam Altman have all said [GBI is] worth exploring." In a Harvard University commencement speech on May 25, 2017, Facebook founder Mark Zuckerberg said, "Every generation expands its definition of equality. . . . Now it's time to define a new social contract for our generation. We should have a society that measures progress not just by economics metrics like GDP, but by how many of us have a role we find meaningful. We should explore ideas like universal basic income to make sure everyone has a cushion to try new things." On January 29, 2018, the mayor of Stockton, California, announced plans to begin a basic income pilot program consisting of a five-hundred-dollar-per-month payment to one hundred families below the poverty line. Based on results, that program could expand to as many as seventy-five thousand individuals in a city of three hundred thousand residents.

The idea for a UBI or GBI also enjoys wide and growing popular support. A poll commissioned by the *Huffington Post* in January 2014 reported only 35 percent of Americans supported GBI. That support grew to 48 percent by February 2018, according to a Gallup poll. This 37 percent increase in support by Americans for GBI in just four years during an economic expansion with steady job creation shows the appeal of GBI, independent of recession or downturns in the business cycle. These poll results reflect increasing support for GBI among millennials, now coming of age and entering the workforce. If these trends hold, which is likely, GBI will command the support of a majority of American adults in the run-up to the 2020 presidential election.

Applying the Van Parijs-Vanderborght formula to the United States, for a GBI consisting of 25 percent of GDP distributed on a per-capita basis, amounts to a new U.S. government entitlement costing $4.8 trillion dollars per year at a time when the United States is already facing $1 trillion and greater annual budget deficits for years into the future, while the U.S. debt-to-GDP ratio is the highest in over seventy years, not including contingent liabilities for existing entitlements. Even a single year of such a program would push the U.S. debt-to-GDP ratio past 125 percent. Two years of the program would put the U.S. debt-to-GDP ratio at 140 percent, higher than any economy in the world except Greece, Lebanon, and Japan.

The political feasibility of such a program given existing entitlements and debt burdens is nearly nil, despite growing popular support.

In response to these hurdles, politicians and public intellectuals from left and right are proposing modifications to the pure form of GBI to make it politically palatable. From the right, Charles Murray proposes a GBI of thirteen thousand dollars per year, with three thousand dollars automatically directed to the purchase of health-care insurance and the remaining ten thousand for use as the recipient sees fit. However, his GBI would be paid to adults only, not to all Americans, and would replace almost every existing entitlement, including Social Security, Medicare, Medicaid, welfare, farm subsidies, and corporate tax benefits. By eliminating all of these government handouts and the inefficient bureaucracies that administer them, Murray's plan costs less than the existing income security system and reduces the U.S. budget deficit slightly. Murray makes a case similar to Van Parijs and Vanderborght, that his proposal is based on human freedom and dignity and empowers individuals to make personal choices rather than live lives confined by the narrow boundaries of existing entitlement programs. He also gives specific examples of how individuals with jobs who can save the GBI payment and invest it at market rates with compound returns can fund a retirement income greater than existing Social Security benefits. Murray's succinct summary of his proposal is, "Here's the money. Use it as you see fit. Your life is in your hands."

Despite the financial and philosophical attractions of Murray's proposal, it is also a political nonstarter. Politicians cannot even discuss let alone reach compromise on modest adjustments to existing entitlements that would slow America's headlong charge into unsustainable debt. That those entitlements would be scrapped entirely, even with a GBI replacement, is inconceivable. Murray deserves praise for advancing the debate and showing what's possible. Still, his solution is not a solution susceptible to political support.

The American left, in contrast to the European left, has taken a pragmatic approach to the issue. Opposition to GBI is potent and predictable. Movement conservatives, talk radio, and alt-right media will take to the barricades to denounce GBI as a handout to those too lazy to work and a free ride on a shrinking number of Americans who are working. The attack on GBI will include allegations that, far from providing a stable base from which to pursue work, it destroys incentives to work at all. While the GBI movement has received notice and commentary from think tanks and public intellectuals, it has gone largely unobserved by the right-wing electoral base precisely because of the assumed remoteness of its coming to pass. The minute GBI advances to a prominent place in the progressive policy agenda, the right will mobilize to destroy its chances. The left knows this.

Instead of a guaranteed basic income, the left will propose a government-guaranteed job—the acceptable face of universal income security. Once a job guarantee is in place, pay scales and benefits can be calibrated to provide a guaranteed basic income. The work itself can be nominal in substance and meager in productivity; that doesn't matter. The work is merely an interface between public spending and guaranteed income. Yet the presence of a work requirement separates this program from the more radical basic income proposals of Van Parijs and Vanderborght, who insist that GBI be unconditional. The work requirement neuters objections based on free riding and laziness. As soon as the debate pivots away from bumper-sticker sentiments on laziness to more technical factors such as labor productivity, the public loses interest and the advocates win.

The only politically potent objections to a government-guaranteed job are the ongoing costs and the impact of those costs on deficits and debt-to-GDP ratios. It is precisely this point in the debate when progressive MMT factions rise to the defense of government-guaranteed jobs. If central bank balance sheets, government debt, and money supply are infinitely elastic, as MMT claims, then the cost of government-guaranteed jobs is a red herring and progressive advocates sweep their conservative opposition off the board.

In April 2018, MMT's leading lights—Kelton, Tcherneva, L. Randall Wray, Scott Fullwiler, and Flavia Dantas—coauthored a manifesto titled "Public Service Employment: A Path to Full Employment." The timing of their publication during the run-up to the 2018 midterm elections, and the 2020 presidential election campaign that began the morning after the midterms, was no coincidence. The public service employment plan was clearly intended as a touchstone for every progressive candidate for public office from Bernie Sanders on down. Obama won by offering Americans "hope and change." Trump won by offering to "make American great again." Bernie Sanders and his supporters are out to win in 2020 by offering Americans the one thing they care about most—a decent job at decent wages. With that, a host of social issues from family cohesion to student loans start to self-repair.

Kelton, Tcherneva, and their coauthors of the manifesto begin with a refutation of official employment numbers along the lines described above. They then turn to a succinct description of the PSE program:

> We propose the creation of a Public Service Employment (PSE) program that would offer a job at a living wage to all who are ready and willing to work. This is a "job guarantee" program that provides employment to all who need work by drawing from the pool of the otherwise unemployed during recessions and shrinking as private sector employment recovers. Federally funded but with a decentralized administration, the PSE program would pay $15 per hour for both full- and part-time positions and offer benefits that include health insurance and childcare. In addition to guaranteeing access to work on projects that serve a public purpose, the PSE program establishes effective minimum standards for wages and benefits.

The political appeal of PSE compared to GBI is obvious. PSE effectively sets a national minimum wage of fifteen dollars per hour (which presumably would be adjusted for inflation through the legislation authorizing PSE). Technically, employers could pay less under existing minimum-wage legislation, but those employers would lose employees to the PSE jobs as individuals sought the higher wages available under PSE. This would force private employers to match the fifteen-dollar-per-hour rate, effectively putting a floor under wages. The same holds true for benefits.

The most clear-cut objection to PSE is the expense. Even the PSE proponents acknowledge that the impact on the U.S. budget deficit would be over 1.5 percent of GDP in the early years (2018–22) and over 1.0 percent of GDP in later years (2023–27). Using current GDP levels, PSE would increase the deficit by $300 billion per year in fiscal year 2019, and by higher amounts thereafter. This deficit hit would come on top of projected deficits in excess of $1 trillion per year, even without PSE.

This is where MMT fits in. It's no coincidence that Kelton, Tcherneva, and their coauthors are also leading economists in the MMT school. A program such as PSE is exactly what MMT preaches—improve public welfare and don't worry about deficits. PSE advocates point to a number of benefits that mitigate the deficit damage, including mystical "multiplier effects," as well as improvements in state and local government finances since they would be able to tax payments going to PSE recipients. They also cite lower social costs related to health care, crime, and drug addiction as benefits from PSE, compared to the alternative of no work for millions of adults. PSE jobs would be focused on "projects that serve a public purpose," presumably improvements in infrastructure and public amenities.

Even allowing that some of these benefits are real, it is likely most of the benefits will prove illusory and costs will be greater than anticipated. The fact is, jobs are plentiful today even without PSE. The employment problem facing the millions of missing workers is the result of a mismatch of skills, family dysfunction, drug addiction, motivation, and the welfare trap of existing benefit programs. GBI might address some of those issues, but PSE does not. More to the point, the Reinhart-Rogoff research shows that the U.S. economy is past the point of no return when it comes to multiplier effects. Once the debt-to-GDP ratio exceeds 90 percent, additional spending impedes rather than stimulates growth. By adding $300 billion per year to the national debt, PSE makes the problem of secular stagnation worse. PSE offers work to those willing to work, but those willing to work can already find jobs. PSE is not a solution for unmotivated workers. It is a politically attractive way to raise the minimum wage and improve benefits through the back door. Despite this critique, it's unwise to dismiss PSE as just another progressive chimera. PSE commands near majority support without a sustained campaign on its behalf. Once the 2020 presidential election cycle is under way, the campaigns of Bernie Sanders, Cory Booker, Elizabeth Warren, and other prominent Democrats will become a full-time platform to promote the positive aspects of PSE. Majority support will then emerge. Even the mercurial Donald Trump may become a supporter because he is not bound by the conventions of movement conservatives or mainstream Republicans. PSE could rank with FDR's New Deal as the pinnacle of progressive policy in the past hundred years.

Yet there's a hidden danger in PSE or GBI that even conservative critics and debt doomsters like Reinhart and Rogoff have elided. The danger is inflation. Given the headwinds to growth identified by the Reinhart-Rogoff thesis, the persistent secular stagnation highlighted by Larry Summers, and the millions of missing workers described by Eberstadt, the prospect of inflation seems remote. The Federal Reserve has been trying to create inflation for ten years without success. The Bank of Japan has been trying to create inflation for thirty years, also without success. These cases should lay to rest the central bankers' mantra that inflation is caused by increases in the money supply; it's not. Money is a necessary condition for inflation, but it's not sufficient. Inflation is a psychological phenomenon driven by consumer behavior and expectations. The result of the dot-com meltdown in 2000, the mortgage meltdown in 2007, and financial panic in

2008 was to traumatize a generation of savers and investors. The effects of that trauma may last thirty years or more, as happened after the stock market crash of 1929 and the Great Depression that followed. A powerful catalyst is needed to overcome investor trauma and transform expectations about inflation. Either PSE or GBI could be that catalyst.

The reason has to do with the concept of marginal propensity to consume, or MPC. The concept is simple. If you give a billionaire a thousand dollars, she will probably spend none of it because she already has everything she wants and has no need to spend more. If you give someone below the poverty line a thousand dollars, he will probably spend all of it on food, rent, repairs, gas for the car, and other necessities of life. In technical terms, the MPC of the billionaire is 0 percent (she spends nothing), while the MPC of the poverty-level person is 100 percent (he spends it all). It's the act of spending and the resulting increase in the velocity or turnover of money that gives inflation a jolt.

The increased money velocity resulting from a PSE or GBI program will crash headlong into the real-growth constraints theorized by Reinhart and Rogoff. Higher money velocity increases *nominal* GDP. Meanwhile growth in *real* GDP is constrained by debt. If nominal GDP rises faster than real GDP, the difference is inflation, pure and simple. Progressive politicians may accomplish in the next two years what central bankers have been unable to accomplish in the past two decades—higher inflation. Central bankers who have been hoping for inflation should be careful what they wish for. They may get it, in the words of H. L. Mencken, "good and hard."

Investment Secret #5: Low productivity may mean inflation . . . or deflation.

How does an investor prepare for a world that could be inflationary or deflationary?

The solution is called the barbell portfolio. On one side of the barbell you have inflation protection consisting of gold, silver, land, and other hard assets. On the other side of the barbell you have deflation protection consisting of 10-year Treasury notes, utility stocks, and technology companies that continually reduce costs. Connecting the two sides of the barbell is an allocation of cash. The cash reduces the overall volatility of the portfolio and provides optionality to pivot toward inflation or deflation protection if either becomes dominant.

Today's debt-and-growth trap is the continuation of the crisis that began in 2007. It's the slow-motion phase of the ongoing crisis, but it could turn into a bang point any time. It could also lead to a whimper consisting of decades of slow growth.

Regardless of the outcome, investors are not helpless. The barbell portfolio offers a way to preserve wealth in all states of the world.

CHAPTER SIX
THE MAR-A-LAGO ACCORD

— — — — — — — — — —

How often do we hear references to the notion that we live in a rules-based global trading system? . . . In January 2017, British Prime Minister Theresa May praised liberalism, free trade, and globalization as "the forces that underpin the rules-based international system." . . . Chinese President Xi Jinping likewise extolled the virtues of a rules-based economic order at Davos. . . . But could someone please explain: What exactly are those rules?

—Judy Shelton, "The Case for a New International Monetary System" (2018)

Collaboration or Chaos?

It has been over thirty years since the last major international monetary conference, at the Louvre in Paris on February 22, 1987. The conference included the finance ministers and central bank heads of the United States, United Kingdom, France, West Germany, Canada, and Japan. A new international monetary conference will be needed soon to restore order to an incoherent system. A conference could produce another monetary "reform and evolution," in the classic formulation of scholar Kenneth W. Dam, or a "global monetary reset," in the newer formulation of casual observers. For over a century, the elite catchphrase for the world's monetary workings has been "the rules of the game." Whatever tag attaches, a new regime is coming. The unknown is whether this conference is launched in an orderly way by a convening power or in the midst of chaos in response to a new financial crisis. The former is preferable; the latter more likely.

International monetary conferences were rare before the 1920s. The international monetary system as it existed prior to the First World War was the product of evolution, not design. Gold had long been the leading form of money. Central banking only began with the creation of the Sveriges Riksbank in Sweden in 1668 and the Bank of England in 1694. Those and other central banks issued banknotes backed by gold, although redemption into gold was suspended on occasion during times of war.

When two currencies are pegged to gold they are also pegged to each other by the transitive law. As individual national gold standards spread in the nineteenth century, a global system of fixed exchange rates emerged spontaneously. For example, from 1900 to 1914, the official price of gold in the United Kingdom was £4.25 per ounce, and the official price in the United States was $20.67 per ounce. Using an ounce of gold as the common denominator meant that £1 sterling expressed in dollars was worth $4.87. There was no treaty or other agreement between the United Kingdom and the United States to fix this cross-exchange rate; it was simply the mathematical result of each nation fixing its own currency to gold. A lively physical gold trade between private banks in London and New York, led by the House of Morgan on the U.S. side, maintained the $4.87 sterling/dollar parity through arbitrage, taking into account transportation and insurance costs, relative interest rates, and the time value of money. These non-gold factors were called "gold points." When the points made gold "cheap" on one side of the ocean, a bank would buy gold, ship it to the other money center, and sell it in local currency, pocketing a nearly risk-free profit. These transactions were conducted using then new telephone tech-nology. There was no top-down or centralized enforcement mechanism; this was the free market at its best.

Between 1870 and 1914, widespread adoption of individual national gold standards led to the emergence of an international system of fixed exchange rates despite the absence of a treaty or an institution resembling the International Monetary Fund. The United States was one of the last major trading nations to formally adopt a gold standard under the Gold Standard Act of 1900, although the Coinage Act of 1873 allowed redemp-tion of banknotes for gold at a fixed rate at the option of the noteholder. A global gold standard and system of fixed exchange rates simply emerged by common consent, without direction or treaty.

The classic gold standard collapsed catastrophically in August 1914, the advent of the First World War. Belligerent nations suspended citizens' gold redemption of banknotes, either de jure or de facto. The United States, a neutral party until 1917, remained on a gold standard and became a magnet for much of the world's official gold as the United States exported arms and agricultural produce to embattled trading partners, principally the United Kingdom and France, and settled the resulting balance of pay-ments surplus in gold.

The difficulty after the First World War was how and when to resume a gold standard. War reparations imposed on Germany by the Treaty of Versailles combined with war debts incurred by the United Kingdom, France, and Belgium, among others, left those developed economies awash in unpayable debt after the war. Gold shipments to the United States for war matériel left insufficient gold in Europe to reconstitute the prewar system. The adversaries had greatly expanded their money supplies to fi-nance the war effort. Excessive debt, excessive money printing, and an acute gold shortage made the return to a true gold standard problematic at best. The question was ripe for a multilateral solution. The age of the inter-national monetary conference was born.

The first formal meeting was the Genoa Economic and Financial Conference of 1922. Thirty-four nations participated in the conclave held in the Palazzo di San Giorgio in Genoa, Italy. The agenda for the Genoa Conference was far broader than just the gold standard and included economic reconstruction in Europe, the status of reparations, and relations with the relatively new Soviet Russian regime that replaced the Russian Empire. An objective to return to the gold standard was expressed, with implementation left to individual sovereign participants. The gold shortage was addressed in part by schemes to conserve on the amount of gold needed to support the money supply. These schemes included removing gold coins from circulation, melting the coins and recasting them as 400-ounce bars kept in vaults. This made the physical exchange of gold impractical and caused citizens to become accustomed to paper money, with a vague if misplaced belief that there was sufficient gold behind the paper. Participants also agreed to accept major currencies such as French francs and pounds sterling in settlement of their balance of payments. This meant that foreign exchange was held as reserves in addition to physical gold.

This gold-exchange standard exhibited signs of failure almost from the start. The United Kingdom, France, and Belgium returned to gold over the course of 1925 through1926. France and Belgium returned at greatly devalued rates compared to the prewar parity. The United Kingdom, led by then Chancellor of the Exchequer Winston Churchill, took the opposite course and returned to gold at the prewar parity of £4.25 per ounce. This required a drastic reduction in the money supply to maintain the old parity, which proved deflationary and plunged the United Kingdom into depression several years before the world at large was affected in 1928–1929. The system then broke down completely with successive devaluations by the United Kingdom (1931), the United States (1933), and the United Kingdom and France combined (1936), before gold shipments and convertibility were once again suspended with the outbreak of the Second World War in 1939.

The next major international monetary conference was the most meaningful—the July 1944 United Nations Monetary and Financial Conference of forty-four nations held at the Mount Washington Hotel in Bretton Woods, New Hampshire. Bretton Woods featured a struggle between two principal plans. John Maynard Keynes, representing the United Kingdom, advanced a plan to establish a gold-backed form of world money called the bancor as the primary reserve currency to be issued by an international monetary fund and used to settle the balance of payments among nations. Harry Dexter White, representing the United States, advanced a plan that would establish the U.S. dollar, valued at one thirty-fifth of an ounce of gold, as the primary reserve currency. Other currencies were pegged to the dollar and only indirectly pegged to gold. Devaluation of other currencies against the dollar was possible under agreed procedures, while the dollar itself was firmly fixed to gold. Given U.S. dominance in geopolitics, commerce, and finance in the final days of the Second World War, it was not surprising that the U.S. plan carried the day despite Keynes's best efforts. Ironically, Harry Dexter White was a Stalinist agent inside the U.S. Treasury, whose hidden agenda was to hasten the demise of the British Empire by marginalizing sterling and highlighting the U.K.'s gold shortage. White's plan succeeded brilliantly as U.K. decolonization from 1947 to 1964 amply illustrates.

President Nixon's August 15, 1971, decision to "temporarily" suspend redemption of dollars for gold bullion by U.S. trading partners was not intended at the time as the end of the Bretton Woods system. It was intended as a kind of time-out, during which a new international monetary conference would be convened to devalue the dollar against gold, realign fixed exchange rates, and relaunch the old system at the new valuations. The conference called to implement these changes met at the Smithsonian Institution in Washington, D.C., in December 1971, the third great international monetary conference of the twentieth century. A Group of Ten (G10) nations consisting of the United States, the United Kingdom, France, West Germany, Sweden, Italy, the Netherlands, Belgium, Canada, and Japan signed the Smithsonian Agreement, which devalued the dollar by raising the price of gold from $35.00 per ounce to $38.00 per ounce and revaluing exchange rates of the currencies of the other signatories from 7.5 percent to 17 percent each. The Smithsonian Agreement failed even faster than the gold-exchange standard of the Genoa Conference. The dollar was devalued by an additional 10 percent on February 14, 1973, before eventually settling at today's official value of $42.22 per ounce of gold. One by one, major trading nations abandoned both the gold standard and fixed exchange rates and adopted floating exchange rates determined by the marketplace. Gold still existed in central bank vaults, yet no longer played a role in establishing the value of currencies.

Floating exchange rates were favored by academic economists at the time, most famously Milton Friedman, because they allowed nations to smoothly and continuously adjust unit labor costs and maintain favorable terms of trade without the devaluation shocks and foreign exchange crises that characterized the later years of the Bretton Woods system. As usual, the academics' pet theories ignored the hidden costs of floating exchange rates, including increased uncertainty on the future value of foreign direct investment, hedging costs, unrealistic pegs, market manipulation, and currency wars. These flaws came to the fore in the volatile years following the final demise of the Bretton Woods system and abandonment of the Smithsonian Agreement in 1973.

The Smithsonian Agreement was not the last landmark international monetary conference. Despite the rise of floating exchange rates after 1973, it was still possible to target if not precisely peg cross exchange rates through concerted market interventions by the major trading powers. For this purpose, a meeting of the G5 finance ministers representing the United States, the United Kingdom, France, West Germany, and Japan was convened at the Plaza Hotel in New York City in September 1985. The dollar had appreciated 50 percent between 1980 and 1985 due to Fed chair Paul Volcker's high-interest-rate policies and President Ronald Reagan's fiscal stimulus. U.S. exporters from the agricultural and manufacturing sectors were suffering from the Volcker-Reagan "King Dollar" policy. Rather than act in a unilateral or confrontational manner, the United States, led by Treasury secretary James Baker, convened the G5 at the Plaza Hotel to reach a consensus on dollar devaluation enforced through coordinated currency interventions by the G5 central banks and finance ministries.

The resulting Plaza Accord signed on September 22, 1985, was too successful. The desired dollar decline began almost immediately, and by early 1987 started to become disorderly. A new international monetary conference was convened in Paris in February 1987 to agree on steps to halt the dollar decline and stabilize exchange rates at mutually agreed levels. The Paris group included the Plaza Accord's G5, plus Canada. This new G6 signed the Louvre Accord in Paris on February 22, 1987, stabilizing the dollar against the currencies of major U.S. trading partners. This stability lasted until the 2008 global financial crisis and the start of a new currency war in 2010.

The 105-year era since the collapse of the classic gold standard in 1914 witnessed five major international monetary conferences: Genoa (1922), Bretton Woods (1944), Washington (1971), New York (1985), and Paris (1987). That's an average of one conference every twenty-one years, although the chronology is not evenly spaced. The last major conference was thirty-two years ago. There were important multilateral meetings to address international monetary issues in the meantime. However, none of these meetings resulted in fundamental changes to the rules of the game as seen in the five landmark conferences. On form, the world is overdue for a new international monetary conference to implement a true global monetary reset. The most pressing question for monetary elites is whether a conference is convened proactively with a view to creating a coherent system, or convened reactively in the midst of a new global financial crisis likely to produce a draconian response. A crucial moment in monetary history has arrived. A unique opening has been offered to President Donald J. Trump.

Former Fed chair Alan Greenspan made these remarks, comparing the current unanchored system with the benefits of the former gold standard, in a February 2017 interview with *Gold Investor* magazine:

I view gold as the primary global currency. It is the only currency, along with silver, that does not require a counterparty signature. Gold, however, has always been far more valuable per ounce than silver. No one refuses gold as payment to discharge an obligation. Credit instruments and fiat currency depend on the creditworthiness of counterparty. Gold, along with silver, is one of the only currencies that has an intrinsic value. It has always been that way. No one questions its value, and it has always been a valuable commodity, first coined in Asia Minor in 600 BC. . . . Today, going back onto the gold standard would be perceived as an act of desperation. But if the gold standard were in place today we would not have reached the situation in which we now find ourselves. We cannot afford to spend on infrastructure in the way that we should. . . . We would never have reached this position of extreme indebtedness were we on the gold standard, because the gold standard is a way of ensuring that fiscal policy never gets out of line.

The current managing director of the International Monetary Fund, Christine Lagarde, issued this warning at the 2018 Spring Meeting of the IMF:

Global debt is at an all-time high. It stands at $164 trillion, which is 225 percent of GDP. . . . Public debt in advanced economies is at levels not seen since World War II. And in low-income countries, if recent trends continue, many, not all, will face unsustainable debt burdens. . . . Financial vulnerabilities have increased due to high debt, rising financial market volatility, and elevated asset prices. A sudden tightening of financial conditions could lead to market corrections, unsustainable debt, and capital flow reversals.

The admonitions being sounded are not those of fringe critics or perennial gold bugs. Greenspan and Lagarde are pillars of the international monetary elite. They are forewarning that the system is nonsustainable, that a reset is coming, with gold possibly part of a reset discussion even if gold is unlikely to be an elite's first choice. The call for a new international monetary conference was also limned by prominent economist Judy Shelton in her 2018 article, "The Case for a New International Monetary System," in which she wrote, "Today there are compelling reasons—political, economic, and strategic—for Trump to initiate the establishment of a new international monetary system." Again, the only issue is whether a proactive convening power, possibly Trump, takes the lead, or whether a new hysteria emerges and forces the elites' hands under highly adverse conditions.

If Trump were to take the initiative to convene a new international monetary conference, his venue is ready-made—the Mar-a-Lago resort in Palm Beach, Florida, built by Marjorie Merriweather Post in 1927, now a National Historic Landmark owned by Trump. There would be some irony in the selection of Mar-a-Lago, since the Mount Washington Hotel in New Hampshire, site of the Bretton Woods Conference in 1944, is also a U.S. National Historic Landmark and was owned at the time of the conference by New Hampshire senator Charles Tobey, a personal friend of Franklin Roosevelt. Before the Bretton Woods location was decided, John Maynard Keynes implored his U.S. counterpart, Harry Dexter White, not to have the conference in Washington, because Keynes had a bad heart and in an age before air-conditioning the summer heat in Washington was insufferable. Keynes's request was accommodated by the selection of a site in the cool White Mountains of New Hampshire. If Keynes were alive today he would no doubt approve of the cool sea breezes of Mar-a-Lago as well. The ornate gilded halls of Mar-a-Lago also bear a passing if ersatz resemblance to Italy's thirteenth-century Palazzo di San Giorgio, site of the Genoa Conference in 1922.

Views of the Monetary Elites

To argue that no global monetary reset is in the cards is to argue that the global elites have achieved a permanent state of monetary nirvana. This is false. The international monetary system today is a patchwork of floating exchange rates, hard pegs, dirty pegs, currency wars, open and closed capital accounts, with world money waiting in the wings. It is unanchored. It is incoherent.

"Incoherent" is the exact word used by both former Fed chair Ben Bernanke and John Lipsky, former acting managing director of the IMF, in separate conversations with me. I spoke to Bernanke in Seoul, South Korea, on May 27, 2015, and to Lipsky just a few months later in New York City. Each used the word to describe the international monetary system. I've never heard either one of them use the word publicly. I'm also sure the word was neither rehearsed nor coincidental. The fact that two of the top monetary elites used the same word in this context shows that view is a live topic of discussion in elite circles.

By incoherent, both Bernanke and Lipsky meant that there was no anchor for the system, no universally agreed reference point or metric by which to judge currency values. You can judge *every* currency in relation to another currency, yet there's no way to judge *any* currency by an objective standard under current rules.

The problem of an anchor or objective standard for valuing currencies was solved centuries ago by the gold standard. Prior to the seventeenth century, gold and silver were money and there was no need to reference paper currencies (except for ancient Chinese paper money regimes, which failed catastrophically). Beginning in the seventeenth century, paper money backed by gold and gold coins circulated side by side. Eventually the gold backing was withdrawn. As we've seen, this happened in stages between 1914 and 1971, so that everyday citizens barely noticed. Private gold was made illegal in the United States for citizens in 1933 and commercial banks were forced by law to hand over their gold to the central bank in 1934. Yet the United States remained on a gold standard with its foreign trading partners, and the Federal Reserve was required to back the currency with at least 40 percent gold. Gold backing, called "cover," was reduced to 25 percent in 1945. In 1965, the gold backing was eliminated entirely for Fed deposits, and in 1968 the gold cover was reduced to zero for Federal Reserve notes. Finally, in 1971, Nixon ended gold convertibility of dollars by foreign trading partners.

Neither Lipsky nor Bernanke favor a return to the gold standard. In fact, there's scarcely a mainstream economist in the world today who favors a gold standard. This begs the question, If you're not using gold, yet you want an anchor for major reserve currencies, then what anchor do you propose? This is where the discussion breaks down. Those who criticize incoherence have no answer to the conundrum of how to invent a suitable anchor for the international monetary system.

On February 15, 2017, I met privately with former Treasury secretary Tim Geithner at a small gathering in New York City. I asked him directly about the game plan for the next monetary crisis, including aspects of a possible global monetary reset. I suggested the Fed had done little to reduce its balance sheet after the last crisis in 2008; the balance sheet in early 2017 was still around the $4.2 trillion level reached in late 2014. I expressed doubt the Fed would be able to quadruple its balance sheet in a new crisis as it did after the 2008 crisis. I asked Geithner point-blank if he believed the IMF would print trillions of special drawing rights, or SDRs, to reliquefy the international monetary system if needed. That would require consensus by major members of the IMF, a process that could itself constitute a version of an international monetary conference.

To my surprise, Geithner poured cold water on the idea of the IMF saving the world. He said, "We tried that after 2008 and it didn't work very well." Geithner was right. In August and September 2009, almost a year after the most acute phase of the 2008 panic, the IMF issued SDR182.7 billion (worth $255 billion at today's SDR/USD exchange rate). Most market participants barely noticed the issuance and it did little to stimulate world economic growth. Part of the problem was that the issuance came long after the panic subsided, and even after the U.S. recovery commenced. Also, the amounts involved were small relative to $10 trillion of currency swaps arranged between the Fed and the ECB and other central banks, and the $1 trillion of money printing the Fed commenced under QE1 and later QE2. Still, this did not mean that SDRs could not be effective, merely that the timing had been slow and the amounts insufficient.

I pressed Geithner further. I asked, "Well, if the Fed can't expand its balance sheet and IMF issuance of SDRs is ineffective, how will the Fed and other central banks deal with a new global liquidity crisis?" Geithner paused, looked at me, and said, "Guarantees." In other words, Geithner expected that in a new crisis the Treasury or Fed would stop a run on the banks and money market funds by guaranteeing deposits and account balances.

Geithner was forthcoming, yet I was highly skeptical of his proposal. Guarantees worked in 2008 because there was a run on *private* credit and the government was able to use *public* credit and guarantees to backstop private credit. The next crisis will be different. The investing public and market participants take it for granted today that the government will bail out banks (even if it means using new "bail-in" rules to convert deposits to equity). But who bails out the government? The next crisis will feature a loss of confidence in government itself, central banks, and fiat currencies. How can the government guarantee itself when the government's own credit is called into question?

Finally, on May 31, 2018, I enjoyed an hour-long one-on-one discussion in Hong Kong with John Lipsky, the only American ever to lead the IMF. This was my third meeting with Lipsky after my 2015 conversation in New York and a later occasion in Washington, D.C., and it was by far my most in-depth discussion. Lipsky is not as well known as Geithner, yet he was arguably more powerful than Geithner because for a time he controlled the IMF's world money printing press, which produces SDRs.

Lipsky is a Ph.D. economist from Stanford University. He began his career in 1974 at the IMF and spent ten years there, where he became the IMF's top expert on exchange rate surveillance. In 1984, he moved to Salomon Brothers (today part of Citi), where he worked with the legendary Henry Kaufman, known as "Dr. Doom," eventually becoming chief economist. In 1997, he left Salomon to become chief economist of JPMorgan. In 2006, he returned to the IMF to serve a five-year term as the first deputy managing director.

The first deputy's role is the result of an unwritten power-sharing agreement between Europe and the United States, arrived at during the Bretton Woods Conference in 1944. The Bretton Woods institutions and arrangements, including the IMF and World Bank, were structured along lines desired by the United States. The belief was the United States had too much economic power and needed to share that power with Europe. The informal agreement was that an American would run the World Bank, but an American would *never* head the IMF. The top job at the IMF, managing director, was reserved for Europeans. A second-in-command position, first deputy managing director, was created to be held by an American. In effect, the first deputy was America's eyes and ears at the IMF, while the top job went to a European. In his role as first deputy, Lipsky was an important part in the issuance of the SDR182.7 billion of world money in 2009.

This arrangement remained in place until IMF managing director Dominique Strauss-Kahn was arrested by the NYPD in New York City on May 14, 2011, on sexual assault and attempted rape charges. Strauss-Kahn resigned as managing director a few days later, on May 18. As Strauss-Kahn's departure was so abrupt, the IMF's Executive Committee did not have time properly to consider a successor. Instead, John Lipsky was elevated from first deputy to acting managing director, becoming the first and only American ever to run the IMF. Lipsky retired from the IMF at the end of August 2011, and continued his career in academia.

My May 2018 meeting with Lipsky in Hong Kong was fascinating. No one in the world knew more of the IMF's inner workings and use of SDRs to provide global liquidity in a global monetary reset. I was getting the reset playbook from the source.

Prior to 2009, the IMF had not issued SDRs since 1981, despite severe emerging-markets crises in 1982, 1994, and 1997. A cynic might suggest the IMF never issued SDRs to save emerging markets, yet issued SDRs to save developed markets in 2009. Lipsky emphasized the difficulty of achieving consensus inside the IMF on SDR-related matters. SDR issuance as part of a global monetary reset was unlikely except in a crisis. In other words, the IMF would not *proactively* push for a reset at a new monetary conference, but might *reactively* orchestrate a reset in the midst of a new panic.

I asked Lipsky about Geithner's critique of the 2009 SDR issuance and his dismissal of the IMF's ability to be useful in a crisis. John practically shouted, "Have you read his book?" Lipsky added, "Geithner was at the IMF between his time at the Treasury and when he moved to the Fed. I'm not sure what happened, but he had a bad experience and has nothing good to say about the IMF."

Geithner was president of the Federal Reserve Bank of New York from 2003 to 2009 and became Treasury secretary on January 26, 2009. He served a prior stint at Treasury as under secretary for International Affairs from 1998 to 2001. From 2001 to 2003, Geithner was at the IMF. That period at the IMF was the one Lipsky referred to.

Lipsky was right. Geithner's book *Stress Test* (2014) includes this excerpt:

> The IMF was a more formal and less fun place to work than Treasury. The meetings were endless, with crushing bureaucracy, an intrusive and fractious executive board, an appalling amount of paper, and a lot of factional conflict among various fiefdoms. . . . The pace was much slower than I was used to. . . . The IMF was full of smart and dedicated people, but not many had experienced the

burden of making policy decisions as government officials. There was a lot of paper and bureaucracy and talking.

That's just a small sample of Geithner's scathing critiques of the IMF, going back to the 1997–1998 emerging-markets crisis during his time at Treasury.

It's never enough to study documents and theorize on the future of the SDR. When speaking one-on-one with policymakers like Ben Bernanke, Tim Geithner, and John Lipsky, the picture they paint privately is unsettling in its implications for how a global monetary reset will evolve. Given Trump's self-proclaimed nationalist, America First views, it is unlikely that he has any higher opinion of the IMF than Geithner; he almost certainly has a lower opinion and would be disinclined to provide emergency funding to the IMF in a liquidity crunch or to partner with the IMF in a global financial crisis. If Trump were to convene a new international monetary conference, it seems more likely he would appeal directly to global leaders rather than working through institutional channels at the IMF. This approach is more in keeping with Trump's ad hoc personal style, which abjures red tape and elevates the personal over process.

What my conversations with global monetary elites revealed is that institutions like the Treasury, Fed, and IMF are powerful on paper, yet they are dysfunctional and slow in practice. None of the leaders I spoke with sees a global monetary reset coming. At the height of a new global financial panic, no one will be in charge. Solutions that emerge in that environment are more likely to be ad hoc than thoughtful.

The ideal outcome would be a Mar-a-Lago monetary conference convened by Trump and attended by the ten largest economies (United States, China, Japan, Germany, United Kingdom, France, India, Italy, Brazil, and Canada), who comprise 80 percent of global GDP and about half the world's population. Additional seats would be available for gold or oil powers, including Russia, Mexico, Nigeria, Indonesia, Netherlands, and Saudi Arabia; these countries add another 700 million to the population represented. A larger group of countries could be invited, but the dialogue would be controlled by the "Gang of Sixteen" listed. The agenda would be to establish an anchor for the global monetary system other than a single currency or group of currencies. This anchor could be gold, SDRs pegged to gold, or a new world currency defined by a commodity basket (the "neo-bancor"). Reserves could still be held in leading currencies, but world trade and balance of payments obligations would be calculated and settled in anchor units, removing incentives for devaluation and currency wars. Oil would be priced in anchor units, ending the petrodollar arrangement and dollar hegemony more broadly. Numerous technical issues would have to be addressed that might involve several years of research before the effective date of a final plan. This research hiatus would give participating nations time to adjust to a "shadow anchor" before implementation.

The chances for such a conference are slim in the current environment of trade and currency wars. Paradoxically, the futility of trade and currency wars could be the catalyst for a conference nonetheless. Still, a more likely outcome is continued chaos until an acute crisis emerges. Yet a formal monetary conference is not the only path to reset the system. Alternatives include a digital gold standard, an SDR pegged to gold, and a currency pegged to gold without using gold. What makes these and other alternatives intriguing is they can be pursued unilaterally and covertly, at least in the early stages. These alternatives are surveyed below.

Crypto Gold

The two countries in the world that have been most explicit about their desire to overthrow the rule of the U.S. dollar are the same two countries that have acquired more gold than any others in the past ten years: Russia and China. Now, their plans to bury the dollar have moved beyond wishful thinking to active measures.

Their approach is straightforward. Russia and China are each developing proprietary cryptocurrencies on a permissioned, heavily encrypted digital ledger. They are well aware that neither the ruble nor the yuan have the needed elements for reserve currency status, including deep liquid bond markets and good rule of law. But these elements can be leapfrogged by creating a new currency that does. Their plan would work as follows:

Russia and China will pool their official gold (about 5,000 tons, or about 15 percent of all official gold in the world), placing it on deposit in a Swiss non-bank vault governed by Swiss law. They will invite other participants in the scheme to do likewise. At the same time, Russia and China will launch a new digital currency on their distributed ledger. This new coin (call it a "Putin-coin" or "Xi-coin," for example) will be pegged at an exchange rate of 1 coin = 1 SDR. Units of the new coin could be expanded based on new deposits of gold or the voluntary creation of credit denominated in the new coin. A board of governors of the distributed ledger would make determinations regarding participation, gold deposits, and money supply.

Trading in goods and services will commence among the members of this pool. As members, North Korea could sell weapons to Iran, China could sell infrastructure to Russia, Iran and Russia could sell oil to China, the Chinese could vacation in Turkey, and so on. These transactions could be billed locally in any currency, but would be converted by the participants' central banks to the new digital currency for balance of payments purposes. Digital coin balances would be netted out and settled periodically. The net balances would be settled in a weight of physical gold at market prices converted from SDRs, using the IMF's daily valuations. The gold could either be flown to the holder of the balance due, or reassigned in the Swiss vault without physical transfer. This system would combine both the oldest form of money (gold) with the newest (e-currency on a distributed ledger). Importantly from the perspective of the Russians, Chinese, and other participants, the dollar is not involved at all.

This distributed ledger monetary system is likely to grow quickly as major economic powers such as India and Brazil are attracted by the ease of use and absence of dollars. China and Russia could boost adoption by requiring smaller trading partners to use the new system. Pressure could be applied to major commodity exporters such as Saudi Arabia and Australia to invoice in the new digital currency. Net trade balances could easily be converted into dollars by selling the physical gold balances if desired. By this means, the new digital system could interface with the existing dollar-based system through the medium of gold.

Russia and China are not alone in pursuing cryptocurrencies on distributed ledgers. A new class of global cryptocurrencies on a permissioned distributed ledger controlled by the IMF and central banks is also in the works. Consider this excerpt from the June 2018 IMF report, "Monetary Policy in the Digital Age":

> IMF managing director Christine Lagarde noted in a speech at the Bank of England last year, "the best response by central banks is . . . being open to fresh ideas and new demands, as economies evolve." . . . Government authorities should regulate the use of crypto assets to prevent regulatory arbitrage and any unfair competitive advantage crypto assets may derive from lighter regulation. That means . . . effectively taxing crypto transactions. . . . Central banks should continue to make their money attractive for use as a settlement vehicle. For example, they could make central bank money user-friendly in the digital world by issuing digital tokens of their own to supplement physical cash and bank reserves. Such central bank digital currency could be exchanged, peer to peer in a decentralized manner, much as crypto assets are.

The IMF report should be understood as a declaration of war on non-government cryptocurrencies and a manifesto calling for government-controlled cryptos. One result is likely to be an e-SDR administered by the IMF that would facilitate swaps and secondary-market trading among IMF members who hold SDRs. In the event of a massive new issue of SDRs to mitigate a global financial crisis, the e-SDR should expedite issuance and speed transfers to adversely affected parties in the way fire engines from one town will race to another if a fire is out of control.

While Russian, Chinese, and IMF-sponsored digital currencies are in the works, other more curious events are unfolding in the sphere of world money.

The SDR and Gold

Has a global monetary reset already happened?

I was alerted to this possibility by a research report sent to my attention from a correspondent named D. H. Bauer based in Switzerland. An explanation of Bauer's research begins with the dollar price of gold: $1,260 per ounce at the date of the report. Following the dollar price of gold, we consider that on a given day gold is "up" or "down" by, say $10 per ounce. When we make this observation we effectively quote a cross rate between U.S. dollars (USD) and one ounce of gold (GOLD) or USD/GOLD.

Next, we observe the U.S. dollar value of the SDR. This cross rate, SDR/USD, is calculated and published daily by the IMF. As of this writing, SDR1 = USD1.406570. That rate changes daily like any floating exchange rate. Bauer took the known rates of USD/GOLD and SDR/USD and applied the transitive law to calculate SDR/GOLD, a price that is not actively followed on trading screens. He then graphed the time series of both prices with trend lines from December 31, 2014, to March 31, 2018. The graph includes a black vertical line corresponding to October 1, 2016. That is the date the Chinese yuan was officially included in the SDR basket of major currencies. The other currencies are sterling, yen, euro, and the dollar. The data and graph show that before China joined the SDR, the dollar price of gold and the SDR price of gold were volatile and highly correlated. After China joined the SDR, the dollar price of gold remained volatile, while the SDR price exhibited far less volatility.

Importantly, the trend line of SDR/GOLD is a nearly horizontal line. Gold denominated in SDRs has been trading in a narrow range of SDR850 to SDR950, an 11 percent band with fluctuations of 5.5 percent above and below the SDR900 central tendency. The price exhibits mean reversion. When gold rallies to SDR950, it quickly falls back toward SDR900. Likewise, when gold sinks to SDR850, it rallies back to SDR900. No prices appear outside the range after October 1, 2016. This price band narrowed in early 2017 and was contained in the SDR875 to SDR925 range, a 5.5 percent total band, 2.75 percent on either side of the target. This narrower band is indicative of a currency peg. A first approximation hints the SDR has been pegged to gold at a rate of SDR900 = 1 ounce of gold. This implies a new gold standard using not dollars, but the IMF's world money. A global monetary reset may have occurred without a formal conference or declaration. SDR900 = 1 ounce of pure gold is the new monetary benchmark.

The advent of low volatility in SDR/GOLD (versus prior high volatility) occurred on October 1, 2016. The near straight-line trend of SDR/GOLD after the Chinese yuan joined the SDR is practically impossible without an intervening factor or manipulation. The probability of this occurring randomly is infinitesimal. The SDR/GOLD horizontal trend line after October 1, 2016, is an example of autoregression. This appears only if there's a recursive function (a feedback loop) or manipulation. In the case of SDR/GOLD, one can rule out a recursive function since gold trades in a relatively free market determined by supply and demand. One can also rule out randomness as statistically highly improbable. That leaves manipulation as the only explanation for the flat trend line in SDR/GOLD.

If the SDR price of gold falls below SDR900 (indicating a strong SDR and a weak gold price), the manipulator buys gold, sells dollars, and buys the non-dollar currencies behind the SDR. If the SDR price of gold rises above SDR900 (indicating a weak SDR and a strong gold price), the manipulator sells gold, buys dollars, and sells the non-dollar currencies behind the SDR. By monitoring markets and intervening continually with open-market operations in gold and currencies, the manipulator can maintain the peg. There are only four parties in the world with the resources to conduct this manipulation in an impactful way: the U.S. Treasury, the ECB, the Chinese State Administration of Foreign Exchange (SAFE), and the IMF. These are the only entities with enough gold and hard currency reserves (or SDRs) to conduct the large-scale open-market operations needed to peg the price.

One can eliminate the U.S. Treasury and ECB as suspects. Both are relatively transparent about their total gold holdings, foreign exchange reserves, and the SDR component of their reserves. (For the ECB we look at the large members, including Germany and France, for this data.) If either the Treasury or ECB were conducting open-market operations of this kind, changes in holdings of gold and SDR component currencies would appear in official reports. No fluctuations of any magnitude appear. That leaves SAFE and the IMF. Both are nontransparent. China has about 2,000 tons of gold, probably more—they don't disclose the excess. China has also acquired SDRs in the secondary market in addition to official allocations provided by the IMF to its members. The IMF owns 2,814.1 metric tonnes of gold and can print SDRs in unlimited quantities subject to executive board approval. The IMF makes loans and receives principal and interest in SDRs that are traded among IMF members through a secret trading desk. Gold is traded surreptitiously by major central banks through the Bank for International Settlements (which also traded Nazi gold in the Second World War). The BIS is furtive and controlled principally by the same nations who control the IMF. China can also conduct gold purchases and sales for yuan or dollars on the open market in Shanghai and London and separately buy or sell SDRs for dollars or yuan through the IMF. China can buy or sell the SDR basket currencies separately through bank foreign exchange trading desks.

The targeted value of SDR900 per ounce of gold is intriguing, with dark implications for the future of the U.S. dollar. Currently a total of SDR204.2 billion are issued and held by IMF members. The IMF owns 2,814.1 metric tons of gold, equal to 90,475,284.87 troy ounces. If the IMF wished to make SDRs the sole global reserve currency backed by gold at a 40 percent ratio, the same gold cover as the U.S. dollar from 1913 to 1945, then the implied SDR price of gold would be equal to the quantity 0.40(204,200,000,000/90,475,284.87), representing the amount of SDRs divided by the amount of IMF gold in troy ounces times 40 percent. *This quantity equals SDR902.8 per ounce, almost exactly the pegged price of SDR900 per ounce.*

There is no evidence the IMF is implementing an SDR/GOLD peg. The IMF's gold holdings have remained constant since 2010 and permission to launch the gold-peg operation is unlikely to have been granted by the United States or Germany. To the contrary, there is strong evidence to support the view that China is behind the peg. This is ironic; when the SDR was created in 1969 it was originally pegged to gold and defined as a weight in gold (SDR1 = 0.88867 grams of gold). That peg was soon abandoned even as the dollar peg (USD1 = 0.02857 ounces of gold) was also abandoned. Now the SDR/GOLD peg has returned, albeit at a much higher price for gold.

Since this SDR peg to gold is informal and unannounced it can be abandoned at will. The peg probably will be abandoned sooner than later because Chinese sponsors of the peg have ignored the lessons of 1925, when the United Kingdom returned sterling to the gold standard at a level that overvalued sterling. The result was a catastrophic deflation in the United Kingdom that presaged the Great Depression. Likewise, the Chinese peg of SDR900 per ounce of gold is too cheap to sustain, given the scarce supply of gold and the growing supply of SDRs. More to the point, the IMF will print trillions of SDRs in the next global financial crisis, which will prove highly inflationary unless the IMF conditions the distribution of SDRs on the receipt of gold. China would have to sell precious gold reserves to maintain an SDR900 price. This would reprise the U.S. depletion of its gold reserves by 11,000 tons from 1950 to 1970 to maintain the Bretton Woods gold peg to an overvalued dollar. Still, this is an historic development. Even if the peg is nonsustainable in the long run, it's a clear short-run signal that China is betting on the SDR and gold, not the yuan or the dollar. An important pillar of a global monetary reset seems already in place.

A Gold Standard Without Gold

An international monetary conference, with or without IMF involvement, or an SDR/GOLD peg are not the only paths to a global monetary reset. Unilateral action by nations seeking stability can create network effects that result in the emergence of a global monetary regime not unlike the classic gold standard that prevailed from 1870 to 1914. Is it possible for a single national currency to adhere to a gold standard when the issuer of that currency has little or no gold? Curiously, the answer is yes, provided the currency is other than the U.S. dollar.

A nation that wishes to peg to gold need only denominate its currency by weight of gold and allow the currency cross rate to the dollar to float freely. A holder of that currency wanting to convert to gold at the pegged rate could sell the currency to the issuer's central bank for dollars, at a cross rate calculated to produce an amount in dollars that would enable the purchase of gold at market rates equal to the weight specified by the peg. There are transaction costs and frictions in this two-step process compared to a simple conversion of the local currency into gold. Still, those frictions could be reduced by prearrangement with a physical gold exchange that offered volume discounts, straight-through processing, and speedy delivery to safe non-bank storage for the account of the currency seller. Intermediation between the local currency and gold need not be conducted in dollars; it could be done in any currency accepted in a liquid market for gold. The Shanghai Gold Exchange, or SGE, would offer this facility. By arrangement, the holder of the gold-backed currency could sell that currency for yuan to the issuer's central bank at a cross rate calculated to produce an amount in yuan needed to buy gold at market rates equal to the weight of gold specified by the peg. SGE would welcome this arrangement because it promotes the internationalization of the yuan while generating more liquidity on the exchange itself. This arrangement would also give the local currency issuer's central bank an attractive alternative to dollars (or euros) for its reserve positions, so long as a liquid market in yuan/gold exists.

I call this de facto gold standard for non-dollar issuers the Malaysia Plan in reference to Mahathir bin Mohamad, former and, at this writing, current prime minister of Malaysia. Mahathir was the original currency warrior, who vociferously confronted George Soros and international bankers at the IMF annual meeting in Hong Kong in September 1997. This high-profile confrontation occurred at the peak of the Asian financial crisis that began the prior June. Sequential run-on-the-bank-style currency collapses were occurring in Thailand, Indonesia, Malaysia, and South Korea, later followed by similar collapses in Russia and Brazil. At the time, Mahathir, a physician, not an economist, inquired of his closest advisers whether fundamental conditions had changed in the Malaysian economy. Mahathir closed Malaysia's capital account to prevent its foreign exchange being depleted by panicked bankers in London and New York after being advised that economic conditions were unchanged. For this he was castigated as a "menace" by Soros and privately disparaged both by IMF officials and developed-economy finance ministers. Yet Mahathir successfully defended Malaysia's fragile foreign exchange reserve position, and its capital account was eventually reopened. A decade after Mahathir defied the conventional wisdom of international monetary elites, the IMF reversed course and said that there were circumstances, such as those confronting Mahathir, when closing the capital account is an appropriate remedy for hot-money stampedes. Mahathir was years ahead of his time in 1997; his actions have been fully vindicated in the meantime.

Mahathir ended his first spell as prime minister in 2003, as the longest serving prime minister in Malaysian history. I celebrated Mahathir's ninetieth birthday with him and a small group of close friends at a private dinner in Kuala Lumpur in July 2015. His interest then was to find the best way forward for Malaysia in a world where it could not dictate the international monetary system yet could be victimized by it. The birthday dinner was part of a three-day closed-door dialogue. I was invited to discuss topics including currency wars, the IMF, and systemic risk.

Using Malaysia as an illustrative case, the Malaysia Plan mechanics would work as follows:

At this writing, the U.S. dollar (USD)-Malaysian ringgit (MYR) cross exchange rate (USD/MYR) is 4.0200. The dollar price of gold is $1,268 per ounce. That yields a price of gold denominated in ringgit of MYR5,100 per ounce. Assume the Malaysian government announces a policy of pegging the ringgit to gold at a fixed price of MYR5,100 per ounce. At that point, Malaysia would be on a gold standard at a fixed exchange rate.

Now assume the dollar price of gold rises to $1,350 per ounce and a ringgit holder wishes to exchange ringgit for gold at the fixed rate of MYR5,100 per ounce. In this scenario, the central bank would have to exchange ringgit for dollars at the USD/MYR rate of 3.7800 (versus the original rate of 4.0200, when the peg was set). This new rate of 3.7800 provides sufficient dollars to purchase one ounce of gold at the higher dollar price of gold, thus preserving the fixed ringgit price of 5,100 per ounce. The central bank does not need gold to preserve the gold peg; it merely needs enough dollars to allow the exchanging party to buy one ounce of gold for every MYR5,100 exchanged.

The objections of conventional monetary elites to this new gold standard are easily stated. Any fixed exchange rate, whether to gold, dollars, or another numeraire, impedes a central bank's ability to steal from citizens through inflation and devaluation. The inflation-theft paradigm is critical to elite efforts to transfer wealth to themselves and their state apparatus in pursuit of a globalist policy agenda. Elites also claim that a fixed exchange rate invites a drain on the hard currency reserves of a currency issuer when the fixed rate is viewed as out-of-line with market prices. A fixed exchange rate arguably eliminates one leg of the Mundell-Fleming triangle, which holds that it's nonsustainable to have fixed exchange rates, independent monetary policy, and an open capital account at the same time. This reduces policy flexibility and forces the local currency issuer either to abandon independent monetary policy or close the capital account to support the peg. Finally, the peg to gold introduces volatility into the local currency's cross rate to the dollar, which could hurt local exporters. In the above example, USD/MYR moved from 4.0200 to 3.7800 in support of the MYR5,100-per-ounce gold peg as the dollar price of gold moved from $1,268 to $1,350 per ounce. That move corresponds to a strengthening of the foreign exchange value of the ringgit.

These objections are easily refuted. Elites' inability to steal from citizens through inflation and devaluation is the allure of the plan, not a fault. Far from inviting a drain on foreign exchange, the stability that results from a peg to gold attracts foreign exchange, as global investors see an opportunity to invest in potentially high-growth economies like Malaysia while preserving wealth through the peg to gold. Investors who will not buy gold directly because it lacks yield or due to other institutional constraints can receive the benefits of gold indirectly by investing in an economy with a currency linked to gold. Consider it back-door devaluation insurance. The Mundell-Fleming objection is a red herring; that model does not apply to gold because there is no central bank of gold and no policy interest rate for gold for hot money to arbitrage. The local currency (in our example, MYR) still floats against the dollar, so an independent monetary policy versus the Fed and an open capital account are entirely feasible under Mundell-Fleming. Volatility in the cross rate between the gold-pegged currency and the dollar is likely to be more the result of erratic Fed policy than changes in the subjective value of either gold or the local currency in question. Finally, the gold peg points the way to an investment-driven rather than export-driven path to growth in emerging economies. A stable currency value measured against gold attracts direct foreign investment and facilitates an exit from the middle-income trap that Asian economies have been stuck in for decades (with the notable exceptions of Taiwan, Singapore, South Korea, and earlier, Japan). Low-value added exports are an economic dead end once an economy pulls itself from poverty to middle-income status. Further progress requires the production of high-value added goods and services that are the fruits of investment, not cheap currencies. In short, the elite critique ignores second-order benefits of a stable currency while elevating the alleged but illusory benefits of inflation and devaluation as substitutes for sustainable growth.

The central bank of a country adopting the Malaysia Plan can mitigate volatility in the local-currency-to-dollar exchange rate by conducting open-market operations in gold. Using the Malaysia example, if the dollar price of gold were to drop precipitously to, say, $1,200 per ounce, resulting in a weaker ringgit measured in dollars (USD/MYR = 4.2500, assuming $1,200-per-ounce gold and a ringgit-gold peg of MYR5,100 per ounce), the central bank could buy gold with its reserves until gold returned to the original dollar level of $1,268 per ounce at the time the peg was established. Those gold reserves could then be sold for dollars when the dollar price of gold surpasses the $1,268 per ounce level. These gold open-market operations seem counterintuitive (they involve expending dollar reserves while the local currency is weak), yet pursued consistently an accretion of dollar reserves would result as the gold trading profits were realized. Those added reserves could then be used in defense of the ringgit-gold peg as needed. Conversely, if the dollar price of gold rises dramatically, open-market operations would be unnecessary because the gold peg is vindicated as the ringgit (or other local currency) remains strong (versus dollars), while the dollar itself is debased (versus gold and the gold-pegged currencies).

An important benefit to countries adopting the Malaysia Plan is that when two countries peg to gold, those countries' currencies will be pegged to each other by a simple transitive property. In the above example, the

Malaysian ringgit is pegged to gold at MYR5,100 per ounce. If Indonesia took the same approach and pegged their currency, the rupiah (IDR), to gold at IDR17.9 million per ounce of gold (using exchange rates at this writing of IDR/USD = 0.000071, and $1,268 per ounce of gold), then the MYR/IDR exchange rate would also be fixed at 0.000285 ringgits per rupiah. This de facto pegged exchange rate between ringgits and rupiah would obviate currency wars, lower transaction costs, and facilitate cross-border trade and investment between these two important emerging economies. If this practice were to spread to a group of thirty or forty countries, something like the pre-1914 gold standard would emerge, with two important differences. Almost no gold is needed by the participants themselves; instead the market provides the gold for settlements intermediated through dollar-gold transactions. The United States would not participate. In effect, the world would return to a gold standard by free riding on deep, liquid, dollar-denominated markets in gold, and using those markets to intermediate the local currency-gold peg. The world would be betting that the United States cannot long maintain a strong dollar (measured in gold) with high real interest rates, given lackluster growth, near record debt-to-GDP ratios, and adverse demographics. That's a good bet. The Malaysia Plan's success would be self-fulfilling, as institutional investors allocated their assets toward economies using gold-pegged currencies and away from those that must out of necessity create inflation to alleviate non-sustainable debt burdens. Currencies of plan participants would constitute a pool of synthetic world money; their fixedness to one another makes them interoperable and alleviates fears of devaluation and currency wars.

The Malaysia Plan is a bottom-up self-help model that does not rely on reserve currency central banks or the IMF for implementation. The plan is a way for emerging economies to get out from under IMF hectoring and dollar hegemony, while at the same time offering an attractive investment environment for institutions. The plan shifts the burden of price adjustment from the poor to the rich (through the dollar-gold exchange) and protects the poor from confiscation through devaluation.

This chapter has identified various ways in which a global monetary reset could occur. These include a new international monetary conference (either cooperative or chaotic), crypto SDRs, gold pegged SDRs, and gold pegged local currencies. There are other ways for a reset to play out, including fiat SDRs, or an autarkic outcome with no global reserve benchmark at all. The global monetary reset is coming. What's missing is leadership and foresight.

Investment Secret #6: Prepare for asset-backed currencies with physical gold.

John Pierpont Morgan was called to testify before Congress in 1912, in the aftermath of the panic of 1907, on the subject of Wall Street manipulations and what was then called the "money trust," or banking monopoly, of J. P. Morgan & Co.

In the course of his testimony, Morgan made one of the most profound and lasting remarks in the history of finance. In reply to questions from the congressional committee staff attorney, Samuel Untermyer, the following dialogue ensued:

> **Untermyer:** I want to ask you a few questions bearing on the subject that you have touched upon this morning, as to the control of money. The control of credit involves a control of money, does it not?
>
> **Morgan:** A control of credit? No.
>
> **Untermyer:** But the basis of banking is credit, is it not?
>
> **Morgan:** Not always. That is an evidence of banking, but it is not the money itself. Money is gold, and nothing else.

Morgan's observation that "money is gold, and nothing else" was right in two respects. The first and most obvious is that gold is a form of money.

The second and more subtle point, revealed in the phrase "and nothing else," was that other instruments purporting to be money were really forms of debt, unless they were redeemable into physical gold.

The intermediate-term forecast is that gold will reach ten thousand dollars per ounce in the course of the current gold bull market, which began in December 2015. Investors should keep 10 percent of their investable assets in physical gold, with room left in the portfolio for "paper gold," in the form of ETFs and mining stocks if desired.

The first step is to determine investable assets. This is not the same as net worth. Investors should exclude home equity, business equity, and other illiquid or intangible assets that constitute your livelihood. Do not take portfolio market risk with your primary income source or the roof over your head. Once you've removed those assets, whatever is left are your investable assets. You should then allocate 10 percent of that amount to physical gold. This gold should not be kept in a bank safe-deposit box or bank vault. There is a high correlation between the time you'll want your gold the most and the time banks are closed by government order. Keep your gold in safe, non-bank storage.

The next step concerns the ten-thousand-dollar-per-ounce forecast for the dollar price of gold. This is straightforward. Excessive Federal Reserve money printing from 2008 to 2015, combined with projected U.S. government deficits after 2018 of over $1 trillion per year for the foreseeable future and a U.S. debt-to-deficit ratio of 105 percent rising to over 110 percent in a few years, leave the U.S. dollar vulnerable to a collapse of confidence on the part of foreign investors and U.S. citizens alike. That collapse of confidence will not happen in a vacuum. It will coincide with a general loss of confidence in all major reserve currencies. This loss of confidence will be exacerbated by malicious efforts on the part of Russia, China, Turkey, Iran, and others to abandon dollars entirely and to bypass the U.S.-dollar payments system. The evolution of oil pricing from dollars to IMF SDRs will be the last nail in the dollar's coffin.

At that point, either the United States acting on its own or a global conference resembling a new Bretton Woods will turn to gold to restore confidence. Once that route is chosen, the critical factor is to set a non-deflationary price for gold that restores confidence but does not lead to a new depression. The United States, China, Japan, and the Eurozone have a combined M1 money supply of $24 trillion. Those same countries have approximately 33,000 tons of official gold. As noted, a successful gold standard historically requires 40 percent gold backing to maintain confidence. Forty percent of $24 trillion equals $9.6 trillion of gold required to support the money supply. Taking the available 33,000 tons of gold and dividing that into $9.6 trillion gives an implied gold price of just over nine thousand dollars per ounce. Considering that the global M1 money supply continues to grow faster than the quantity of official gold, this implied price will rise over time; ten thousand dollars per ounce is a reasonable estimate of a balanced relationship between gold and central bank money. The portfolio recommendation is to put 10 percent of investable assets into physical gold as a diversifying asset allocation and as portfolio insurance. The following example demonstrates that insurance aspect.

For purposes of simplification, assume the overall portfolio contains 10 percent gold, 30 percent cash, and 60 percent equities. Obviously those percentages can vary and the equity portion can include private equity and other alternative investments. Here's how the 10 percent allocation to gold works to preserve wealth:

If gold declines 20 percent, the impact on your overall portfolio is a 2 percent decline (20 percent x 10 percent). That's not highly damaging and is offset by equity outperformance. Conversely, if gold prices go to ten thousand dollars per ounce, that's a 650 percent gain from current levels. That price spike gives you a 65 percent gain on your overall portfolio (650 percent x 10 percent). There is a conditional correlation between a state where gold goes up 650 percent and where stocks, bonds, and other assets are declining. For this purpose, assume a scenario similar to the worst of the Great Depression from 1929 to 1932, where stocks fell 85 percent. An 85 percent decline in stocks making up 60 percent of your portfolio produces a portfolio loss of just over 50 percent.

In this scenario, the gains on the gold (650 percent separately and 65 percent in your portfolio) will more than preserve your wealth against an 85 percent decline in stocks comprising 60 percent of your portfolio (85 percent separately and 50 percent in your total portfolio). The 30 percent cash allocation holds wealth constant.

If 60 percent of your portfolio drops 85 percent (equal to the stock market drop in the Great Depression), and 10 percent of your portfolio goes up 650 percent (gold's expected performance in a monetary reset), you lose 50 percent on your portfolio of stocks, but you make 65 percent on your portfolio on gold. Your total wealth is preserved and even increased slightly. Total portfolio performance in this new depression scenario is a gain of 15 percent. That's the insurance aspect at work. Investors without an allocation to gold will be hurt badly. Those with a 10 percent allocation will survive the storm with their wealth intact.

CHAPTER SEVEN
GODZILLA

— — — — — — — — — —

A finite time singularity simply means that the mathematical solution to the growth equation . . . *becomes infinitely large at some finite time.* . . . This is obviously impossible, and that's why something has to change.

—Geoffrey West, *Scale* (2017)

JPMorgan versus Godzilla

I've been a Godzilla fan since I saw the 1954 film version of *Godzilla* on television as a child. Godzilla was a prehistoric sea monster awakened by nuclear radiation after the Second World War. Godzilla initially destroys several Japanese fishing boats at sea. Later he is spotted ashore by villagers on a remote island. The Japanese navy sends frigates and uses depth charges to destroy Godzilla. Still, he survives. Finally, Godzilla comes ashore near Tokyo and uses his sheer size and "atomic breath" to wreak havoc on the city before retreating back into Tokyo Bay. Japanese scientists use an advanced oxygen deprivation device to kill Godzilla at sea. Still, their scientists fear radiation from continued nuclear weapons testing may cause a new Godzilla to arise.

Godzilla's commercial success led to a long line of sequels from Japanese and U.S. studios, including *Godzilla Raids Again* (1955) and the classic *King Kong vs. Godzilla* (1962). King Kong, a gigantic gorilla, was unveiled in the movie *King Kong*, a 1933 black-and-white film. Both monsters have enduring popularity. In all, thirty-nine Godzilla films and nine King Kong films have been produced.

How tall was Godzilla? The answer depends on which film version you reference. Godzilla was 164 feet tall in the original 1954 film, then grew to 197 feet in the 1998 remake. The tallest Godzilla yet was the 387 foot tall supermonster portrayed in the 2016 film titled *Godzilla: Resurgence.*

How tall was King Kong? The answer also depends on which film you use. The original King Kong was 24 feet tall when he was in New York, yet strangely was only 18 feet tall on Skull Island, his original home. By the time of Dino De Laurentiis's 1976 remake, *King Kong*, the gorilla had grown to 55 feet. The biggest King Kong ever was 147 feet tall, as portrayed in *King Kong vs. Godzilla*. It seemed the film producers needed King Kong to bulk up a bit to combat the larger lizard, Godzilla.

Behind these film versions of giant lizards and gorillas lies an intriguing question in physics and biology. Can a real King Kong or Godzilla ever emerge on the earth? The tallest land animal on earth, the giraffe, can reach a height of 20 feet, although 15 feet is more typical. Among sea creatures, the blue whale is the largest animal ever known, at 100 feet in length. Among extinct animals, brontosaurus was up to 72 feet long and tyrannosaurus measured 40 feet from head to tail and stood 12 feet tall at the hips. Since these creatures are all real, why not a 147-foot King Kong or a 387-foot Godzilla?

It turns out creatures over twenty feet tall or one hundred feet in length are physically impossible; cardiovascular systems cannot function beyond that scale. The blue whale is the largest creature we have ever seen or ever will. A look at the science of scale behind this conclusion points to questions about the scale of capital markets. The answers may save us from ruin if acted upon soon.

Let's start with the size constraint. The math and analysis are straightforward. Large land creatures stand on two or four legs. The legs are supported by bones. How much weight can bones support?

For analytic ease, we'll look at a simple wooden construction such as a house, although the analysis applies to all structures, from steel skyscrapers to human bodies. The strength of structural support in a wooden beam increases by the *square* of an increase in the lengths of the sides of a cross-sectional area, regardless of the length of the beam. For example, if you double the sides of of a 2" x 4" beam, its strength is increased by a factor of 4. This increase in strength is calculated by the square of the increase in size, or $2^2 = 4$.

Increases in volume are governed by a different function. When a structure increases in size, that increase involves three dimensions of height, width, and breadth. Likewise, when a creature grows in size, its body expands in three dimensions of height, width, and breadth; total volume increases. If you double the size of an object, the resulting volume is measured by the *cube* of the increase, or $2^3 = 8$.

Based on these relationships, the problem is obvious. When an object doubles in size, strength increases at a rate of 2^2 while volume increases at a rate of 2^3. If volume is increasing faster than strength, it's only a matter of time before a building or animal collapses of its own weight. Two superlinear functions increasing by different exponents are what determine the maximum size and height of natural or man-made objects.

Leading physicist Geoffrey West makes this point in his book *Scale*:

> Consider increasing the height of a building or tree by a factor of 10 keeping its shape the same; then the weight needed to be supported increases a *thousand*fold (10^3) whereas the strength of the pillar or trunk holding it up increases by only a *hundred*fold (10^2).

Thus, the ability to safely support the additional weight is only a tenth of what it had previously been. Consequently, if the size of the structure, whatever it is, is arbitrarily increased it will eventually collapse under its own weight. There are limits to size and growth.

This is why the tallest skyscrapers taper near the top. The taper reduces the volume increase relative to the height increase somewhat, and allows the structure to support greater height with a smaller exponential increase in volume. Still, the cubic volume increase is greater than the square of the beam cross-section increase, so scaling limits based on strength and volume are eventually reached.

What of the length of the largest creature? Whales have bones but they do not support weight in the same manner as a land creature. The buoyancy of a whale in the water does a great deal to support the weight. Still, there are limits to growth. Why can't a blue whale be two-hundred- or three-hundred-feet long?

For this answer, physicists introduce the idea of the "terminal unit." A terminal unit is the interface between the larger biological organs (or building structure) and units of energy delivered at the smallest scale. For a living creature such as a blue whale or a human being, the terminal unit is the blood cell. It's at the level of the individual blood cell that energy in the form of oxygen is transferred to muscles and waste is removed. A blue whale may weigh two thousand times a typical human, yet the blue whale and human blood cells are the same size. Regardless of the size of an organism, the terminal unit (the blood cell) is the same size. This rule applies in buildings also. The terminal unit is the standard wall outlet into which lamps, computers, chargers, and printers are plugged. Whether you are considering a one-story house or a one-hundred-story skyscraper, the terminal unit (the wall outlet) is the same size. Skyscrapers do not have gigantic wall sockets; they're the same size as the ones in your apartment.

While the terminal unit may be the same, the distance from the energy source to the terminal unit is not the same. In larger structures or creatures, there are exponentially more tubes, wires, arteries, or channels through which the energy flows to get from the central source to the place where the energy is needed. Passage through those channels, especially at branches, uses energy. As the creature expands in size, the amount of energy used to move blood to all parts of the body (the terminal units) exceeds the energy available. At that point, the creature dies for lack of oxygen to all of its tissues. Evolution solves this problem by insuring creatures don't grow that large to begin with, since they won't survive. This evolutionary feedback loop is another limit to growth.

This can be illustrated by the circulatory system of the blue whale. The whale's heart is the central pump. When blood leaves the heart it flows quickly and smoothly through large blood vessels, like the aorta. Yet the blood vessels must eventually shrink to the size of capillaries that can reach the terminal units of tissue that receive the oxygen in the blood. All parts of the body must receive these blood cells or they die from oxygen depletion. The larger the creature, the more junctions or splits are needed as the blood flows from the aorta to a wide network of capillaries. At each junction, there is some resistance or impedance to the flow (in effect, the heart is pumping against itself) and more energy is required. The large network of arteries and capillaries also causes friction, which puts more stress on the heart and uses more energy. As the energy needed to pump the blood exceeds the energy available in the blood, the whale starts to die of hypoxia. Scientists have estimated that given the distance and energy loss from the heart to the capillaries, the maximum size of a mammal is approximately 250,000 pounds, about the size of a typical blue whale. Stated simply, the blue whale is the largest creature ever seen because it is the largest creature that can ever exist given the constraints of energy outputs, inputs, and hypoxia. Again, there are limits to growth.

What do these biological and structural insights have to do with finance? The creatures and structures studied by Geoffrey West and his colleagues are examples of complex dynamic systems. Such systems include animals, forests, businesses, cities, and the cosmos. Capital markets are one of the best examples of a complex dynamic system. Capital markets exhibit the behaviors and constraints of other biological and man-made complex systems. Limits on size, as represented by the blue whale, also apply to ships, buildings, friendships, nature, and finance. Snow piles up on a mountainside for only so long before the snowpack destabilizes and collapses into an avalanche. A vessel can only be so large before it capsizes and sinks. A bank balance sheet can only be so leveraged before confidence is lost and the bank tumbles into failure. West and others have identified scaling metrics and limits to growth in sundry systems. What are the limits to growth in finance?

While complex systems have unique characteristics (a snowpack is different from a patch of moss, which is different from a whale's bloodstream), they all have certain dynamics in common. They exhibit diversity, communication among parts, interaction among parts, and adaptive behavior. They exhibit emergent properties; behavior arises that cannot be inferred from perfect knowledge of the system components. They exhibit scale invariance; subunits are near perfect replicas of larger units, like a stream and a river, or a branch and a limb. Energy inputs scale faster than energy outputs, so that new sources of energy (or efficiency) are constantly needed. Most important, the risk of extreme behavior or a systems collapse is a superlinear function of scale.

These complex system dynamics have been expressed theoretically and shown empirically in myriad systems. West and his colleagues have shown how the number of gas stations in a city scales in relation to the population of a city. The slope of the logarithmic power curve that compares population size to the number of gas stations is 0.85. This means that when you double the population size, you increase the number of gas stations by 85 percent. That's a 15 percent reduction compared to doubling the number of gas stations—an example of economies of scale. Each gas station handles more customers. The scope of the 0.85 exponent is illustrated by the fact that it applies to all cities in all countries, regardless of size. If you inform West of the name and size of a city anywhere, he can tell you how many gas stations that city has with a high degree of accuracy, based solely on the slope of the power curve. There are countless similar examples in natural and man-made systems.

In the gas station case, scientists had a scaling metric (population size of the city) and a specified slope of the power curve (0.85 based on empirical research). What if you had neither? What if you had a complex dynamic system based on composition and behavior but no agreed scaling metrics and no empirical research on the frequency of extreme behavior? That is roughly the situation facing financial risk management today. Capital markets are certainly complex dynamic systems; they exhibit all of the conditions of complexity, including diversity, communication, interaction, and adaptive behavior in the right middling proportions. Capital markets can be scaled up or down, as we saw in 2007 to 2009, and are prone to serious collapse, as we saw in 1987, 1994, 1998, 2000, and 2008. What is unknown is the best way to measure scale and the exponent of the slope of the power curve that links scale to collapse.

Candidates for measuring capital markets' scale include bank asset size, gross notional value of derivatives, concentration of assets in fewer banks, contingent liabilities (clearinghouse credit, guarantees, options, etc.), non-bank lenders, trading volumes, SWIFT message traffic, and other gross metrics. A weighted blend of numerous factors may prove best. Risk factors that could trigger a market collapse include leverage ratios, government debt-to-GDP ratio, government deficit-to-GDP ratio, real interest rates, real growth, nominal growth, contagion, trade wars, currency wars, credit spreads, and geopolitical shocks. A forecaster using predictive analytic science looks for a critical state measured by scale combined with a catalyst of two or more triggers acting as force multipliers in a feedback loop (such as excessive leverage and declining asset values). The difficulty is that while most of these factors are tracked on an individual basis by specialists, there is no effort to synthesize the factors into a mosaic that captures unexpected emergence, amplification, feedback, and contagion. The most challenging dynamic is the extent to which the capital market interacts with itself.

Which brings us back to Godzilla. In studies of scaling limits based on variable exponents for volume versus strength and the branching needed to reach terminal units, West was always careful to specify that the scaling limitations applied, "provided, of course, that the materials they're made of don't change so that their densities remain the same." In other words, a one-hundred-foot Godzilla can be compared to a three-hundred-foot Godzilla (the first is barely possible, the second is impossible) only if the same organic body parts are involved. If the three-hundred-foot Godzilla is a robot made of titanium and copper wire, then a different factor analysis is required. Or, perhaps a three-hundred-foot Godzilla could pose upright if lashed to a steel scaffold.

Are there hidden scaffolds in finance?

A large financial institution like JPMorgan is a complex entity, like capital markets more broadly. It has the markers of diversity, communication, interaction, and adaptive behavior. It exhibits emergent properties such as the sudden appearance of $6 billion in trading losses in May 2012, attributable to actions by a trader, Bruno Iksil, known as the London Whale. Iksil's trading in credit derivatives expanded for over a year with poor supervision before losses unexpectedly emerged—behavior typical of complex systems.

Just as a blue whale has a terminal unit, the blood cell, a bank has a terminal unit, which is the client. Deals can be for $100 at an ATM or $100 billion at a corporate closing, but in each case the bank faces off with a client. A bank's blood is money. Just as blood flows through arteries and capillaries, so money flows through payment systems all the way down to cash dispensers. Blood carries energy in the form of oxygen and nutrition and removes waste. Likewise, money is stored energy. You expend energy as labor or capital to earn money, and use money to release energy by hiring workers or investing in plant and equipment. Money is stored energy that powers a capitalist economy. Banks provide the cardiovascular system to move the money around.

Godzilla cannot exist because he would fall of his own weight. No creature larger than a blue whale can exist because the energy needed to move its blood is greater than the energy available. Skyscrapers have different height-volume equations than Godzilla because they substitute steel for bone. Still, they too have limitations on absolute height and volume. What are the limitations of size and scale for a bank? In what way can a bank fail due to excessive scale in the way an oversized mammal can collapse of its own weight or suffer hypoxia and die?

We don't have exact metrics on excessive scale in banks because the scaling factors have not been specified and empirical testing has not been conducted. So-called stress tests imposed on banks by the Treasury are mostly for show and involve static capital adequacy, which is never sufficient in extreme stress. The fact that banks can fail due to excessive size has been demonstrated repeatedly. In 2008, Bear Stearns, Fannie Mae, Freddie Mac, and Lehman Brothers failed successively between March 18, 2008, and September 15, 2008, due to overleverage, contagion, and credit spreads—three of our scaling metrics. After Lehman Brothers' bankruptcy, Morgan Stanley was days away from failure and Goldman Sachs and other major banks were next in line to fail. This is evidence that the individual banks, and the system as a whole, were suffering the institutional equivalent of hypoxia. They were out of oxygen and dying off. Only government intervention in the form of deposit guarantees, money market guarantees, term-lending facilities, and trillions of dollars of currency swaps propped up what was left of the banking system. Think of the big banks as collapsing Godzillas and the Federal government as a steel scaffold put in place to prop up the bloated banks.

Once the scaffolding around the banks is in place it cannot be removed unless the banks shrink or the risk of collapse is accepted. The Fed cannot escape the room. Reduced derivatives exposure does not reduce systemic risk when bank derivatives are simply moved to a clearinghouse whose credit is backed up by the same banks. Increased bank capital does not mitigate risk when leverage is still too high and credit risk is understated by flawed models. At most, the added capital buys a few days to work out a rescue. The Fed scaffold around banks like JPMorgan cannot be removed. Worse, it allows Godzilla banks to grow larger, to the point when they collapse of their own weight and take the scaffold down with it.

Middle Class Agonistes

How often have peers lamented the "death of the middle class"? The terms "death" and "middle class" are not defined, yet everyone gets the point. The rich are undeniably richer. The poor are struggling to make ends meet. Meanwhile, the middle-class member works hard, supports a family, pays the majority of all federal income taxes, gets little federal support during her working years, and seems to bear the weight of society.

The middle class is not disappearing, there may be 100 million members of the U.S. middle-class depending on the definition. Yet they are struggling to hold onto their status; members feel that they are clinging to middle-class rank by their fingernails. This insecurity of the U.S. middle class holds warnings for investors. The economic prognosis is poor for members of the middle class and the broader society. The ability of individual members of the middle class to reverse this trend is limited by a lack of political power and elite indifference.

There is no standard definition of middle class. Still, several academic models stand out. One model, developed by Leonard Beeghley in his work *The Structure of Social Stratification in the United States* (2016), breaks U.S. society into four groups: the rich (5 percent), the middle class (45 percent), the working class (40 percent), and the poor (10 percent). In this ontology, the status of the rich (annual incomes over $350,000) and the poor (living below the poverty line) are self-evident. However, the two middle categories might all be considered middle class by some analysts.

The rich have a net worth of $1 million or more. However, most of that is in illiquid home equity. Individuals with home equity of $1 million likely consider themselves "upper middle class" if not quite rich, depending on their zip code. Likewise, Beeghley's working class includes those making $40,000 per year, a group that might consider itself "lower middle class." If these expanded definitions are used, the middle class might be 89 percent of the population with a 1 percent super-rich group and 10 percent in poverty.

Another ontology is offered by William Thompson, Mica Thompson, and Joseph Hickey in their work *Society in Focus* (2017). The Thompson, Thompson, and Hickey rankings adhere more closely to the foregoing revised version of the Beeghley rankings. Thompson, Thompson, and Hickey have an upper class (1 percent) and a lower class (20 percent). In between are an upper middle class (15 percent), lower middle class (32 percent), and a working class (32 percent). The upper class has incomes of $500,000 per year or more. The upper middle class earns between $75,000 and $499,000 per year. The lower middle class earns between $35,000 and $74,000 per year. The working class earns between $16,000 and $35,000 per year. The lower class has little earned income; they receive government transfer payments or are in poorly paid positions.

Finally, Dennis Gilbert offers a third ontology in his book *The American Class Structure in an Age of Growing Inequality* (2015). Gilbert offers six levels of society instead of the customary five. He describes a capitalist class (1 percent), an upper middle class (14 percent), a lower middle class (30 percent), a working class (30 percent), the working poor (13 percent), and the underclass (12 percent). Gilbert relies on job descriptions and educational attainment rather than income levels to identify his classes, although it's straightforward to attach estimated income levels to each group. The capitalist class consists of CEOs and politicians. The upper middle class consists of professionals and middle managers. The lower middle class consists of semiprofessionals and craftsmen. The working class consists of blue-collar workers. The working poor consists of low-level clerks. The underclass is generally not in the labor force and receives government transfer payments.

There are various other income distribution studies available and other class definitions used by economists and social scientists. The most common way of approaching the problem is to divide society into five tiers or quintiles, where each tier has exactly the same number of members and the tiers are divided by income levels without regard to job descriptions or education. This method shows that as of 2016, the highest 20 percent of U.S. households received 51.5 percent of total income. The next 20 percent of households received 22.9 percent of total income. The middle 20 percent received 14.2 percent of total income. The next 20 percent received 8.3 percent of total income, and the bottom 20 percent of households received 3.1 percent of total income. Put differently, the top 40 percent of households receives 74.4 percent of the total income while the bottom 60 percent of households receives only 25.6 percent of total income.

This quintile analysis shines a harsh light on several realities of income distribution in the United States today. The first is that these figures represent household income, which depends on the size of the household. If these figures were computed for individuals, income concentration would be even more skewed in favor of the rich. The second reality is that the U.S. trend is toward *greater* income inequality. The lowest 60 percent of households earned 32.3 percent of total income in 1970 versus 25.6 percent of total income today. That's a stunning 21 percent drop in the share of the lowest 60 percent in the past forty-eight years. Meanwhile the highest 20 percent saw a 19 percent gain in their share (from 43.3 percent to 51.5 percent) in the same time period. In the United States today, the adage that the rich get richer and the poor get poorer has seldom been more true.

Whether you analyze the U.S. economy by quintiles, income brackets, job descriptions, or on a highly granular basis with regard to the top 0.01 percent, the result is the same—incomes and net worth in the United States exhibit a high degree of concentration of income and assets among the wealthiest, with a far larger group struggling to hang on to their piece of the American dream.

This data can be used to develop a simpler definition of middle class. Divide the population into rich, upper middle class, lower middle class, working class, and poor. The rich are the top 1 percent, with incomes of $500,000 per year or more. The upper middle class have incomes from $100,000 to $500,000 per year. The lower middle class have incomes from $35,000 to $100,000 per year. The working class have incomes from $15,000 to $35,000 per year. The poor have incomes below $15,000 per year and receive government assistance. This class structure shows the middle class is 85 percent of the total population or 270 million Americans.

Several clarifications are needed. The first is that the figure of 270 million persons includes homemaker spouses and children. With an average family size of 3.5 persons, the number of middle class *workers* is closer to 80 million, still a large number but only 25 percent of the total U.S. population. The second clarification involves taxation. The income numbers cited above are pretax. When a 30 percent statutory marginal tax rate is applied, the after-tax income figures drop considerably from the pretax levels. A $200,000 income drops to $140,000 after tax, and a $100,000 income drops to $70,000 after tax. Those after-tax numbers are far more modest than the pretax figures.

The pre-tax–after-tax distinction is important because the tax burden falls disproportionately on the middle class. Pew Research Center data reveals that the middle class (as defined above) pays over 60 percent of all income taxes. The poor pay almost no income tax because of low rates, exemptions, and credits. The rich pay 38.3 percent of all income taxes, yet make over 50 percent of total income. This lower effective tax rate compared to the middle class is due to income deferral plans and preferential rates on capital gains. The middle class is right to feel overtaxed relative to both the rich and the poor.

A struggling middle class has more to do with the future than the present. While today's numbers testify to the presence of a large middle class, their mood is pessimistic. There is a feeling that children will not do as well as their parents. There is a feeling of job insecurity. There is a feeling of overtaxation relative to other echelons of society. Above all, there is a feeling of a rigged game in which the rich share inside information, the poor are subsidized, and the middle class does all the work and receives no respect from elites or political leadership. None of these feelings is misplaced. Burdens placed on the middle class have never been greater, even as society's rewards are snatched by super-rich investors or recipients of government assistance.

There is no clearer example than the course of the 2008 financial crisis. In the years leading up to the crisis, Alan Greenspan and the Federal Reserve kept interest rates artificially low. This enabled bankers to originate subprime mortgage loans and to package those loans into highly rated securities for sale to institutional investors. The bankers made billions of dollars in origination and servicing fees and billions more in underwriting fees and trading revenue. These mortgages and mortgage derivatives were rated AAA in many cases, due to flawed risk models, venality, and malfeasance by the major rating agencies such as S&P, Fitch, and Moody's. Bank regulators were ignorant of the risks involved because of their own flawed models and obtuse oversight. Inevitably, mortgage default rates rose; the first reports of these defaults emerged in the spring of 2007. This was called to the attention of Federal Reserve and U.S. Treasury officials. Ben Bernanke assured the Federal Reserve Board in March 2007 that the situation was manageable and losses would abate. The U.S. Treasury had no interest in intervening or even requesting information, despite the fact than any distress would land in their lap.

By the late summer of 2007, financial dominoes began to fall. Two Bear Stearns mortgage hedge funds collapsed. Several money market funds sponsored by BNP Paribas closed their doors to stop a flood of redemptions. Markets stabilized by December 2007 as major sovereign wealth funds in Singapore, China, Abu Dhabi, and Kuwait were prevailed upon by the Treasury to bail out major banks, including Citibank, Morgan Stanley, and Merrill Lynch. Then panic reemerged with the Bear Stearns failure in March 2008, the collapse of Fannie Mae and Freddie Mac in June 2008, and finally the Lehman Brothers bankruptcy in September 2008. In late September 2008, stock markets crashed, bank runs began, and the United States was days away from a sequential collapse of all major banks. Intervention by the Federal Reserve and FDIC, including unlimited deposit insurance, guarantees on all money market funds, massive money printing, and multitrillion-dollar currency swaps with the European Central Bank were needed to alleviate the panic. Finally, by March 2009 the stock market bottomed and a long, slow recovery began.

The middle class watched these developments with a mixture of fear and disbelief. Investors knew panics happen from time to time and stock market booms don't last forever. The middle class might have been resigned to their losses if they had seen some trace of accountability on the part of elite bankers, CEOs, and regulators. That never happened. In fact, no bank CEOs or senior executives were ever held accountable. They kept their jobs or moved seamlessly to other financial firms. After two years of increased scrutiny, the bank CEOs resumed the practice of awarding huge bonuses and options, which rose on a stock market propped up by the Fed. Treasury secretary Tim Geithner secretly communicated with Attorney General Eric Holder at Obama's Department of Justice with a request to refrain from prosecution of bankers because prosecutions could hurt confidence and destabilize the financial system. Holder agreed. There were no penalties, prosecutions, or terminations related to the crash among the top bank elites at all.

The middle class was decimated. Members lost half their savings and many lost their jobs and homes. It was the worst economic setback since the Great Depression. These financial and career losses for the middle class were on top of emotional stress that resulted in higher suicide rates, increased divorce rates, and a wide opioid epidemic. There was a social and emotional collapse in addition to the financial collapse, a phenomenon rarely discussed on happy-talk financial TV. The middle class might have borne the burden of the financial crisis as they had borne burdens from the Great Depression to the Second World War. Yet this crisis was different. The burden was not equally shared by all. In fact, the burden was placed exclusively on the middle class while elites escaped responsibility.

The leading bank CEOs in 2008 were Jamie Dimon of JPMorgan, Lloyd Blankfein of Goldman Sachs, Brian Moynihan of Merrill Lynch (now Bank of America), John Mack of Morgan Stanley, Larry Fink of BlackRock, and Vikram Pandit of Citi. Every one of them and various of their subordinates are either still in those positions or retired recently with dynastic fortunes in bonuses and stock options. Meanwhile, the middle class is still in shock. It's true that stocks later rallied to new highs after a ten-year recovery from the lows. Still, ten years is a long time to wait for your money back.

Middle-class investors were not lucky enough even to enjoy the protracted recovery. They sold near the lows in 2009 in a desperate attempt to preserve what was left of their capital. They refused to reenter markets based on a legitimate fear that a new collapse could happen at any time. In short, the rich got richer and the middle class got crushed by the big money.

This scenario of the rich getting richer and the middle class falling behind is playing out in areas besides investing. Inequality is true in college admissions, where the wealthy continue to send their sons and daughters to elite schools while the middle class are restrained by sky-high tuitions and the burden of student loans. It's true in the housing market, where the rich picked up mansions on the cheap in foreclosure sales while the middle class were frozen in place by negative equity. It's true in health care, where the rich could afford all the insurance they needed while the middle class were handicapped by unemployment and the loss of job-related benefits. These disparities also affected the adult children of the middle class. There are no gold-plated benefits packages in the gig economy.

The extent of this income redistribution toward the rich and away from the middle class is revealed in recent research from Deutsche Bank. Their work shows the percentage of children earning more than their parents at age thirty by date of birth over time. The research shows that fewer than 50 percent of all children age thirty today earn more than their parents at the same age. This 50 percent figure compares with 60 percent who earned more in 1971 and 80 percent who earned more in 1950. The American Dream of each generation earning more than the prior generation is collapsing before our eyes.

With this and similar data in mind, we repeat the original question. Is the middle class disappearing? The answer is no, but it is struggling and is increasingly disadvantaged in relation to powerful elites. The middle class is getting poorer on a relative basis and it is lagging farther behind the rich, whose incomes absorb an increasing share of total GDP. This result is discouraging for the middle class and creates a headwind for growth, in the form of lower productivity. Why work harder if the gains are not distributed fairly?

The manner in which the rich become rich in the first place is highly variable. It could be simple luck, as when two farmers buy adjacent parcels of land and one strikes oil while the other doesn't. It could be the result of smart choices in matters such as personal health care, marriage, and higher education. It could be the result of hard work, invention, or entrepreneurship. The initial sources of wealth are not necessarily unfair in a capitalist system.

Problems arise with the way in which the rich *stay* rich, become *more* rich, and pass wealth to their children and grandchildren. Techniques for preserving wealth are supported by customs, laws, and regulations mostly promoted by the rich themselves to perpetuate and expand their wealth. This is what gives rise to the rigged system of which the middle class rightly complains.

The first set of abuses arises in the tax code. On paper, the rich pay higher taxes than the middle class. But that's a mirage based on a quick glance at progressive tax tables. The reality is far more complicated. Much of the wealth of the richest Americans is *never* taxed because they hold on to real estate and stocks and pass them to their beneficiaries tax-free. When the media points out that Amazon CEO Jeff Bezos is worth over $100 billion, it's important to bear in mind that most of that $100 billion is in the form of Amazon stock on which Bezos has paid no income tax, except for the shares he has sold. Even when Bezos sells some stock, he is treated to capital gains tax rates, which are lower than normal income tax rates. The same analysis applies to Mark Zuckerberg at Facebook and Elon Musk at Tesla. An average upper-middle-class professional pays a higher effective tax rate than the richest people on the planet. Holding on to stock is not a cash-flow burden, because billionaires can easily borrow cash using the stock as collateral. There is no income tax on loan proceeds.

The second tax dodge is the use of foundations. The ultrawealthy can donate their stock to a foundation (for which they receive a tax deduction against other income) and then appoint themselves or their spouses as heads of the foundation. They can then remain in control of the money by making the minimal statutory grants to favored causes while investing foundation assets in a portfolio of their choosing. The foundation itself pays no income tax. In effect, the billionaires remain in control of vast fortunes that are effectively tax-free. Middle-class individuals do not have the cash flow and the resources for legal fees to set up similar arrangements.

Other tax dodges abound, including offshore income, deferred income plans, transfer pricing between taxable and nontaxable entities, and inflated valuations on charitable gifts. The result is always the same—the rich dodge taxes while the middle class pay more than their share.

Other preferences include the impact of social networks on opportunities for jobs, school admissions, and investment opportunities. Many of the most profitable new investments of the past twenty years were shared among a tightly knit crew of Silicon Valley and Wall Street insiders who tipped each other off about new companies like Google, Amazon, Uber, Airbnb, and others long before the companies went public (in many cases the companies still have not gone public). Middle-class investors get crashing valuations in companies like Snap Inc. (formerly Snapchat), which has fallen from $20.75 per share in early 2018 to $9.15 per share as of this writing. The Silicon Valley founders captured the higher valuation in the IPO while the middle class is left with the lower valuation today. The best stock tips are passed around by the wealthy at country clubs and private equity firms before middle-class investors are even aware these companies exist.

College admissions at elite schools have always carved out a significant portion of each entering class for "legacy" admissions. If your dad went to Harvard, your chances of admission to Harvard are higher than the typical middle-class applicant. This system is not foolproof or automatic, yet it does give an edge to sons and daughters of the wealthiest Americans and helps their families as a whole to maintain an elite edge. When graduation rolls around, the same network makes sure the graduates who are members of elite families get first crack at top jobs in law firms, investment banks, wealth managers, and other preferred occupations. This passing of the baton from one elite generation to the next helps the elites to keep a stranglehold on wealth and privilege. Middle-class graduates with brains and talent are not shut out completely; they just have a harder time cracking the code.

Finally, the student loan debacle is one of the most powerful discrimination factors between the rich and middle class. The sons and daughters of rich families breeze through college and emerge with little or no debt. The middle-class families borrow extensively from government student loan programs to graduate from the same schools. The difference shows up upon graduation, when the elites enter careers debt-free while the middle-class students may easily have a hundred thousand dollars in student loan debt.

This debt burden in a gig economy quickly results in missed payments. As we've seen, bad payment history then impacts the FICO credit scores of the recent graduates. Poor FICO scores stand in the way of good jobs, leases on attractive apartments, or mortgages on starter homes in good neighborhoods. Student loans constitute a form of indentured servitude in the case of middle-class graduates who work hard to pay them off, but fall further behind in doing so. Meanwhile, the rich graduates are getting promotions, raises, and buying new homes with ease. The stage is set for another generation of the rich getting richer and the middle class getting left behind.

Is there a public policy solution to this increasing inequality in income distribution? Walter Scheidel's book *The Great Leveler* (2017) examines income inequality since the agrarian age. He reached several important conclusions that are critical to understanding the income inequality society faces today.

Scheidel's first conclusion is there is no shortage of proposed remedies for income inequality. The list of solutions varies with the stage a society has reached. The usual remedies are land redistribution, progressive income taxation, higher estate taxation, free education, greater access to good schools, support for preschool programs, free lunches and improved nutrition, universal health care, an end to preferential legacy school admissions, an end to discrimination in hiring, and greater diversity in the management of large companies.

Scheidel's second conclusion is that none of these remedies has any chance of becoming law on a large enough scale to have a material impact on income inequality. Reasons for this failure of implementation are diverse, but the most prominent reason is that legislatures and courts are effectively controlled by elite bankers and lawyers who stand in the way of policies that erode their clients' elite status. In short, the wolves are in charge of the hen house.

This does not mean that income inequality is never leveled or reversed. Periodically society experiences what Scheidel calls a "leveling," in which income distribution is compressed and gaps between rich and poor are greatly reduced. That's the good news. The bad news is that leveling is achieved only through death and violence as a result of mass mobilization warfare, extreme revolution, pandemic plague, or a systemic collapse. A classic example is the Black Death in fourteenth-century Europe, in which over one third of the population died. Surviving workers received higher wages because of resulting acute labor shortages. This phenomenon is well documented. Still, plague is a tough way to get a raise.

Prospects for a reduction in income inequality and improvement in the relative well-being of the middle class are dismal absent the appearance of one of these violent four horsemen in the form of warfare, revolution, plague, or systemic collapse. No one is rooting for those outcomes, yet no one should expect a reduction in income inequality without them.

Despite this embedded unfairness, those on the wrong side of the income inequality distribution should not assume all is well with the superwealthy. The rich may not be concerned with paying bills, but they are concerned with survival if, as many expect, current social disorder spreads into social collapse. This is the impetus for luxury bombproof bunkers built in former missile silos, and expansive estates in New Zealand loaded with rations and good wine. Even these precautions don't ease their minds, because it leads to the next worry, which is how to get to the shelters in a panic and how to insure the loyalty of their guards and private-jet pilots as society unravels. These second-order fears are on full display in this excerpt from an article by theorist Douglas Rushkoff, describing a private encounter with superrich clients:

> After I arrived, I was ushered into what I thought was the green room. But instead of being wired with a microphone or taken to a stage, I just sat there at a plain round table as my audience was brought to me: five super-wealthy guys—yes, all men—from the upper echelon of the hedge fund world. After a bit of small talk . . . they edged into their real topics of concern. . . . The CEO of a brokerage house explained that he had nearly completed building his own underground bunker system and asked, "How do I maintain authority over my security force after the event?"
>
> The Event. That was their euphemism for the environmental

collapse, social unrest, nuclear explosion, unstoppable virus, or Mr. Robot hack that takes everything down. . . .

They knew armed guards would be required to protect their compounds from the angry mobs. But how would they pay the guards once money was worthless? What would stop the guards from choosing their own leader? The billionaires considered using special combination locks on the food supply that only they knew. Or making guards wear disciplinary collars of some kind in return for their survival. . . .

When the hedge funders asked me the best way to maintain authority over their security forces after "the event," I suggested that their best bet would be to treat those people really well, right now. They should be engaging with their security staffs as if they were members of their own family. . . . All this technological wizardry could be applied toward less romantic but entirely more collective interests right now.

Rushkoff's advice to treat people decently is worthy, yet seems to have escaped the hedge-fund crowd. A more practical answer is to pay your guards in gold or silver, always money good. The fact that this solution never occurred to the hedge-fund mavens shows even the richest are estranged from the concept of real money.

As if to validate elite worries, one need only point out that the 2008 global financial crisis is not over. In fact, it has barely begun. Economic downturns historically run in a V-shaped pattern. Growth declines during the recession stage and then bounces back to the trend line quickly. The lost growth in the recession is made up by a steep rebound. Once growth returns to trend, the lost wealth is recovered and the economy continues on its historic growth path. That never happened in the 2008 crisis. Growth declined, but it never bounced back. Growth never returned to the trend line and never made up the losses. Instead, growth resumed on a new trend line well below the old trend and on a more shallow trajectory.

Not only was there no V-shaped recovery, the new trend falls further away from the old trend over time. The gap between the old higher trend and the new lower trend is referred to as the wealth gap, the difference between how rich we would be if there were a strong recovery after 2008, and how rich we are based on the historically weak recovery that occurred. That wealth gap today is *over $4 trillion dollars*. What's worse is the wealth gap keeps getting larger because the new trend line is not as steep as the old one. The old and new trend lines don't run parallel; they diverge, so the wealth gap keeps growing.

Still, the wealth gap is only part of the reason America remains in crisis. As weak as growth is, the United States purchased that paltry growth with nonsustainable debt. Since the global financial crisis, America's national debt roughly doubled from $10 trillion to $20 trillion. That debt is set to grow another $5 trillion in the next five years due to the Trump tax cuts, repeal by Congress of spending caps, and a wave of student loan defaults. That projection assumes no recession. If a recession strikes, analysts add another $2 trillion of debt on top of the projected $5 trillion because of lower tax collections, higher benefits for unemployment and food stamps, higher student loan default rates, and higher disability payments.

This phenomenon of slow growth, high debt, and a wealth gap is not confined to the United States. It's a global phenomenon. The situation is worse in China, Japan, and Europe. There has been persistent growth in global debt for the past twenty years. This debt cancer began before the 2008 global financial crisis and continued afterward. The crisis itself had no lasting impact on the growth of debt. The idea that the world deleveraged or the banking system became stronger since the crisis is a myth.

While there was a slight decline in the developed economy debt-to-GDP ratio between 2012 and 2017, from 387 percent to 382 percent, the absolute size of the debt still increased from $170 trillion to $174 trillion. The decline in the ratio was due to slightly improved growth in major economies, especially the United States, after 2012. Meanwhile, the increase in emerging-markets debt from $42 trillion in 2012 to $63 trillion in 2017 and the increase in the emerging-markets debt-to-GDP ratio from 171 percent to 210 percent over the same period more than offset the mild reduction in the developed economy ratio. Combining the developed economy and emerging-markets data results in an increase of total debt from $212 trillion to $237 trillion, and an increase in the debt-to-GDP ratio from 310 percent to 314 percent between 2012 and 2017. These levels are unsustainable; the trend is ominous for investors.

Investment Secret #7: Allocate wealth to alternative assets.

We're all familiar with the so-called run on the bank. Runs begin quietly, with a few depositors getting nervous about the solvency of the bank. They line up to get their cash before the bank closes its doors. Soon word spreads and the line gets longer. The bank projects an air of confidence and gives cash to depositors who request it as long as they can, but soon the cash runs out. Today, a bank run is unfolding at the Federal Reserve Bank of New York. What's different is that the run on the bank involves gold, not cash.

The New York Fed will never run out of cash because it can print all it needs. Still, they could run out of gold. Until recently, the New York Fed had 6,000 tons of gold stored in its vaults on Liberty Street in Lower Manhattan. That gold does not belong to the United States. The Fed gold belongs to foreign countries and the International Monetary Fund. Beginning a few years ago, central banks demanded the return of their gold to their home countries. Germany was the most prominent example, yet there were others, including small holders such as Azerbaijan. One of the largest holders, Turkey, is asking for its gold back also. The process is difficult because the Fed bullion consists of old bars, some stacked up since the 1920s, that don't meet today's standard for purity and size. This doesn't mean the gold is bad, just that the bars have to be melted down and re-refined to meet the new standards. The gold stash in New York is dwindling and global behavior is coming to resemble a run on the gold bank. The reason is an expectation that gold prices will surge due to U.S. inflation, combined with a view that the Fed may be unwilling to release the gold in a future financial panic.

Before the run on the Fed hits a manic stage, what can investors do to decide if gold is at an attractive price? If gold is just another form of money (it is), then the dollar price of gold can be analyzed as if it were a currency cross rate. The all-time high for gold was $1,900 per ounce in early September 2011, and the low since then was $1,050 per ounce in December 2015.

Volatility in the dollar-gold cross rate says more about the dollar than it does about gold. When gold is $1,050 per ounce, the message may be that the dollar is too strong. When gold rallies to $1,900 per ounce, the message may be that the dollar is excessively weak. In either case a simple cross rate is a useful way to consider dollars versus gold. Still, it's not a particularly sophisticated way to understand gold's role in the broader monetary system and the macroeconomy. What other metrics can we use?

One metric is the market value of gold as a percentage of the monetary base for a given country. This alternative measure asks how much gold a country owns relative to its base paper money supply. Even the most ardent gold standard supporters don't argue for more than 100 percent coverage of money with gold. As we've seen, some coverage ratio between 20 percent and 40 percent has been sufficient since it's unlikely that all dollar holders will want their physical gold at the same time.

The U.S. Treasury holds over 8,000 tons of gold and the U.S. Federal Reserve System holds gold certificates issued by the Treasury as assets in approximately the same amount. Neither dollars (Fed liabilities) nor the Fed's gold certificates (Fed assets) are redeemable into gold, although citizens are free to buy gold with dollars at market prices. Gold's existence in the system is officially ignored by all parties. Gold is not a day-to-day operating reality of the system. That said, the gold-to-paper-money ratio is a thermometer that reveals the monetary health of the U.S. economy. In

1936 and 1980, when the value of official gold exceeded the base money supply, the U.S. economy was unhealthy, in the former case because of depression and in the latter case because of borderline hyperinflation.

How is the economy today? The short answer is not well. The gold-to-paper-money ratio is again at an extreme level that does not reflect an overvaluation of gold, but an *undervaluation*. The gold-to-paper-money ratio is around 10 percent, well below the 20 percent to 40 percent range historically considered adequate for a gold standard, let alone the 100 percent range deemed necessary by Austrian School economists and other hard-shell gold standard advocates.

The U.S. money system has never had less backing by gold than today and has never been more vulnerable to a loss of confidence. If confidence in paper money were lost due to an extreme economic event or excessive debt creation, and authorities had to turn to gold to restore confidence, the ability to do so has never been more impaired. This suggests the United States should follow China and Russia in acquiring more physical gold. This prospect makes it attractive for individuals to do likewise.

CHAPTER EIGHT

AFTERMATH

––– ––– ––– ––– ––– ––– –––

Reduced to essentials, history has known only two . . . modes of
wealth acquisition: making and taking.

—Walter Scheidel, *The Great Leveler* (2017)

Rosewood

The Rosewood hotel on Sand Hill Road off Route 101 in Silicon Valley is
home away from home for high-end visitors to the tech capital of the
world. It's a short drive from the Rosewood to Google and Apple headquarters and other castles of computation. The hotel is expensive, but
worth it; amenities are excellent. Still, the scent of privilege is strong. Marc
Andreessen of Netscape fame has his venture capital firm in an office suite
adjacent to the hotel, connected by slate walkways lined with trimmed
hedges and flowing fountains. The grounds are eerily quiet. The scene
might be mistaken for a spa or meditation retreat but for the signage and
security guards.

The hotel design is enviro-modern with low-rise, flat-roofed, stylish parallel lines done in tan, wood, and slate with greenery. The rooms are like connected bungalows; the doors lead directly outside, no hallways, no long rows of numbered portals.

The lobby lounge has the only signs of life. Low-backed sofas, lounge chairs, and ottomans in the ubiquitous earth tones are occupied by cosmetological blondes and fiftysomething men, tanned, lean, in jeans, expensive tees, Nike Dunk Low sneakers or Italian loafers, no socks, and the occasional hopsack jacket. The body language says, "I'm rich, I'm invested here, I belong, who are you?" The habitués were tethered to devices, tapping away, sipping Sauvignon Blanc, and staring blankly at the fake fireplace.

I arrived at the Rosewood early evening in late April 2018 for a one-night stay after a flight from JFK to San Francisco and a short drive down to the Valley. My two prior Valley trips were off the run. One was to lead a complexity science seminar at Singularity University, a pop-up college on the grounds of NASA's Ames Research Center in Cupertino. Singularity's educational role is a thin veil over what is really a speed-dating venue for big brains and billionaire backers of the next big thing.

My second Valley visit was to address a larger audience at the Ritz-Carlton in Half Moon Bay. It was Silicon Valley with surf. The Ritz-Carlton was dripping with money like the Rosewood, yet more in your face, more boisterous, more Dallas than digital. There was a golf tournament going on with a tented Cadillac prize on display for the winning round. I thought the Half Moon Ritz-Carlton must be the go-to hotel for Valley visitors, but I was wrong. The Rosewood was the real deal. Despite its elitist aura, I liked the Rosewood; the quiet was built in, ideal for a writer. I could get some writing done before my business the next day.

I was at the Rosewood for a conclave with the board of directors of Morgan Stanley, one of the most powerful banks in the world. The board was meeting off-site on a trip that included visits to tech giant clients. I was invited by Morgan Stanley's head of technology investment banking, Drew Guevara, to engage in a colloquy with the board on capital markets and geopolitical risk. The board met privately during the day, took a break, and reconvened for drinks and dinner. I was the after-dinner event to round out the day.

Drew was a bit nervous about his decision to invite me. On the one hand, he was intrigued by a scientific approach to risk and thought the board would benefit from the discussion. On the other hand, he was worried about my critique of "elites." He said, "Jim, I just want you to understand, these people *are* the elites. I don't want my directors throwing chairs at the stage." I replied, "I get it, Drew, I do this all the time. I always respect the audience, especially this board. Their biggest problem is they live in a thought bubble. They need to hear voices like mine. They'll thank you when we're done." I appreciated the fact that he had invited me. Still, it wasn't a risk-free decision; I have made edgy remarks, including the time I told a Fed governor her central bank was broke on a mark-to-market basis. She demurred, then stalled, then finally agreed.

I did my homework on the board members before the event. Their résumés were familiar, but I had met only one in person prior to this event. The directors all knew each other, so this wasn't a name tag event. I would have to repeat the names under my breath. James Gorman, the CEO, was obviously the easiest.

Twilight arrived. "Showtime," I thought. The way from my room to the cocktail venue was outdoors until the end. The path consisted of a flight of steps and a promenade on an open-air mezzanine with a trimmed lawn on one side and a twenty-foot drop on the other. As I turned from the stairs onto the walkway, a jet-black raven alighted on the fence at the far end and perched stock-still like a sentinel. I flashed back to Poe's classic poem, "The Raven," and to *The Raven of Zürich*, an out-of-print work that inspired my book, *The Road to Ruin*. Ravens have symbolized prophecy since antiquity. This raven didn't say "Nevermore," but I heard it in my head as I walked past the avian specter. I didn't look back.

Drinks were served on a patio with a pit fire. Dress was business casual; no jeans, no ties either. It was the directors' turn to relax even as I was getting ready to work. I grabbed a Diet Coke with a lime wedge from the bar and mingled among those with a Scotch or Chardonnay. Drew greeted me and began to introduce me to the board members. I shook hands with Gorman and thanked him for inviting me. He's tall, fit, brilliant, with zero tolerance for drivel. Gorman was a successful lawyer from Melbourne before his transition to investment banking. His demeanor was relaxed. Aussies are always down to earth, even when they rise to the top. It spoke well of Morgan Stanley that a lawyer was in charge, not a trader or quant. Lawyers are trained to see both sides and be good listeners and good advocates. "This is good," I thought. "Good idea to keep quants in their place."

Next came Colm Kelleher, Morgan Stanley's president. He's shorter than Gorman, but with a more powerful build. Without much ado he said, "I'm going to knock you down when we get inside." I thought to myself, "Tough Irishman, typical Wall Streeter. Watch out for this one." I wasn't wrong.

The person I went out of my way to meet was Jami Miscik. She had a long career at CIA and rose to the rank of deputy director of intelligence. She was in charge of the Directorate of Intelligence, the analytic branch that receives intelligence collections from all sources, responsible for integrating that into analyses and reports. It also undertakes strategic studies to look at future threats and new analytic techniques. The Directorate of Intelligence is one of the CIA's two main pillars, alongside the Directorate of Operations, which runs the clandestine service. The Directorate of Operations consists of case officers who handle spies in the field as well as black ops and deceptions. Miscik was well informed on those operations to conduct her analytic role. She was the highest-ranking woman in CIA history prior to Gina Haspel's appointment as director in May 2018.

I knew her on sight and walked up to introduce myself. Miscik had been my big boss at CIA when I worked on Project Prophesy. Although she ran the group I worked for, we never met at the agency. That's typical of the compartmentalization that is part of agency culture. Still, we knew many people in common, including intermediate officers between my project and her office. The conversation was relaxed until I brought up insider trading in advance of the 9/11 attack. She abruptly pivoted and walked away to join another conversation. Old habits die hard.

Companies as powerful as Morgan Stanley have equally powerful directors, but not all boards have the same discernment. Some boards are so large that each director's impact is diluted. Some big-name directors are just that, names, who float from board to board as figureheads. Morgan Stanley's board was different. Each member was distinguished, the board was small enough to be effective, and every director seemed highly engaged. Morgan Stanley was fortunate to have two female superstars in Miscik and the brilliant Hutham Olayan, heir to a Saudi engineering dynasty. Gorman did an admirable job putting the group together.

Now it was time for dinner and my presentation. The format was relaxed, round tables of eight with a small stage and two barstools, one for me and one for Drew, who would introduce me and moderate the discussion. I nibbled, waited, and then took the stage on cue. My intro consisted of a video clip on a wide-screen TV showing my last interview before the 2016 presidential election. It was an appearance on Bloomberg TV, recorded live at 4:00 A.M. New York time on Election Day, broadcast to a European audience. Michael McKee, the Bloomberg economics correspondent, said, "We'll all be in bed by ten P.M. tonight, Hillary will win it that easily. She'll do even better than her husband did in 1996, she'll win it in the East." The anchor, Francine Lacqua, turned to me and said, "Jim, what do you think?" I said we'd be up late, but Trump would win in a close race. Francine seemed momentarily flabbergasted. She's brilliant, but it was hard even for her to process a Trump victory forecast. She asked me about polls and turnout and I dissected both to support my prediction. Then the clip ended. I thought, "Well, that's a good start."

Most of my presentation consisted of points I've made many times in the past. Capital markets are not equilibrium systems; they're complex systems. Risk is not normally distributed; it's distributed along a power curve. Events are not random; they're path dependent. The most catastrophic outcome is not a linear function of scale; it's a superlinear function. I summarized by saying that capital markets and the banking system were vulnerable to a collapse of unprecedented proportions because of the scale of the system, the dense interconnectedness of megabanks, and flawed risk models.

The point was not that I was saying something new, it's that I was speaking to an audience that (mostly) had never heard it before. One who had heard my statistical analysis was Keishi Hotsuki, the chief risk officer. Hotsuki was not a board member, but it's typical to invite nonboard senior managers to attend board meetings to inform decisions or as grooming for further advancement. Hotsuki said, "Jim, your presentation is music to my ears; I've been saying the same thing for years." He gushed, "I'm so glad you gave this analysis. I want to hug you!" Gorman, the tough Aussie, stood up and quipped, "Keishi, I've been paying you millions for a decade and you've never offered to hug me." Soon there were man hugs all around. An old saying goes, "Science advances one funeral at a time." Maybe the science of risk management can advance one hug at a time.

Now it was question time.

Gorman began, "I read your book," a reference to *The Road to Ruin*. I knew he meant it. People pay lip service to authors by complimenting their books, but a writer knows within seconds whether they've read more than a few pages. It's an instinct. Gorman's gambit meant a critique was coming next.

He pointed out that Morgan Stanley's capital adequacy had grown significantly since the last crisis, that certain risky trading strategies were no longer allowed, and that compliance and risk management had been greatly strengthened. He strongly disagreed with my assessment that Morgan Stanley and other securities firms were more vulnerable than ever to a financial collapse.

Gorman's points were correct in a narrow sense, but missed a deeper reality. I told a story of an encounter with legendary Citibank CEO Walter Wriston in 1981, at a time when confidence in the U.S. dollar was waning and oil-rich Arabs were rumored to be pulling petrodollars from U.S. banks, including Citi. Wriston explained to me the banking system was a closed circuit. Arabs could pull deposits from banks and buy other assets, including gold, but the sellers of those assets would put the money on deposit with another bank, which lent it back to the original bank in the interbank deposit market. There were small costs in terms of rates and fees, yet the money ended up where it started. Wriston told me, "Banks don't need capital; they just need to borrow from other banks."

The truth is, banks don't need capital when markets are calm, interbank liquidity is readily available, and collateral is well-bid. Yet the opposite is true. In a panic, when liquidity dries up, when assets go no-bid, and when everyone wants his money back, no amount of capital is enough. Banks, even good banks, are leveraged and it only takes modest declines in asset values on a leveraged balance sheet to wipe out capital. My point to Gorman was that his improved capital cushion was more than enough for most market conditions, but far from enough for a replay of 2008 on a larger scale.

Kelleher had been biding his time and now pounced. He repeated Gorman's points about capital adequacy and risk, but went further. He asserted that derivatives exposures had declined significantly (I asserted the opposite). Even under my complexity analysis, diminution in derivatives notional amounts should result in a nonlinear reduction in risk that made the system safer. Kelleher was tough, but his analysis was expert.

The gross notional value of all derivatives held by banks, typically off-balance sheet and disclosed only in footnotes, had declined since 2008 as Kelleher asserted, according to comprehensive statistics reported by the BIS. This was because the banks assigned swaps and other derivatives to centralized clearinghouses, which net out offsetting exposures as urged by the G20 leaders in September 2009. When clearinghouse footings are included, the gross notional value of derivatives has increased since 2008, consistent with my claim. Clearinghouses provide transparency and netting, and in a panic, problems are spotted more readily. Still, derivatives risks have not disappeared; they have simply been moved from banks to clearinghouses, which raises the question of their capital adequacy. What happens if a major clearinghouse participant is in financial distress and cannot perform its obligations? It's not comforting to know that the major clearinghouses, including CME, ICE, and the London Clearing House are using the same flawed VaR and stress-test risk-management methods that missed the coming catastrophe in 2008. Mutualization of losses among all clearinghouse members is the prescribed remedy when a member defaults, but this simply acts as a conduit for contagion. It's as if a patient with an infectious deadly disease escaped from quarantine and spent the day at Starbucks. As with AIG in 2008, net exposure rapidly morphs into gross exposure once counterparty performance is in doubt.

Gorman's and Kelleher's critiques suffered from what Keynes called the fallacy of composition; that components of a system can be added up to describe the system as a whole. This is not true in complex systems, where scaling metrics means emergent properties come out of nowhere and cannot be inferred from perfect knowledge of the system's parts.

I leaned forward, looked straight at Kelleher, and said, "Look, Colm, you're right. Morgan Stanley is safer. *Still, the system is not.* Morgan Stanley is part of the system; when the system collapses, Morgan Stanley goes with it. It's not enough to look at your own balance sheet; you have to look at the global balance sheet. It's all connected." Of course, there was no need to single out Morgan Stanley. The same could be said of all the big banks. Their balance sheets were safer in a narrow sense. Yet they were more vulnerable than ever to systemic risk.

It was almost time to head back to the bar. Jami Miscik asked the smartest question of the evening: "What would you do if you were in my position as a director of Morgan Stanley?" I said I would work with colleagues to break up the big banks, including Morgan Stanley, ban most derivatives, and adopt Bayesian statistics and complexity theory as new risk-management tools. Like the CIA veteran she was, Miscik showed no reaction. Still, she clearly understood every point.

I sympathized with the reality that a bank director has a duty to that bank and its stockholders, not to the system as a whole. Systemic risk is more the purview of central banks, finance ministers, and the IMF. Still, directors and CEOs are powerful. If they urged a risk-reducing agenda on government policymakers, the policymakers might listen. There's no evidence this is happening. Inertia rules.

Glaciers

In writing and public speaking, I frequently use a snowflake-avalanche metaphor to describe complex system dynamics and the way systems collapse. Capital markets are complex systems, but their workings are incomprehensible to everyday citizens. Attentive investors know if the Dow Jones index went up or down or if their 401(k) balance showed a gain or loss from the last monthly statement, but that's all. People are busy; unless they're finance professionals, there's no reason they should know more than the latest prices. When one explains how complex systems work and why capital markets are vulnerable to total breakdown, people are intrigued, yet their eyes glaze over at the mention of density functions, power curves, and hypersynchronicity. That's understandable and is why the avalanche metaphor is useful. It begins with the buildup of an unstable snowpack on a mountainside. Billions of individual snowflakes form an interconnected lattice. A new snowflake falls, it hits the snowpack in a way that shakes loose a few other snowflakes, those snowflakes begin to slide, the slide gains momentum, and soon the entire snowpack rips loose from the mountain and buries the village below. The image is vivid and more than a metaphor; the math and dynamics behind the avalanche are exactly the same as a capital markets collapse, adjusted for the idiosyncrasies of snowflakes versus live traders. Breaking up unstable snowpacks with dynamite to reduce danger has the same rationale as breaking up big banks.

Yet an avalanche is not the only metaphor that might apply to capital markets. In some cases, a glacier is a better way to describe the economic processes that drive securities prices, exchange rates, and interest rates. A glacier is a complex dynamic system, yet glaciers move more slowly and cause more lasting change than an avalanche. Glaciers gouge valleys, move boulders, and push obstacles aside with ease.

While glaciers are reputed to move slowly, they can also surge. In 1956, the Muldrow Glacier near Denali in the Alaska Range surged at a pace of fifteen hundred feet per day. Surface ice levels dropped three hundred feet as the ice moved rapidly to lower elevations. The glacier moved four miles down the mountain by the end of the surge.

Events shaking capital markets today are better likened to glaciers than avalanches. They are unrelenting and slow, yet sometimes produce dramatic surges. They are less dramatic than avalanches in the short run, but more destructive in the end. Some of the glaciers grinding down the system today are Chinese debt, trade wars, Fed monetary finesse, and an emerging-markets debt debacle. There are other threats, but these are among the greatest. What follows is a précis of some glaciers gaining ground to push capital markets into a new Ice Age and leave us in the aftermath.

China Is Madoff

1 percent, 1 percent, 1 percent, 1 percent, 1 percent . . .

That's a close approximation of the time series of monthly returns reported by Bernie Madoff over the twenty years he ran his wealth management business.

When you gain 1 percent per month, that compounds to 12.7 percent per year, year after year. That return more than doubles your money in six years, and doubles it again in another six years. After eighteen years, about the time between the birth of a child and when she goes off to college, you would have made eight times your money with Madoff. One million dollars invested with Madoff in 1990 would have been worth $8 million by 2008.

There was only one problem. It was all a fraud. There was no pool of investable assets. There were no above-average returns, no compounding, and no profits. It was all fake accounting and looting by Madoff. Sometimes new money was used to cash out old money that wanted to redeem, but most of the money stayed in. Madoff's Ponzi collapsed in 2008.

The amount lost in the Madoff fraud varies depending on one's calculation method. If you use the amount the investors believed they had, even though the account statements were bogus, the losses were about $65 billion. If you use the amount of invested money that was lost without counting fake profits, the loss was $17 billion. Either way, Madoff set the record for the biggest Ponzi scheme in history.

The fraud was discovered in conjunction with the financial panic of 2008. Global investors were losing money in stocks, mortgages, derivatives, and other asset classes. Leveraged investors were getting hit with margin calls. Money market funds and banks experienced runs as investors tried to get their money back any way they could. It was the worst global liquidity crisis in history.

In this panicked environment, Madoff's investors knew they could count on Bernie as a liquidity source. They began to make redemptions from Madoff's fund. That's when the Ponzi unraveled. Madoff didn't have the funds to meet the redemptions, he began to default, rumors spread, the SEC and FBI moved in, and the rest is history. On June 29, 2009, Bernie Madoff was sentenced in federal court to 150 years in jail.

Readers familiar with the Madoff story may also know there were numerous suspicions and warning signs as early as the mid-1990s that Madoff might be running a Ponzi. These warnings were never properly investigated by the SEC or other agencies.

The most famous warnings were given by forensic analyst Harry Markopolos. What first tipped Markopolos off to the fact that Madoff might be a fraud? It was those steady returns, the 1 percent, 1 percent, 1 percent month after month, year after year. A graph of Madoff's returns over time rose at a near perfect 45-degree angle. Markopolos knew *it's impossible to produce those returns in finance.*

It is possible to produce positive returns on an annual basis over long periods of time. Some of the best hedge-fund managers have done it, although most have not. But even superstar hedge-fund managers have a bad month or a bad year now and then. And the positive years are not all the same. You might be up 10 percent one year, 25 percent the next year, then down 3 percent, and up 7 percent in year four. That's a pretty good track record, but it's not repetitive and it doesn't move in a straight line.

The technical name for a time series of returns similar to what Madoff was reporting is serial correlation or autocorrelation. This happens when a signal contains a feedback function that causes it to produce the same signal over and over, sometimes with amplification. Serial correlation exists in physics, mathematics, and acoustics, but it does not exist naturally in finance. Markets are complex dynamic systems with emergent properties that disrupt the steady feedback needed to produce serial correlation. The fact that Madoff reported returns exhibiting autocorrelation was a dead giveaway to Markopolos. Unfortunately, the SEC did not understand what Markopolos was saying.

Here's another time series of economic returns: 1.8 percent, 1.7 percent, 1.5 percent, 1.8 percent, 1.8 percent, 1.6 percent, 1.4 percent, 1.8 percent. That's the time series of quarterly growth in China's GDP from the second quarter of 2016 to the second quarter of 2018. It's not as smooth as Madoff's returns, but it's close. It's also impossible. China can only produce those returns by cooking the books, the same as Madoff. China reports steady, positive returns quarter after quarter, like clockwork. Those numbers aren't real; they're manufactured to appease gullible investors, policymakers, and the media.

What does a real economy look like? Here's the annualized U.S.

growth rate for GDP for the same eight quarters as the China example: 1.9 percent, 1.8 percent, 1.8 percent, 3.0 percent, 2.8 percent, 2.3 percent, 2.2 percent, 4.1 percent. Notice that the U.S. growth rates exhibit far more variance than China's from a high of 4.1 percent to a low of 1.8 percent. Notice that weak quarters, like 1.8 percent, are adjacent to strong quarters, like 3.0 percent.

If you take the time series back even further you discover that China has not had a negative quarter in over five years, while the United States has. In short, the U.S. data exhibits the mix of weak, strong, and negative quarterly data that one expects from a complex economy, while China exhibits the autocorrelation that one expects from a financial fraud.

There is no question that China is manipulating its growth data. Real growth in China is closer to 5.5 percent per year than the 6.8 percent per year China claims. Growth is even lower once wasted investment is stripped out. The policy question is why China feels compelled both to lie about the data and present it as an improbable autocorrelated time series.

The reason is that China is a Ponzi like Madoff. China has trillions of dollars in external dollar-denominated debt, wealth management products, bank loans, intercompany loans, and other financially engineered arrangements that can never be repaid. If everyone with a claim on China wanted her money back, China couldn't come close to satisfying even a small portion of those seeking liquidity.

This doesn't mean China does not have a real economy. It does. It's just that the real economy is tangled in a web of leverage, unpayable debt, bogus accounting, and the vain hope that Communist Party leadership can keep a lid on dissent until the global economy improves.

That's not happening. The global economy is sinking into trade wars, currency wars, and fights over intangibles such as intellectual property. Shooting wars in the South China Sea, Taiwan Strait, Korea, and the Middle East may not be far behind.

China cannot win a trade war because it exports far more than it imports, especially on a bilateral basis with the United States. Trump wants the U.S.-China bilateral trade deficit reduced by several hundred billion dollars. China cannot easily do that without hurting its economy, so the trade wars will drag on and get worse.

China does have one financial weapon it can use to alleviate the pressure from the trade wars: currency devaluation. China has about $3 trillion in reserves. About $1 trillion is illiquid; invested in hedge funds, private equity, and other alternative assets that cannot easily be redeemed. Another $1 trillion is held as a precautionary reserve to bail out the banking system when the time comes. That leaves only $1 trillion to defend the currency peg with the dollar. It's not enough. In 2016, China used up $1 trillion in reserves defending its currency. China was losing reserves at the rate of $80 billion per month at one point. It would have been broke by the end of 2017 if it had not closed its capital account and trapped the reserves inside China.

By devaluing its currency, China can take pressure off the capital outflows, buy time, import inflation to reduce the value of local currency debts, and make its exports more attractive. Devaluation is a simple solution to China's financial imbalances. Imagine if Madoff had been able to "devalue" his liabilities to investors. He might still be in business. China will still be in business a century from now, but that doesn't mean there won't be enormous investor losses and global economic disruptions along the way.

China's risks go far beyond liquidity and exchange rates. It is now reaping the bitter fruit of its one-child policy of the 1980s, 1990s, and early twenty-first century. The ban on two children, sometimes enforced by drowning newborn girls in bedside buckets, has left China with a rapidly aging population and insufficient younger workers to maintain growth or provide benefits for retirees. Relaxing the policy as China has done recently will not have an impact on workforce participation or productivity for another twenty years. Labor-force participation and productivity are all there is to economic growth. China has shortsightedly truncated its labor force and lags badly in productivity. Apart from borrowed money, wasted infrastructure investment, and fictitious accounting, there is no Chinese economic growth miracle. In short, China is growing old before it grows rich. In the end, it is just another emerging-markets economy stuck in what the IMF calls the middle-income trap with no easy way out.

These economic and demographic headwinds come on top of an increasingly confrontational geopolitical relationship between China and the United States. This confrontation, referred to by experts as the "gray rhino," is summed up by University of Hong Kong scholar Andrew Sheng:

> In addition to structural and cyclical risks, China must address the "gray rhino" (highly likely, but often ignored) strategic risks arising from the intensifying Sino-American geopolitical rivalry. Here, the emerging trade war is just the tip of the iceberg. The U.S. and China are set to become immersed in a long-term competition for technological and strategic supremacy. To stay ahead, they will use every kind of leverage and instrument at their disposal. If this competition is left unchecked, it will surely have far-reaching spillover effects.

Introduction of the geopolitical struggle is critical to the analysis because it marks a change from the era of globalization, when economic growth trumped all other policy considerations. Wars are not free, even cold wars, and if the price of containing Chinese ambition is slower growth, that is a price the United States is prepared to pay to protect its intellectual property and national security. This is a rude awakening for younger bankers and scholars who have known only a golden age of globalization (1989–2017). More senior analysts acquainted with the first Cold War (1947–89) will find the elevation of geopolitics over growth to be familiar ground.

Trade Tango

In May 2018, a high-level delegation of Trump administration officials traveled to Beijing for a critical round of negotiations intended to avoid an all-out trade war between the two largest economies on the planet.

The U.S. delegation consisted of Treasury secretary Steve Mnuchin, U.S. trade representative Robert E. Lighthizer, director of the National Economic Council Larry Kudlow, and White House trade director Peter Navarro. This delegation included every senior U.S. official with line responsibility for trade issues except Commerce secretary Wilbur Ross. The composition of the delegation was President Trump's way of announcing the negotiations were of the utmost importance. Wits have compared this delegation to the bar scene in the original *Star Wars* film, where an eclectic group of characters speaking different languages mingle, and trouble is never far from the surface—an apt comparison.

Lighthizer is a trade war veteran with public service going back to the Reagan administration and over thirty years in the private practice of trade law, representing major corporate clients including U. S. Steel. Navarro is a trade hawk also, but from academia and without Lighthizer's deal-making experience. Kudlow is well liked yet is seen as a free-trade cheerleader. Mnuchin has not shown any particular interest in trade issues, is more aligned with the globalist agenda, but does favor a cheap dollar, which is another way to improve the U.S. trade deficit. Officially, the delegation was led by Mnuchin because he has the highest Cabinet rank of those present. That said, there's no doubt that Lighthizer was the most important official in the trade delegation.

In a closed-door meeting during an earlier visit to Beijing with high-level Chinese trade and political officials, Lighthizer leaned forward across the table, engaged with his counterpart, and unleashed a detailed chronology of Chinese cheating on trade issues. The trade deception litany recited by Lighthizer started in 1994, when China engaged in an overnight 33 percent maxi-devaluation of the yuan, taking it to 8.7 yuan to $1.00. That devaluation was a declaration of a currency war and trade war at the same time, since the cheap currency helped Chinese exports at the expense of its trading partners. Lighthizer went on to recite further instances of currency manipulation, theft of intellectual property, subsidies to state-owned enterprises, development of excess capacity in tradeable goods, dumping, ignoring environmental costs, forced labor, and willful violations of World Trade Organization, or WTO, rules over nearly a quarter century, from 1994 to 2017. When Lighthizer was done he paused, looked directly at the top Chinese delegate, and said, "You've been lying to us for twenty-five years. Why should we believe you now?"

The Chinese were shocked. They had never witnessed anything like Lighthizer's bluntness, combined with his complete mastery of the facts. There was no more to say at the meeting, yet a message was delivered. The United States would no longer accept vague promises and delayed deadlines that never seemed to arrive. From now on, the United States would insist on substantial actions delivered in verifiable ways.

Upon learning of this trade tour de force, President Trump asked Lighthizer for the notes he used in describing the Chinese trade violations. Trump thought it would be useful in building his own stump speeches on the subject.

"Sir, I didn't use notes," replied Lighthizer.

"Okay," said Trump, "I understand. Just give me your outline or bullet points, then."

"Sir, I didn't use bullet points," Lighthizer informed the president.

Trump smiled and nodded. He realized that Lighthizer kept it all in his head, had lived through these trade issues for decades, and could repeat the litany of Chinese cheating anytime and without preparation. Trump liked that because he too is an intuitive presenter who uses notes or teleprompters infrequently. Trump knew he had made the right choice for trade representative.

Lighthizer enjoys Trump's full support in his trade confrontation with

China and in pending rounds of negotiation with Canada, the EU, Japan, Brazil, and other trading partners. For his part, Lighthizer rarely does interviews, is not in the limelight, and does not leak to the press. He is fine with Peter Navarro doing rounds of high-profile interviews and being the public face of the trade wars. In the Trump White House, there's more downside than upside when you upstage the boss or contradict some real-time tweet you haven't even seen. Lighthizer avoids these dangers with his low-profile demeanor. Trump likes that too.

Lighthizer lives in Palm Beach, Florida, not far from President Trump's getaway estate at Mar-a-Lago. This makes it convenient for Trump to invite Lighthizer aboard Air Force One when he leaves Washington, D.C., for a weekend visit to Palm Beach. Lighthizer takes Trump up on his offer as frequently as possible. This gives him valuable one-on-one time with the president outside the White House glare that most Cabinet officers and West Wing advisers can only dream about.

Lighthizer developed the Trump trade approach to China using a hardline playbook he developed in confrontations with Japan during the Reagan years. In the early 1980s, the U.S. automobile industry was reeling from cheap Japanese imported cars. Lighthizer realized the Japanese manipulated their currency to lower their unit labor costs when converted to dollars. He worked with Reagan to impose steep tariffs on imports of Japanese and European cars. This forced the Japanese and Germans to jump the tariff wall by locating auto plants in the United States. Today most "German" BMWs and "Japanese" Hondas are built in Alabama, South Carolina, Tennessee, and elsewhere in the South and Midwest. The result was thousands of high-paying manufacturing jobs in the United States. Lighthizer and Trump are ready to run this playbook again on the Chinese.

In early 2018, Trump announced tariffs on Chinese solar panels, washing machines, steel, and aluminum under Section 272 of the Trade Act of 1974. Trump also announced tariffs on $50 billion of Chinese imports under Section 301 of the act as punitive action for Chinese theft of U.S. intellectual property.

The Chinese promptly announced tariffs on $50 billion of U.S. imports, including agricultural goods such as soybeans and sorghum, in retaliation for the U.S. Section 301 tariffs. Like a shrewd poker player with a large stack of chips, Trump announced tariffs on *another* $50 billion of Chinese imports on top of the original $50 billion, as retaliation for the retaliation. It was as if China said, "I'll see your fifty billion dollars," and Trump said, "I'll raise you fifty."

Initially, the stock market took these announcements in stride, betting that Trump's announcements were a negotiating bluff and China's response was simply to avoid loss of face. Wall Street had high confidence that after the initial threats were hurled the two sides would negotiate their differences, lower tariffs, and reduce the trade deficit pragmatically, with larger purchases of U.S. soybeans by China.

As usual, the Wall Street forecast was an unrealistic, rosy scenario. In fact, the initial tariffs went into effect by September 2018 and additional rounds of tariffs were then imposed by Trump. China did not back down, and announced its own additional rounds of tariffs on U.S. exports to China. However, China was fighting a losing battle. U.S. imports from China are almost $300 billion greater than Chinese imports from the United States. China was simply running out of space to match the U.S. tariffs dollar for dollar because it did not buy enough from the United States. By late 2018, China's only recourse was to cheapen its currency so that lower production costs measured in dollars might offset some of the higher costs imposed by tariffs. As in the 1930s, currency wars and trade wars were working side by side.

China feels that its economy is sufficiently strong and resilient enough to weather a trade war with the United States. China can always buy soybeans from Canada and aircraft from Airbus. It is betting that the United States has more to lose than China if the trade war escalates. China is wrong in its estimate. Both sides may lose in a trade war, but China has far more to lose. Trade is a materially larger component of Chinese GDP than it is for the United States. Trump weaponized CFIUS to prevent Chinese acquisitions of U.S. technology firms. China is living atop a mountain of debt. Any forced decline in China's trade surplus with the United States will slow the Chinese economy, increase unemployment, jeopardize debt service, and possibly lead to the kind of social unrest the Communist Chinese most fear. While Mnuchin is not a trade hawk, he is a currency hawk and can unleash a cheaper dollar to complement Trump's tariffs and make American purchases of Chinese goods more expensive. In short, Trump has more trade war weapons than China, and Lighthizer is as skilled as a four-star general when it comes to using them.

The U.S.-China trade war has far to run. The United States will win, but there will be collateral damage in markets. The dollar will head lower both in order to mitigate trade damage and to maintain maximum pressure on China.

Fed Fantasia

Is the Fed ready for the next recession?

The answer is no.

Economic research shows that it takes 300 to 500 basis points of interest-rate cuts by the Fed to pull the U.S. economy out of a recession. One basis point is 1/100 of 1 percentage point. Five hundred basis points of rate reduction means the Fed would have to cut rates 5 percentage points. As of January 2019, the Fed's target rate for Fed funds, the so-called policy rate, is 2.5 percent. How do you cut rates 3 percent to 5 percent when you're starting at 2.5 percent? You can't.

What about more quantitative easing? The Fed ended QE in late 2014 after QE1, QE2, and QE3, from 2008 to 2014. What about QE4 in a new recession? The problem is that the Fed never normalized its balance sheet from QE1, QE2, and QE3, so their capacity to implement QE4 is in doubt. During that period, the Fed expanded its balance sheet from $800 billion to $4.4 trillion. The Fed used the $3.6 trillion of newly printed money to purchase long-term Treasury securities to suppress interest rates across the yield curve. Resulting higher valuations for stocks and real estate would create a wealth effect that would encourage more spending. The higher valuations would also provide collateral for more borrowing. This expected spending and lending was intended to put the U.S. economy on a sustainable path to higher growth.

This theory was another failure by the academics. The wealth effect never emerged and the return of high leverage by consumers never returned in the United States. The only part of the Bernanke plan that worked was higher asset values, but those values now look dangerously like bubbles waiting to burst. The result is that almost all of the leverage from QE is still on the Fed's balance sheet. The $3.6 trillion of new money was never mopped up by the Fed; it's on the Fed's books in the form of bank reserves. The Fed began a program of balance-sheet normalization in 2017, yet that program is not far along. The Fed's balance sheet today is still almost $4 trillion. That makes it highly problematic for the Fed to start QE4. When the Fed started QE1 in 2008, the balance sheet was $800 billion; if the Fed started a new QE program today, it would be starting from a much higher base. The policy question is whether the Fed could take their balance sheet to $5 trillion or $6 trillion in the course of QE4 or QE5. In answering that question, bear in mind the Fed has only $40 billion in capital. With current assets of $4 trillion, the Fed is leveraged 100:1, a ratio that is problematic for banks and brokers and unheard of among hedge funds.

Modern monetary theory (MMT), led by left-wing academics like Stephanie Kelton, see no problem with the Fed printing as much money as it wants to monetize Treasury debt. MMT is almost certainly incorrect about this. There's an invisible confidence boundary beyond which everyday Americans suddenly lose confidence in Fed liabilities (aka dollars) in a hypersynchronous phase transition. No one knows exactly where the boundary is, but no one wants to find out the hard way. The confidence boundary certainly exists, possibly at the $5 trillion level. The Fed seems to agree, although they won't say so. The Fed is trying to reduce its balance sheet today so that it can expand again in future without destroying confidence. If a recession hit tomorrow, the Fed would *not* be able to save the day with rate cuts because they'd hit the zero bound before they could cut enough to make a difference. They would *not* be able to save the day with QE4 because they're already overleveraged.

What can the Fed do?

All the Fed can do is raise rates (slowly), reduce the balance sheet (slowly), and hope that a recession does not hit before they get policy rates and leverage back to normal, probably around 2021. The odds of the Fed being able to pull this off before the next recession are low. The current expansion started in June 2009 and continues until today. It is the second longest expansion since 1945, currently over 117 months. It is longer than the Reagan-Bush expansion of 1982–1990. It is longer than the Kennedy-Johnson expansion of 1961–1969. It's longer than any expansion except the Clinton-Gingrich expansion of 1991–2001. Probabilistically, the odds of this current expansion turning to recession before the end of 2020 are extremely high.

In short, there's a very high probability that the U.S. economy will go into recession before the Fed is prepared to pull the economy out of it. Once the recession starts, the United States, like Japan starting in the 1990s, may stay near recession levels for decades. Japan has had three lost decades. The United States is just finishing its first and may have more to go.

The situation is even worse than this dire forecast suggests. The reason is that by preparing to fight the next recession, the Fed may cause the recession they're preparing to cure. It's like trying to run a marathon while being chased by a hungry bear. The Fed needs to raise rates and reduce their balance sheet in order to have enough policy leeway to fight a recession. If they move too quickly, they'll cause a recession. If they move too slowly, they'll run out of time and be eaten by the bear.

This conundrum is at the root of the Fed's monetary finesse. This trap was caused by Bernanke's failure to raise rates in 2010 and 2011 when the economy was in a better position to absorb rate hikes in the early stages of an expansion. It was also caused by Bernanke's insistence on QE2 and QE3 despite zero evidence then or now that quantitative easing helps the economy. (QE1 was needed to deal with a liquidity crisis, but that was over in 2009. There's no rationale for QE2 and QE3.)

A recession is coming, the Fed is unprepared, and it's extremely unlikely the Fed will be prepared in time. Investors fear inflation, but if the recession scenario unfolds, deflation will emerge as a greater concern.

Emerging Markets Submerge

Emerging-markets debt crises are as predictable as spring rain. They happen every ten to fifteen years with few variations or exceptions. In recent decades, the first crisis in this series was the 1982–1985 Latin American debt crisis. The combination of inflation and a commodity price boom in the late 1970s had given a huge boost to economies such as Brazil, Argentina, Mexico, Zaire (now the Congo), and many other nations. This commodity boom enabled these emerging-markets economies to earn U.S. dollar reserves in exchange for their exports. These dollar reserves were supplemented with dollar loans from U.S. banks looking to recycle petrodollars that the OPEC countries were putting on deposit after the 1970s oil price explosion.

I discussed the petrodollar recycling process personally with Walter Wriston, Citibank's iconic leader during the energy crisis. In the 1960s, Wriston invented the negotiable eurodollar CD, which was later critical for funding those emerging-market loans. Wriston is considered the father of petrodollar recycling after the petrodollar was created by Henry Kissinger and William Simon in 1974. Citibank made billions of dollars recycling petrodollars and its stock price soared. It was a euphoric phase and a great time to be an international banker.

Then the market boom crashed and burned. Beginning in 1982, the debtors defaulted. They squandered their reserves on vanity projects such as skyscrapers in the jungle, which I saw firsthand on the Congo River in Central Africa. Whatever wasn't wasted was stolen and stashed away in Swiss bank accounts by kleptocrats. Citibank was technically insolvent after these defaults, but was bailed out by the absence of mark-to-market accounting. We were able to pretend the loans were still good as long as we could refinance them or roll them over in some way. Citibank has a long and glorious history of being bailed out, stretching from the 1930s to the 2010s.

After the defaults of the 1980s, reaction set in. Emerging markets had to adopt austerity, devalue their currencies, cut spending, cut imports, and gradually rebuild their credit. There was a major emerging-markets debt crisis in Mexico in 1994, the Tequila crisis, but that was contained by another U.S. bailout led by Treasury secretary Bob Rubin. On the whole, the emerging markets used the 1990s to rebuild reserves and restore their creditworthiness. Gradually, the banks looked favorably on this emerging-markets progress and new loans started to flow. Now the target of bank lending was not Latin America but the Asian Tigers (Singapore, Taiwan, South Korea, and Hong Kong), and the South Asian minitigers.

The next big emerging-markets debt crisis arrived right on time in 1997, fifteen years after the 1982 Latin American debt crisis. This new crisis began in Thailand in June 1997. Money had been flooding into Thailand for several years, mostly to build real estate projects, resorts, golf courses, and commercial office buildings. Thailand's currency, the baht, was pegged to the dollar, so dollar-based investors could get high yields without currency risk. Suddenly a run on the baht emerged. Investors flocked to cash out their investments and get their dollars back. The Thai central bank was forced to close the capital account and devalue their currency, forcing large losses on foreign investors. This sparked fear that other Asian countries would do the same. Panic spread to Malaysia, Indonesia, South Korea, and finally to Russia, before coming to rest at Long-Term Capital Management, a hedge fund in Greenwich, Connecticut. As chief counsel to LTCM, I negotiated the fund's rescue by fourteen Wall Street banks. Wall Street put up $4 billion in cash to prop up the LTCM balance sheet so it could be unwound gradually. At the time of the rescue on September 28, 1998, global capital markets were just hours away from complete collapse.

Emerging markets learned valuable lessons in the 1997–1998 crisis. In the decade that followed, the emerging markets built up their reserve positions to enormous size so they were not disadvantaged in another global liquidity crisis. These excess national savings were called "precautionary reserves" because they were over and above what central banks normally need to conduct foreign exchange operations. The emerging markets also avoided unrealistic fixed exchange rates, which was an open invitation to foreign speculators like George Soros to short their currencies and drain their reserves.

These improved practices meant that emerging markets were not in the eye of the storm in the 2007–2008 global financial crisis, and the subsequent 2009–2015 European sovereign debt crisis. Those crises were mainly confined to developed economies and sectors such as U.S. real estate, European banks, and weaker members of the Eurozone, including Greece, Cyprus, and Ireland.

Yet memories are short. It has been over twenty years since the last emerging-markets debt crisis and ten years since the last global financial crisis. Emerging-markets lending has been proceeding at a record pace. Once again, hot money from the United States and Europe is chasing high yields in emerging markets, especially the BRICS (Brazil, Russia, India, China, and South Africa), and the next tier of nations, including Turkey, Indonesia, and Argentina.

The world is now at the beginning of the third major emerging-markets debt crisis in the past thirty-five years. One critical metric is the size of hard currency reserves relative to the number of months of imports those reserves can buy. This relationship is critical because emerging markets need imports of parts and components in order to generate exports.

They need machinery in order to engage in manufacturing. They need to buy oil in order to keep factories and tourist facilities operating. Most major emerging-markets economies, with the exceptions of Russia, China, and Brazil, have less than twelve months liquidity in their reserve positions.

Another key metric is the gross external financing requirement, or GXFR, calculated as a percentage of total reserves. GXFR shows maturing debt as a percentage of reserves in the coming twelve months. Turkey and Argentina are both over 120 percent, which means they have more maturing debt than reserves to pay that debt. GXFR considers both maturing debt denominated in foreign currencies (including dollars and euros), and any current account deficit over the coming year.

Both metrics show a new crisis in the making. The hard currency import coverage for Turkey, Ukraine, Mexico, Argentina, and South Africa, among others, is less than one year. This means that in the event of a developed economy recession or another liquidity crisis where demand for emerging-markets exports dried up, the ability of those emerging markets to keep importing needed inputs would evaporate quickly. Turkey's maturing debt and current account deficit in the year ahead is almost 160 percent of its available reserves. Argentina's ratio of debts and deficits to reserves is over 120 percent. The ratio for Venezuela is about 100 percent, which is shocking since Venezuela is a major oil exporter.

These metrics don't merely forecast an emerging-markets debt crisis in the future. The debt crisis has already begun. Venezuela defaulted on some of its external debt, and litigation with creditors and seizure of certain assets is under way. Argentina's reserves have been severely depleted defending its currency and it has turned to the IMF for emergency funding. Ukraine, South Africa, and Chile are also highly vulnerable to a run on their reserves and default on their external dollar-denominated debt. Russia is in a relatively strong position because it has little external debt. China has huge external debts, but also has huge reserves, over $3 trillion, to deal with those debts.

The problem is not individual sovereign defaults; those are bound to occur. The problem is contagion. History shows that once a single nation defaults, creditors lose confidence in other emerging markets. Those creditors begin to cash out investments in emerging markets across the board and a panic begins. Once that happens, even stronger countries such as China lose reserves rapidly and end up in default. In a worst case, a full-scale global liquidity crisis commences, potentially worse than 2008.

A full-blown emerging-markets debt crisis is likely soon. It will spread from Turkey, Argentina, and Venezuela to other overleveraged nations, including Indonesia, South Africa, and Mexico. The panic will then affect Ukraine, Chile, Poland, and the other weak links in the chain. The IMF will run out of lending resources and will have to pass the hat among the richer members. But the Europeans will have their own problems and the United States under President Trump is likely to reply, "America First," and decline to participate in bailing out the emerging markets with U.S. taxpayer funds. At that point, the IMF may resort to printing trillions in special drawing rights to reliquefy a panicked world.

This coming crisis is as predictable as spring rain.

An Asset for All Seasons

From the Black Death in the fourteenth century, to the Thirty Years' War in the seventeenth century, to the world wars of the twentieth century, gold has been a reliable store of wealth. There is no reason to believe that existential events are no longer a danger.

The reader needs no reminder of the litany of risks present today. The United States is determined to prevent Iran from obtaining nuclear weapons. Iran is equally determined to develop them. Iran's neighbors such as Saudi Arabia have said that if Iran obtains nuclear weapons, they will quickly do the same. In that case, Turkey and Egypt would follow suit. The choices boil down to a conventional war with Iran or a wider nuclear arms race in a highly volatile region.

North Korea already has an arsenal of nuclear warheads with a yield approximately the size of the Hiroshima atomic bomb, 15 kilotons of TNT, but it has tested larger weapons. It has also developed intermediate-range ballistic missiles (IRBMs) and has tested intercontinental ballistic missiles (ICBMs). Denuclearization discussions are ongoing between the United States and North Korea, yet Trump has made it clear that he will attack North Korea if it advances further toward its stated goal of having a deliverable nuclear weapon that can reach the United States. If the United States does attack North Korea, it is likely that North Korea will unleash devastating force on South Korea, and possibly launch a nuclear weapon aimed at Japan.

Venezuela is a political and humanitarian catastrophe and is approaching the level of a failed state, which could result in civil war, riots, mass refugees, and a cutoff of its oil exports, 3 percent of the world total today. Other hot spots around the world include Syria, Ukraine, Israel and its confrontation with Hamas and Hezbollah, the Saudi war with Iranian-backed Houthi rebels in Yemen, and conflicting claims in the South China Sea.

Natural disasters abound from the extreme flooding of Hurricanes Harvey and Florence to the lava flows of Kilauea on Hawaii. The Ebola virus recently reemerged in the Congo four years after a prior epidemic in West Africa caused ten thousand deaths. Other threats are ubiquitous.

New threats are emerging that are not traditionally geopolitical or natural. These include power-grid collapses, cyberwarfare, hacking, data theft, and misuse of big data, including examples such as Russian interference in U.S. elections. Killer robots, swarm attack drones, and rogue artificial intelligence applications are here or coming soon.

An investor would not be blamed for saying "So what?" The threats mentioned have been festering for years. Going back further in time would produce a different list of threats, most of which never came to fruition. Americans in particular seem safe from the worst of these threats, except for the temporary effects of a bad storm or wildfire in a specific area. To most Americans, these threats are background noise. Complacency rules the day.

Yet here's an interesting bit of math, somewhat simplified, that might break investors out of their complacency. Let's consider the much discussed "one-hundred-year flood," which can literally be a one-hundred-year flood like Hurricane Harvey or a metaphorical rare event; a so-called black swan. Let's call P the probability of a one-hundred-year flood in a known flood zone, and consider the odds of the flood happening or not happening each year in a succession of years. Mathematicians express this situation as:

P(100-year flood) = P(F) = 1% = 0.01

P(no 100-year flood) = $P(F^1)$ = 1-0.01 = 0.99

P(no flood for 2 years) = $P(F^1) \cdot P(F^1) = P(F^1)^2 = 0.99^2 = 0.9801$

P(no flood for X years) = $P(F^1)^X$

Therefore, P(no flood for 30 years) = $P(F^1)^{30} = 0.99^{30} = 0.7397$

This means that over a thirty-year period, the probability of no one-hundred-year flood is approximately 74 percent, and the probability of one one-hundred-year flood is 26 percent, or *more than one chance in four*. This math is called a Bernoulli process. It's a standard statistical formula. The point is that disastrous events with tiny probabilities of happening in a short time span are *almost certain to happen* over a longer horizon.

Let's take the above math and consider four separate catastrophes, each equivalent to a one-hundred-year flood, with no correlation to each other. If the odds of each individual event happening in thirty years are 26 percent, the chance of any one happening in the same period is 100 percent. As we consider a longer list of one-hundred-year floods, the time frame of one event happening with 100 percent certainty goes from thirty years, to twenty years, to ten years, etc. In other words, the next one-hundred-year flood is waiting right around the corner.

Real-world experience bears out this math. When we consider recent financial catastrophes affecting U.S. investors only, without regard to other disasters, we have major stock market crashes or global liquidity crises in 1987, 1994, 1998, 2000, and 2008. That's five major drawdowns in thirty-one years, or an average of once every six years. The last such event was over ten years ago. This does not mean you race to your fortified bunker and curl up in a ball. We wake up every morning and face the day. But the crashes mean we need to overcome cognitive biases about the future resembling the past, and calm as a good forecast for the future.

The best way to preserve wealth in the face of an extreme event is with a modest portfolio allocation to physical gold bullion. When the one-hundred-year flood does hit, it's too late to buy flood insurance. Likewise, when the next financial crisis hits it will be too late to buy gold at today's prices. The best time to buy flood insurance is when the sun is shining. The best time to buy gold is now, before the wall of complacency crumbles.

CONCLUSION

The essence of dramatic tragedy is not unhappiness. It resides in the solemnity of the remorseless working of things.

—Alfred North Whitehead, *Science and the Modern World* (1925)

In his embarrassment, all he came to understand was the one reliably sound thing to do with money: spend it on someone else.

—Lionel Shriver, *The Mandibles* (2016)

Doomsday Clock

One of the most famous passages in American literature occurs in chapter 13 of Ernest Hemingway's *The Sun Also Rises*. The dialogue takes place in a café in Pamplona, Spain, during the running of the bulls.

Bill Gorton, a friend of the protagonist, Jake Barnes, has just arrived from New York. Bill is in the café talking with Mike Campbell, an upper-crust Englishman, now fallen on hard times, but keeping up appearances. In the course of telling a story about his tailor, Mike casually mentions his bankruptcy. Here's the dialogue:

> "How did you go bankrupt?" Bill asked.
>
> "Two ways," Mike said. "Gradually and then suddenly."
>
> "What brought it on?"
>
> "Friends," said Mike. "I had a lot of friends. False friends. Then I had creditors, too. Probably had more creditors than anybody in England."

You've probably seen variations of Mike's phrase "Gradually and then suddenly." It's often misquoted as "Slowly at first, and then quickly." The short version is offered as a warning that a slow, steady debt accumulation with no plan for repayment can continue longer than expected, and then suddenly descend into full-blown financial distress and a rapid collapse.

I selected the longer version to give the short quote context. The debtor, Mike, didn't just go bankrupt. He had a lot of "friends" who relied on him for his generosity and support, with no willingness to pay him back or help him in distress.

He also displayed a lack of control with regard to his financial situation. Most debtors can see problems coming and either cut back spending or take other steps to deal with the debt. Either course brings the situation to a head sooner than later. It's the lack of control that allows the debtor to reach the point of nonsustainable debt, the "gradually" part, and then have a crisis thrust on him all at once, the "suddenly" part. It's how the inevitable still comes as a surprise.

This is the situation in which the United States finds itself. The U.S. national debt has accumulated slowly for decades. There is no plan to make it sustainable, just a vague wish that creditors keep expanding the debt or rolling it over. The United States has a lot of "friends," both at home and abroad, who expect benefits in the form of entitlements, foreign aid, government contracts, or tax breaks. The café scene is complete.

The question is whether the United States is now at the point of suddenly going bankrupt. Of course, the United States won't go bankrupt; it can print all the money needed to pay off its debts in nominal terms. Yet when does that money printing become necessary?

The "gradually, and then suddenly" dynamic is well known to physicists and applied mathematicians. In physics, it is known as a phase transition. A good example is a pot of water being boiled and then turning to steam. The flame can be applied to the pot for quite awhile with no change visible to the naked eye. The water temperature is rising, yet hot water looks like cold water. Suddenly the water's surface becomes turbulent and quickly after that the bubbly surface bursts into steam. The water has been transformed. If no more is done, the entire pot evaporates.

In mathematics, the same dynamics are known as hypersynchronicity. That's a technical term for everyone suddenly doing the same thing at the same time. A run on the bank is a perfect example. A bank run begins with just a few people demanding cash at the teller counter (or the digital equivalent of withdrawing deposits or redeeming money market funds). Soon word spreads, people panic, everyone wants his money back at once, and there's not enough money to meet the demand for liquidity. This is exactly what happened in September 2008 following the Lehman Brothers bankruptcy. That crisis had been on a slow boil since August 2007, then suddenly in September 2008 the whole world wanted its money back.

I've been a Hemingway fan for decades, and have read almost every word he ever published, including letters and incomplete manuscripts, as well as a number of well-researched biographies. I've seen no evidence that he took much interest in physics or mathematics. Yet there's ample evidence that Hemingway was a close observer of human nature and an excellent armchair economist. Hemingway learned an enormous amount about foreign exchange, inflation, and national insolvency as an expatriate reporter living and traveling in Europe in the 1920s. He saw the 1925

French hyperinflation firsthand. As an American with a dollar income, he could live in a decent apartment and afford the best wines in the best cafés because the French franc drastically devalued. His dollars were a natural hedge against franc devaluation. The French themselves suffered the consequences of hyperinflation because they were paid in francs, not dollars.

What if the dollar suddenly became as unwanted as the French franc in 1925?

Consider the evidence that the United States is now dangerously close to the "suddenly" stage of Hemingway's bankruptcy scenario:

- Congress enacted the Trump tax cut in late 2017. This legislation blows a $1.5 trillion hole in the budget deficit. The belief that tax cuts stimulate enough growth to pay for themselves is an unsubstantiated surmise shared by Larry Kudlow, Art Laffer, and few others.
- Congress removed discretionary spending caps on domestic and defense spending that have been in place since 2011. At the same time, Congress reinstated "earmarks" that allow members to spend money on pet projects. These two acts add another $300 billion per year to the U.S. deficit.
- Student loan defaults are now running at 15 percent per year and student loan volume exceeds $1.6 trillion, far more than the amount of junk mortgages in 2007, and with a much higher default rate. Covering these losses adds another $200 billion per year to federal deficits for years to come.
- The U.S. debt-to-GDP ratio is over 105 percent. This is well past the 90 percent danger zone identified by economists Ken Rogoff and Carmen Reinhart. Once in the danger zone, further borrowing causes growth to decline rather than acting as a stimulus.
- Russia, China, Iran, Turkey, and other U.S. adversaries are stockpiling thousands of tons of gold as a hedge against the inflation they expect as the United States tries to print its way out of its nonsustainable debt.

There are other signs that the day of reckoning on the U.S. debt situation is arriving faster than experts believe. Like Hemingway's expatriates, fiscal policy is characterized by complete indiscipline.

Hemingway's point was that bankruptcy comes faster than anyone, especially the bankrupt himself, expects. The United States is closer to an inflection point than the Congress and the White House realize. The pot is beginning to boil. The time to hedge against the worst outcomes is now.

Riding the Bull

Seasoned stock investors know how to deal with bull markets. They increase their allocations to stocks, use margin accounts and other forms of leverage, ride out the drawdowns, buy the dips, and hopefully move to cash before the bull runs out of steam.

Investors also know how to deal with bear markets. They rotate into defensive sectors like consumer nondurables and utilities, increase allocations to cash, unwind leverage, avoid catching a falling knife, and wait patiently for clear signs of a bottom before moving back into stocks.

The one condition investors *don't* know how to deal with is the situation we have now. Consider this recent tale of the tape.

The Dow Jones Industrial Average started 2018 at 24,719 and ended March 2018 at 24,103, a modest 2.5 percent loss. If that's all the information you had, you might assume that not much had happened. Of course, investors know otherwise.

Stocks went on a tear in January 2018, rising over 7.6 percent before hitting an interim high at 26,616 on January 26. Then the stock market party, which had been going strong through all of 2017, suddenly came to an end. Stocks plunged 12 percent to 23,446 intraday by February 9, a full-scale correction, the first since 2016.

Then a recovery rally took the Dow up almost 10 percent to 25,760 on

February 27, 2018. This was quickly followed by another drawdown, this time a 6 percent decline to 24,270 on March 2. The Dow bounced back almost 5 percent to 25,415 on March 12, only to suffer another 7.4 percent decline to 23,533 on March 23. Then the Dow staged a modest recovery to 24,103 to finish out the first quarter.

The year 2018 ended with an even more extreme performance, including the "Christmas Eve Massacre" (Dow down over 650 points), and a Boxing Day gain of over a thousand points in the next trading session. Even this overview does not tell the full story. In the course of these rallies and drawdowns there were attempted rallies and minicrashes, including a series of five-hundred-plus point intraday rallies and skids. Volatility surged.

What happened?

Investor uncertainty is part of the answer. Markets can adjust to good news and bad news, but have no easy way to price true uncertainty. Still, there's more to the market's behavior than that. The factors affecting the market are not only uncertain, they are contradictory. The market is attempting to discount multiple inconsistent stories with no easy way to reconcile the inconsistencies. The market rallies or falls day to day based on rumors, tidbits, and tweets, with no more ballast than that to steady the ship.

There are four major factors driving the market. The factors are growth, trade wars, geopolitics, and technology regulation. Each of the four factors has its own internal contradictions, in effect a binary outcome for each factor. This means there are sixteen possible paths the market might follow ($2^4 = 16$). It's unsurprising that markets are confused.

With regard to growth, the bulls expect a boost from the Trump tax cuts. They are also anticipating inflation due to strong job creation, rising labor-force participation, and a low unemployment rate. They expect interest rates to rise, yet consider this more a sign of economic strength than a cause for concern. Strong growth is good for corporate earnings, and a little inflation is usually good for nominal stock prices, at least in the early stages. The bull case for growth is a curious mixture of the Phillips Curve and the Laffer Curve.

Bears point to an economic slowdown in the fourth quarter of 2018. This is consistent with the dismal average of 2.2 percent growth since the end of the last recession in June 2009. Stronger growth is impeded by demographic and debt headwinds and the impact of Chinese labor and technology on global pricing power. Tax cuts are not expected to help because the drag on growth caused by increased debt outweighs the stimulus from lower taxes.

The Fed is giving a weak economy a double dose of tightening in the form of rate hikes and the unprecedented destruction of base money as they unwind QE. The Fed pushed the economy to the brink of recession before they got the message and paused rate hikes. This bearish view combines the Reinhart and Rogoff thesis on debt death spirals, with a return visit to the Fed policy blunders of 1929 and 1937.

The trade wars are another conundrum. There is little doubt that a true trade war will reduce global growth. Are we facing a prolonged trade war or a series of negotiating postures by Donald Trump as he pursues the art of the deal? Initially, Trump imposed Section 232 tariffs on steel and aluminum imports and then immediately carved out exemptions for Canada and Mexico, pending progress on NAFTA. Next the president trumpeted a trade deal with South Korea that imposed quotas on steel imports, then almost immediately said that deal was conditional upon South Korean help in dealing with North Korea. South Korea did offer help and by September 2018 the new Korea-United States trade deal (KORUS) went into effect.

Trump threatened over $50 billion of Section 301 penalties on China for theft of U.S. intellectual property, then within days China and the United States calmed market fears by announcing plans for bilateral trade negotiations. The China-United States negotiations initially proved fruitless, and by September 2018 the tit-for-tat tariffs escalated to cover over

$450 billion of goods shipped between China and the United States. By late 2018, the reality of an extended trade war between the United States and China sank in, yet the economic impact on global growth was surprisingly muted. The stock market continued performing as if the trade war had never happened.

Geopolitics are another on-again, off-again market driver. A strong case can be made for a coming war with North Korea. Decades of North Korean development of nuclear weapons and ballistic missiles and a rapid increase in the operational tempo of tests in recent years reveal that North Korea is determined to build an arsenal of nuclear-armed ICBMs, which pose an existential threat to the United States. For its part, the United States made it clear that North Korea will not be allowed to acquire or possess these weapons. These two views are irreconcilable and point toward war. At the same time, a rapid round of diplomacy, involving summits among North and South Korea, China and North Korea, and Japan and North Korea, all leading to the June 2018 Singapore summit between Donald Trump and Kim Jong Un, point to a possible peaceful resolution of the impasse. If you believe Kim Jong Un is dealing in good faith, you'll be encouraged by these developments. If you believe Kim Jong Un is dealing in bad faith and playing for time as he perfects his weapons technology, then you'll expect that war is just a matter of time.

The final factor confounding markets is the potential for technology regulation. Investors need no reminder of the outsized impact of the FAANG stocks (Facebook, Apple, Amazon, Netflix, and Google) on markets overall and the NASDAQ 100 in particular.

Suddenly Facebook is facing scrutiny because of misuse of personal customer data and acting as an accessory to Russian meddling in U.S. elections. Amazon is under scrutiny on possible antitrust grounds, alleged government subsidies for shipping, and for Trump's visceral dislike of the "fake news" *Washington Post,* owned by Amazon founder Jeff Bezos. There have been congressional hearings on these matters pointing toward legislation. Will Silicon Valley lobbyists dilute the legislation? Will antitrust allegations go up in smoke? Or will populist outrage with the tech giants lead to a sea change and aggressive enforcement as we saw with the Rockefeller trusts in the early 1900s? The correct answer is no one knows. This will be a battle between corporate lobbyists and populist outrage. Usually the lobbyists win. Still, this time may be different.

None of these four issues will be resolved quickly. It may take six more months of data before the Fed realizes the economy is weak despite tax cuts, or before the bears throw in the towel. Trade wars usually play out over years, not months. If negotiations with China produce results quickly, the trade war concerns will fade, otherwise they will only get worse as retaliation escalates. If Kim Jong Un wants peace, we will know fairly soon. If not, the countdown clock to war, currently paused, will resume ticking. The hearings and legislative process involving technology regulation will also take a year or more to play out. Members of Congress like to milk these issues for campaign contributions from both sides before resolving them, so do not expect quick results.

The problem for investors is they have to wake up every day and commit capital whether they know the answers on these issues or not. If growth is strong, trade wars fizzle, North Korea wants peace, and the tech lobbyists prevail, then Dow 30,000 is in sight. If growth is weak, trade wars escalate, North Korea is dealing in bad faith, and popular outrage hamstrings the tech giants, then Dow 15,000 is in the cards. Of course, other combinations of these factors may emerge. On the whole, the less optimistic, more bearish path is most likely. But it's unwise to go all in on any particular outcome. Now is a time to be nimble.

Mandibles Redux

How bad will the worst-case scenario be?

For many investors, the 2008 financial panic is the benchmark for a worst possible outcome. The Dow Jones Industrial Average fell 54 percent in the seventeen months from October 9, 2007 to March 9, 2009. Major investment firms including Lehman Brothers, Bear Stearns, Fannie Mae, Freddie Mac, and AIG either filed for bankruptcy or were rescued by government intervention after massive losses. Unemployment soared from 4.4 percent in March 2007 to 10 percent in October 2009. The S&P Case-Shiller Home Price Index fell from 182.72 in January 2007 to 133.99 in February 2012, a 27 percent plunge. Housing investors with only 10 or 20 percent equity were wiped out. Numerous hedge funds closed their doors or suspended redemptions. Investor losses were in the trillions of dollars. The contagion spread to Europe and the Middle East. Dubai World went insolvent in November 2009 and a sovereign debt crisis raged in Europe from 2010 to 2015. It was the worst financial crisis since the Great Depression.

The financial damage did not pass quickly. From June 2009 to December 2018, the United States experienced the weakest recovery in its history. Yet the damage did pass. From March 2009 to September 2018, major stock indices more than tripled. Unemployment fell from 10 percent in October 2009 to 3.9 percent in December 2018. The S&P Case-Shiller Home Price Index rallied to 204.44 in June 2018, a new all-time high. Investors who did not sell at the bottom in March 2009 and held their positions recouped all of their losses and made substantial profits by late 2018. A bank CEO or investment maven like Warren Buffett could shrug off the entire episode.

Yet that's not how most investors navigated the meltdown. Investors bailed out of the stock market in late 2008 or early 2009 to preserve what capital they had left. They did not come back to the stock market until years later, if at all, missing out on much of the recovery rally. Homes were foreclosed, denying the previous owners participation in the bounceback that started in 2013. Worst of all was the loss of trust. Investors who suffered heavy losses saw bank CEOs keep their jobs and make multimillion-dollar bonuses by 2016. There were no arrests for fraud, and no accountability among top CEOs. Investors gradually returned to markets but without confidence in Wall Street research or so-called wealth managers. After 2009, investing was a self-help, dog-eat-dog pursuit where cynicism replaced confidence and bitterness replaced trust.

It may be difficult to envision a worse scenario than 2008 and its aftermath, yet such scenarios are not infrequent—they have happened many times in U.S. history. In the Great Depression, major stock indices fell 80 percent from 1929 to 1932. In the Civil War, the Southern economy was decimated and never fully recovered until the 1970s, over a century later. The Second World War imposed massive austerity on the home front and left over 1 million Americans killed or wounded on the front lines. The Dust Bowl drought on the U.S. Great Plains from 1934 to 1939 caused an internal migration of about 3.5 million people, mostly poor, with their few belongings packed into jalopies, from Oklahoma, Arkansas, and Texas to California and other states in search of work. Thousands died from pneumonia or starvation. In short, America has seen far worse than the 2008 financial crisis.

This implies that consideration of a true worst-case scenario must be broader than a 50 percent stock market decline and a few bank failures. The scenario should include financial disruption, yet go beyond that as the consequences of greater scale in capital markets and faster contagion among networked institutions inevitably impact critical infrastructure and, finally, social order.

We can dismiss a few scenarios immediately. Americans have been saturated for decades with film portrayals of zombie uprisings and alien invasions. It's great entertainment but there are no zombies. There may be some unsettled ghosts and spirits here and there, but no zombies. There's also no hard evidence of alien contact. Based on empirical analysis, encounters with aliens are as likely to have a supernatural as intergalactic explanation. That debate need not detain us. Alien spaceship landings on the Mall in Washington, D.C., are not high on my list of bleak scenarios.

More likely is a financial crash associated with some other catastrophic event such as a power-grid collapse or natural disaster. These double catastrophes are not as unusual as many expect; in fact, density functions make them likely. The Fukushima catastrophe in Japan in March 2011 is a perfect example; an earthquake led to a tsunami that killed thousands, disabled a nuclear power plant, and caused a partial meltdown, then finally crashed the Tokyo stock exchange. This was a case of one critical state system (tectonics), triggering phase transitions in other critical state systems (hydraulics, radiation, capital markets), until the chain of criticality ran its course.

Linkages between critical state systems are not merely situational, as in the case of Fukushima; they can also be by design. If China intended to launch an attack on the U.S. power grid, they would not do so on a sunny day. They would wait for a day when stocks were crashing and then attack the power grid, a tactic known as a force multiplier, which heightens fears when the lights go out. Iran might see the chaos at play and decide it's opportune to shut down part of the World Wide Web by disabling key nodes such as the data traffic hub near the airport in Fujairah, UAE. The web and power outages might accelerate the stock market crash, although a more likely outcome is that the stock exchanges would be closed, a condition that further amplifies the panic.

Other catalysts include pandemic, war, and an out-of-the-blue failure of a major bank before the central bank ambulance can arrive at the scene. While each of these is a low probability event, the chance that none of them happens in the next several years is near zero, as illustrated by the Bernoulli process equations in the previous chapter. A catalyst triggers the cascade as one systems failure causes another and the breakdown becomes widespread to the point of paralysis.

Sociologists and historians have documented civilization's thin veneer. Once critical systems break down, civilized behavior lasts three days. After that, the law of the jungle prevails. Citizens rely on violence, money, remoteness, or other forms of coercion to maintain their positions. Loyalty to country is cast aside since the country is no longer holding up its side of the bargain by providing order. Tribes form based on locally shared values. Hurricane Katrina, which overwhelmed New Orleans in August 2005, is a classic example. Day one was the storm. Day two was shock and immediate survival. By day three, looting broke out, although some officials discounted the looting as no more than victims going into survival mode looking for food and water. Then armed vigilante groups formed, that shot some looters but more often shot innocent survivors who happened to end up in the "wrong" neighborhood. Our concern is not with the justice of this, but with the fact that in extreme circumstances it takes only days, not weeks, for armed quasi militias to flood the streets with violence. Civilization is barely skin deep.

Order returns, yet what kind of order? The "barbarians" who invaded Rome in the late fifth century preserved imperial trappings and appealed to the Eastern emperor in Constantinople for legitimacy. Still patrician fortunes were confiscated and patricians were killed wholesale. Bretton Woods was a new world economic order in 1944 that rose from a collapse caused by the currency and trade wars of the 1920s and '30s. Allied troops restored order to defeated Germany after the Second World War using martial law, but the demolished infrastructure, decimated fortunes, and dispirited citizens were all too real. Order returns, but it is not the same order as before the catastrophe. The aftermath is different.

Investors should not focus on the cause of a collapse (it's a long list and the timing is uncertain). The collapse itself will run its course and order will reemerge through coercion, cooperation, or sheer exhaustion. The question is where will you stand in the new order?

The postapocalyptic genre epitomized by Cormac McCarthy's novel *The Road* is compelling and instructive in a metaphorical sense, but is not a case we need consider. McCarthy's world is one that suffered an extinction-level event. Almost all life on earth had ended and the few survivors are cannibals, captives, or those defending a small homestead. This outcome cannot be ruled out. But the term "investor" will have no meaning in the complete absence of a functioning economy or the rule of law. A reversion to a pre-1870s agrarian society without cars, phones, running water, or electricity is more likely than apocalypse, yet still is not a likely case. Someone will turn the lights back on, even if the someone is the U.S. military operating under emergency powers and martial law.

The best depiction of life after a financial collapse is found in *The Mandibles*, a brilliant 2016 novel by the award-winning author Lionel Shriver. The novel offers details of an economic collapse in 2029, but is mostly concerned with the lives of everyday people living in the aftermath. Like Anthony Burgess, Shriver invents words and phrases as needed to convey the unfamiliar. She uses Stone Age to describe a power-grid collapse that preceded the financial crash, and Dryout to describe water scarcity in urban areas.

What is eerie about *The Mandibles* is not that life is apocalyptic, as in *The Road*, nor that life is normal, as Wall Street cheerleaders would have it, but that it's a mixture of both. The United States has defaulted on its debts and is relying on the Federal Reserve to print money to cover interest and principal payments. A new global reserve currency, the bancor, has been launched, but the United States is excluded from this currency system. The Mexican-born U.S. president Alvarado, who delivers his speeches in Spanish, confiscates all private gold in America, a replay of FDR's gold confiscation in 1933. Hyperinflation is 30 percent per week (something I've experienced firsthand traveling in Turkey), so barter is gradually replacing money. Stores still exist, but the shelves are mostly bare. Shoppers don't buy what they want (it's not there); they buy what others may want in the future (hardware and the like) so they can barter it for food. Police are on the streets, but they work for bribes from residents and ignore crimes perpetrated on nonbribers. Routine jobs are still around, but elite occupations in the professions and academia are being eliminated to cut costs. This results in the formerly richest members of the Mandible clan moving in with their poorer relatives, who still have a roof over their heads.

One of the recurring themes in *The Mandibles* consists of elites who insist that the economic collapse is temporary and the economy will soon bounce back as it did after their Stone Age and indeed after the Great

Depression. Except in Shriver's world there is no bounceback; the economy keeps getting worse. Those who cling hardest to recovery chimera end up losing the most. Shriver describes a government plan to eliminate cash in order to crush the black market economy, something Ken Rogoff and Larry Summers endorse today. Some rich Americans survive, but they confine themselves to luxury bunkers prepared before the crisis. Shriver includes a grisly scene in which two of the Mandibles enter one of these bunkers. It turns out that no one killed the rich; they killed each other. Book reviews for *The Mandibles* were largely positive except for one negative review in *The Washington Post,* unsurprising since Shriver has D.C. firmly in the crosshairs of her sniper wit.

What Shriver created in *The Mandibles* is a far more realistic economic scenario than total apocalypse or totalitarian backlash. It's a world where you can go shopping, but the shelves are bare. It's a world where you can use money, but the value is like an ice cube melting in your hand. It's a world where you can have a job, but most don't. It's a world where citizens survive not with machine guns but with wits, hustle, and grim persistence.

While *The Mandibles* has been labeled dystopian, futuristic, and even science fiction, it is actually a realistic portrayal of a postcollapse economy. The day-to-day trials of Shriver's characters would be familiar to civilians behind the lines in the Civil War or getting by in the Great Depression. Those who assume such scenarios won't happen again put too much faith in central banks and too little in the study of history.

Most plans for catastrophe will fall apart in the first five minutes of being needed. Washington, D.C., Beltway traffic is bumper to bumper on a good day. The idea that one could evacuate D.C. in an automobile on short notice is absurd. The superrich have their hideaways in New Zealand. Sounds good, but the tycoons have spent more time picking out a location than they have asking if they can even make it to the airport, whether the airport is operating when they get there, where they can refuel their private jets en route, and whether the Kiwis will be waiting at Auckland Airport with troops if they make it that far. The more blue-collar approach of semiautomatic rifles, stacks of ammo, and cases of freeze-dried food won't fare much better. The bunkers of these wannabe Rambos will be overrun by pop-up militias in minutes, albeit with casualties. A simple device like a bicycle will be more valuable than bullets when the time comes.

This is the point Shriver makes in the climax of her novel. The beleaguered Mandibles decide to leave Brooklyn, where they lately gathered to begin a long march to Gloversville, New York, a small town northwest of Albany in the Adirondack foothills. There a Mandible relative, Jarred, had moved earlier to buy a farm. Jarred developed a survivalist instinct in advance of the meltdown's worst phase, yet his farm was not a bunker, it was a working farm with fruit trees, vegetables, and livestock. He let his extended family know that if they could make it to the farm, he had plenty of need for help and would share the food and shelter. The Brooklyn Mandibles make the trek and, in the end, survive.

The key to survival in a true collapse is not a bunker, rifle, or private jet. The key is community. You will not survive on your own, yet you might just survive in a community that is prepared to share food, fresh water, labor, and artisanal skills. Your skill as a carpenter, dentist, or field hand might be richly rewarded with corn, cheese, milk, and bacon. Cities will break down faster than surrounding countryside because of overreliance on electricity and transportation networks, and their vulnerability to riots, looting, and violent crime. Shriver describes a Brooklyn housejacking that is scary and surreally funny at the same time.

Yet long after cities become uninhabitable, the countryside can function relatively smoothly. This is not the result of weapons, but the result of community. Neighbors will look out for neighbors. Those in need will hire those with skills. Output will stabilize and prices will be steady. The way to envision this is not the barren landscape of McCarthy's *The Road*, but small-town life circa 1901 in Grover's Corners, New Hampshire, as portrayed in the play *Our Town* by Thornton Wilder. For George Gibbs, the boy next door in *Our Town,* as for Jarred Mandible in *The Mandibles,* a farm is more important than a college degree.

What about money and wealth preservation? Both Grover's Corners in 1901 and Shriver's Gloversville in 2029 had money. In Grover's Corners, it was silver coins or gold-backed banknotes. In Gloversville, it was gold and silver bullion, gold-backed notes, or simple barter. What was not money was what we call money today—fiat currency printed by the Fed. In both places, wealth came down to tangible assets and your skills as a laborer, artist, or entrepreneur. Another form of wealth that carries no weight in Grover's Corners or Gloversville is stocks and bonds. This reality is nicely captured by Shriver in a rant by a professor whose portfolio was wiped out in the crash:

> All those pension funds with pie charts of 62 percent equities and 27 percent bonds. . . . All the investment accounts with their contrasting strategies of "growth" or "income." . . . The solicitous questionnaires from Morgan Stanley about the degree of "risk" you'll tolerate—questionnaires that tend to play down the fact there's nowhere on the form to check "zero." . . . The "large cap" versus "small cap" versus "emerging markets." . . . The delicate tweaking. *Maybe we should move a little more into the energy sector and deemphasize pharma.* . . . Well, *all* of those accounts have been flattened. The strategies didn't matter.

In other words, hard assets and hard work are the only stores of value. Stocks and bonds will be worthless because the companies will collapse, the debtors will default, and the nominal value of whatever is left will be wiped out by inflation. The game may start over, but existing players are wiped off the board.

This is not to say that one should not hold stocks and bonds today alongside hard assets. The point is to stay alert and be nimble as conditions deteriorate and risks rise. The time will come in the not distant future when quick decisions will need to be made first to pivot from securities to cash and later from cash to gold . . . and maybe a farm.

Shriver ends *The Mandibles* with a revelation by the then oldest member of the family, who rescues the clan with a gift of the one form of money that survived the chaos against all odds, hidden in a box. I won't ruin the surprise by saying what's in the box. But, if you know my writings, you can probably guess.

ACKNOWLEDGMENTS

Aftermath may not be my last book ever, yet it is the last volume in an international monetary quartet that began with *Currency Wars* (2011) and continued through *The Death of Money* (2014) and *The Road to Ruin* (2016), an eight-year, four-book project in all. The support, encouragement, and patience of my agent, publisher, and editors who were involved for part or all of this personal odyssey were indispensible. My appreciation is commensurate with their great generosity of spirit.

My agent, Melissa Flashman, was the first to see the potential for writings on international economics with a popular flair that avoided the textbook style of most economics books. The entire project would not exist without her. Mel's optimism for *Aftermath* was infectious when my progress was slowed in 2018 by recovery from an injury. She kept me going until we crossed the finish line. She has my heartfelt thanks and deep admiration.

My publisher, Adrian Zackheim, founder of the Portfolio imprint at Penguin Random House, is a vital source of support. Writers work alone so much they can lose sight of the network of editors, publicists, and production staff who stand behind their work. Adrian's presence at the head of the team insured the team was working with the highest standards to turn a manuscript into a finished work shared with readers. *Aftermath* was a longer book that took longer to write than my others. Adrian's support was unwavering. Deputy publisher Will Weisser, who works side by side with Adrian, kept the publication process moving smoothly. Thank you, Adrian and Will.

As a writer of books, articles, and op-eds, I can say categorically I've rarely written a piece that was not improved by great editors. I've been fortunate to work for years with Niki Papadopoulos, editorial director of Portfolio, who applied her considerable talents to *Aftermath* with wit and a smart reader's perspective. If chapter openings are inviting, it's because Niki found gems buried in the text (a bad habit left over from my legal training) and urged me to move them to the front so a reader could engage immediately. Niki was also on the receiving end of my many missed deadline missives, which she handled with understanding and good cheer. Thanks, Niki, and I promise I'll do better next time. Thank you also to Rebecca Shoenthal, part of Niki's editorial team; Stefanie Brody, who handles the publicity duties with diligence and creativity; and copyeditor Jane Cavolina.

My freelance editor, Will Rickards, specializes in spotting my flaws as a writer and fixing them in felicitous ways. The result is a book that is more fluid and offers a better experience for the reader. Will has edited all of my books and is an integral part of the team. Thanks, Will.

Book publicity and marketing begin even before the book is finished. Authors don't write just to put a book on the shelf; it's critical to connect with readers, get the message out, and receive reader and reviewer feedback. The book tour begins while the writer's finishing touches are still being applied. I work daily with my business manager and media adviser, Ali Rickards, to discuss book content and connective threads so we can do the best possible job of bringing the book to the reader. Thanks, Ali, for keeping us ahead of the curve.

I am fortunate to participate in a wide network of correspondents on

Twitter, email, and other channels, who continually offer ideas and insights that challenge conventional wisdom and settled opinion. Thank you to Larry White, Art Santelli, Peter Coyne, Dan Amoss, Ronni Stöferle, Mark Valek, Chris Whalen, Chris Blasi, "TraderStef," Velina Tchakarova, Robert and Kim Kiyosaki, Steven "Sarge" Guilfoyle, Dave Collum, Nomi Prins, Byron King, and Terry Rickard. Please keep those notes, links, and messages headed my way.

The paradox of writing is that it's a solitary activity in search of a mass audience. The bridge between the individual and the group is the small circle of family and friends who support one's work every day on its way to the agora. My writing would not be possible without the continuous support and feedback of my loving wife of forty years, Ann, and our growing family—our son Scott and his wife, Dominique, and their four children Thomas, Sam, James and Pippa; our daughter, Ali; our son Will and his wife, Abby. And the expanded family photo would not be complete without the pups, Ollie and Reese, and kitten Pliny. I'm beyond grateful for all of your support; I couldn't do this without you. I love you all.

As for any mistakes in the book, they're all mine.

NOTES

INTRODUCTION

12 **"In their comments regarding financial markets"**: "Minutes of the Federal Open Market Committee, October 31–November 1, 2017," Board of Governors of the Federal Reserve System, accessed January 7, 2019, www.federalreserve .gov/newsevents/pressreleases/monetary20171122a.htm.

14 **"a chronic condition of sub-normal activity"**: John Maynard Keynes, *The General Theory of Employment, Interest, and Money* (New York: Harvest/ Harcourt Inc., 1964), 249.

14 **Today Truman is ranked by historians:** "Presidential Historians Survey 2017," C-SPAN, accessed January 7, 2019, www.c-span.org/presidentsurvey2017 /?page=participants.

16 **"In Helsinki in 1975"**: Michael Kimmage, "The Surprising Promise of the Trump-Putin Summit," *Foreign Affairs*, July 11, 2018, accessed January 7, 2019, www.foreignaffairs.com/articles/russian-federation/2018-07-11/surprising -promise-trump-putin-summit.

CHAPTER ONE: SCATTERGOODS

21 **"From November 1918 down to the present day"**: Adam Tooze, *The Deluge: The Great War, America and the Remaking of the Global Order, 1916–1931* (New York: Penguin Books, 2014), 418.

24 **"the best museum"**: Transcript of interview with Michael Hayden on *Meet*

the Press, March 30, 2008, accessed January 7, 2019, www.cia.gov/news
-information/press-releases-statements/press-release-archive-2008/transcript
-of-director-haydens-interview-on-meet-the-press.html.

41 **As Giustra put it:** Peter Schweizer, *Clinton Cash: The Untold Story of How and Why Foreign Governments and Businesses Helped Make Bill and Hillary Rich* (New York: Harper, 2016), 24.

43 **publication of the book *Clinton Cash*:** Schweizer, *Clinton Cash.*

45 **the case of William D. Campbell:** Joel Schectman, "Exclusive: Secret Witness in Senate Clinton Probe Is Ex-Lobbyist for Russian Firm," Reuters, November 17, 2017, accessed January 7, 2019, www.reuters.com/article/us-usa-clinton -informant-exclusive/exclusive-secret-witness-in-senate-clinton-probe-is-ex -lobbyist-for-russian-firm-idUSKBN1DG1SB.

46 **Roosevelt supported tariffs in his race:** Patricia O'Toole, "The War of 1912," *Time,* July 3, 2006, accessed January 7, 2019, content.time.com/time/subscriber /article/0,33009,1207791,00.html.

46 **Roosevelt wrote that this kind:** Arthur Lang and Lila Weinberg, eds., *The Muckrakers* (Chicago: University of Illinois Press, 2001), 59.

46 **Roosevelt stormed out:** O'Toole, "The War of 1912."

47 **One of the main planks:** Theodore Roosevelt, *An Autobiography* (New York, Macmillan, 1913), 625.

51 **Reuters reported a decision by CFIUS:** Koh Gui Qing and Greg Roumelitois, "Exclusive: U.S. Puts HNA Deals on Ice Until It Gets Ownership Info—Source," Reuters, January 18, 2018, accessed January 8, 2019, www.reuters.com/article/ us-hna-cfius-exclusive/exclusive-u-s-puts-hna-deals-on-ice-until-it-gets -ownership-info-source-idUSKBN1F80AC.

CHAPTER TWO: PUTTING OUT FIRE WITH GASOLINE

55 **"It appears to have been":** David Hume, *Selected Essays* (New York: Oxford University Press, 2008), 203.

57 **In general, the United States borrowed:** See Robert E. Kelly, *The National Debt of the United States, 1941 to 2008, Second Edition* (Jefferson, NC: McFarland & Company, 2008).

68 **At the Republican nominating convention:** Philip Klein, "How George H. W. Bush's Broken 'No New Taxes' Pledge Changed American Politics and Policy Forever," *Washington Examiner,* December 1, 2018, accessed January 8, 2019, www.washingtonexaminer.com/opinion/how-george-h-w-bushs-broken-no -new-taxes-pledge-changed-american-politics-and-policy-forever.

69 **However, he lost the support:** See Howard Kurz, "The Passion of the New York Post," *The Washington Post,* March 28, 1993, accessed January 8, 2019, www.washingtonpost.com/archive/opinions/1993/03/28/the-passion-of-the

-new-york-post/9b341497-e4eb-46c4-9883-bc119cb818e7/?utm_term=
.b3f4c2b11c2b.

70 **Clinton's closest political adviser:** Robert Burgess, "The Daily Prophet: Carville Was Right About the Bond Market," *Bloomberg BusinessWeek*, January 29,
2018, accessed January 8, 2019, www.bloomberg.com/news/articles/2018-01
-29/the-daily-prophet-carville-was-right-about-the-bond-market-jd0q9r1w.

CHAPTER THREE: FIND THE COST OF FREEDOM

87 **"It is much easier":** Daniel Kahneman, *Thinking, Fast and Slow* (New York:
Farrar, Straus and Giroux, 2011), 3.

90 **Their most influential contribution:** Richard H. Thaler and Cass R. Sunstein,
*Nudge: Improving Decisions About Health, Wealth, and Happiness, Revised
and Expanded Edition* (New York: Penguin Books, 2009).

90 **his Ph.D. thesis:** Richard Thaler and Sherwin Rosen, "The Value of Saving a
Life: Evidence from the Labor Market," in Nestor E. Terleckyj, ed., *Household
Production and Consumption* (Cambridge, Mass.: National Bureau of Economic Research, 1976), 265–302, accessed January 8, 2019, www.nber.org/
chapters/c3964.pdf.

92 **These landmark experiments:** See Daniel Kahneman, Paul Slovic, and Amos
Tversky, eds., *Judgment Under Uncertainty: Heuristics and Biases* (New York:
Cambridge University Press, 1982), and Daniel Kahneman and Amos Tversky,
eds., *Choices, Values, and Frames* (New York: Cambridge University Press,
2000).

94 **As Kahneman wrote:** Daniel Kahneman, "Don't Blink! The Hazards of Confidence," *The New York Times Magazine*, October 19, 2011, accessed January 8,
2019, www.nytimes.com/2011/10/23/magazine/dont-blink-the-hazards-of
-confidence.html.

95 **This is revealed in their book:** Thaler and Sunstein, *Nudge*, 13.

96 **"Decision makers do not make":** Richard H. Thaler, Cass R. Sunstein, and
John P. Balz, "Choice Architecture," *Social Science Research Network*, April 2,
2010, accessed January 8, 2019, papers.ssrn.com/sol3/papers.cfm?abstract_id=
1583509.

97 **They write, "If people are":** Thaler and Sunstein, *Nudge*, 33.

98 **With reference to their book title:** Thaler and Sunstein, *Nudge*, 6.

98 **They subscribe to a process:** Thaler and Sunstein, *Nudge*, 74, footnote.

98 **This is not that difficult:** Thaler and Sunstein, *Nudge*, 53.

98 **With reference to framing:** Thaler and Sunstein, *Nudge*, 37.

98 **They advise, "If you want":** Thaler and Sunstein, *Nudge*, 69.

98 **The authors claim that:** Thaler and Sunstein, *Nudge*, 5.

105 **The patient nearly died:** See Chris Clearfield and András Tilcsik, *Meltdown:*

Why Our Systems Fail and What We Can Do About It (New York: Penguin Press, 2018), 85.

116 **"When Liu Hu recently tried":** Ben Tracy, "China Assigns Every Citizen A 'Social Credit Score' to Identify Who Is and Isn't Trustworthy," CBS New York, April 24, 2018, accessed January 8, 2019, newyork.cbslocal.com/2018/04/24/china-assigns-every-citizen-a-social-credit-score-to-identify-who-is-and-isnt-trustworthy.

119 **The title of his 2016 book:** See Samuel Bowles, *The Moral Economy: Why Good Incentives Are No Substitute for Good Citizens* (New Haven, Conn.: Yale University Press, 2016).

CHAPTER FOUR: THE ALPHA TRAP

123 **"If we were all passive":** Gerry Frigon, "What Would Happen If We Were All Passive Investors?," *Forbes*, June 14, 2018, accessed January 8, 2019, www.forbes.com/sites/forbesfinancecouncil/2018/06/14/what-would-happen-if-we-were-all-passive-investors%E2%80%8B/#3d826c0e40bf.

124 **This was shown by:** See Robert C. Merton, "On Market Timing and Investment Performance. I. An Equilibrium Theory of Value for Market Forecasts," *The Journal of Business* 54, no. 3 (July 1981); and Roy D. Henrikkson and Robert C. Merton, "On Market Timing and Investment Performance. II. Statistical Procedures for Evaluating Forecasting Skills," *The Journal of Business* 54, no. 4 (October 1981).

134 **"To illustrate the idea":** J. B. Heaton, N. G. Polson, and J. H. Witte, "Why Indexing Works," Cornell University, January 14, 2018, 1, accessed January 8, 2019, arxiv.org/pdf/1510.03550.pdf.

137 **"I define a bubble as":** Cody Eustice, "Robert Shiller: Stocks, Bonds and Real Estate Are Overvalued," GuruFocus, May 30, 2015, accessed February 12, 2019, https://www.gurufocus.com/news/338699/robert-shiller-stocks-bonds-and-real-estate-are-overvalued.

148 **"There is an obvious dumbness":** Matt Levine, "Algorithms Had Themselves a Treasury Flash Crash," *Bloomberg Opinion*, July 13, 2015, accessed January 8, 2019, www.bloomberg.com/opinion/articles/2015-07-13/algorithms-had-themselves-a-treasury-flash-crash.

CHAPTER FIVE: FREE MONEY

155 **In his 1925 poem:** T. S. Eliot, *Collected Poems 1909–1962* (New York: Harcourt, 1991), 82.

156 **the "bang" point:** Carmen M. Reinhart, Vincent R. Reinhart, Kenneth S. Rogoff, "Debt Overhangs: Past and Present," National Bureau of Economic Re-

search, NBER Working Paper Series, Working Paper 18015, April 2012, accessed January 8, 2019, www.nber.org/papers/w18015/

158 **Of particular importance:** Carmen Reinhart and Kenneth Rogoff, "Debt and Growth Revisited," VOX CEPR Policy Portal, August 11, 2010, accessed January 8, 2019, voxeu.org/article/debt-and-growth-revisited.

158 **Their main conclusion:** Reinhart and Rogoff, "Debt and Growth Revisited."

158 **Importantly, Reinhart and Rogoff emphasize:** Reinhart and Rogoff, "Debt and Growth Revisited."

158 **For debt-to-equity ratios:** Reinhart and Rogoff, "Debt and Growth Revisited."

158 **Titled "The Real Effects of Debt":** Stephen G. Cecchetti, Madhusudan Joharty, and Fabrizio Zampolli, "The Real Effects of Debt," Bank for International Settlements, BIS Working Papers No. 352, September 16, 2011, 1, accessed January 8, 2019, www.bis.org/publ/work352.pdf.

159 **Another study published:** Cristina Checherita and Philipp Rather, "The Impact of High and Growing Government Debt on Economic Growth—An Empirical Investigation for the Euro Area," European Central Bank, Working Paper Series No. 1237, August 2010, accessed January 8, 2019, ssrn.com/abstract_id=1659559.

159 **That ECB report concludes:** Checherita and Rather, "The Impact of High and Growing Government Debt," European Central Bank, Working Paper Series no. 1237, August 2010, 22, www.ecb.europa.eu/pub/pdf/scpwps/ecbwp1237.pdf.

160 **"After the immediate threat":** Robert Skidelsky, "The Advanced Economies' Lost Decade," Project Syndicate, April 13, 2018, accessed January 9, 2019, www.project-syndicate.org/onpoint/the-advanced-economies-lost-decade-by-robert-skidelsky-2018-04.

162 **In an open letter:** Carmen M. Reinhart and Kenneth S. Rogoff, "Open Letter to Paul Krugman," Carmen M. Reinhart Author Website, May 25, 2013, accessed January 9, 2019, www.carmenreinhart.com/letter-to-pk.

166 **One of the leading treatments:** Rodger Malcolm Mitchell, *Free Money Plan for Prosperity* (Wilmette, Ill.: PGM Worldwide, 2005).

167 **Georg Friedrich Knapp is:** Georg Friedrich Knapp, *The State Theory of Money* (Eastford, Conn.: Martino Fine Books, 2013).

167 **Yet Kelton and other scholars:** Adam Smith, *The Wealth of Nations* (New York: Modern Library, 1994).

167 **In a pellucid piece:** Stephanie Bell, "The Role of the State and the Hierarchy of Money," *Cambridge Journal of Economics*, 2001, accessed January 9, 2019, cas2.umkc.edu/economics/people/facultyPages/wray/courses/Econ601%202012/readings/Bell%20The%20Role%20of%20the%20State%20and%20the%20Hierarchy%20of%20Money.pdf.

167 **"What makes a currency valid":** Bell, "The Role of the State," 155.

168 **As Kelton explains:** Bell, "The Role of the State," 160.

169 **She writes, "Only the state":** Bell, "The Role of the State," 161.

174 **"I have concerns about":** "Transcript of the Meeting of the Federal Open Market Committee on October 23–24, 2012," Board of Governors of the Federal Reserve System, 192, accessed February 13, 2019, https://www.federalreserve .gov/monetarypolicy/files/FOMC20121024meeting.pdf.

175 **At an ad hoc press briefing:** Thomas L. Friedman, "Mideast Tensions; U.S. Jobs at Stake in Gulf, Baker Says," *The New York Times*, November 14, 1990, accessed January 9, 2019, www.nytimes.com/1990/11/14/world/mideast-tensions -us-jobs-at-stake-in-gulf-baker-says.html.

178 **"Economically, declining LFPRs and falling":** Nicholas Eberstadt, *Men Without Work: America's Invisible Crisis* (West Conshohocken, Penn.: Templeton Press, 2016), 150–51.

178 **"While the national unemployment rate":** Pavlina R. Tcherneva, "Unemployment: The Silent Epidemic," Levy Economics Institute of Bard College, Working Paper No. 895, August 7–10, 2017, accessed January 9, 2019, www .levyinstitute.org/publications/unemployment-the-silent-epidemic.

180 **The fullest explanation of:** Philippe Van Parijs and Yannick Vanderborght, *Basic Income: A Radical Proposal for a Free Society and a Sane Economy* (Cambridge, Mass.: Harvard University Press, 2017).

180 **Using 2015 data:** Van Parijs and Vanderborght, *Basic Income*, 11.

181 **"the new wave of automation":** Van Parijs and Vanderborght, *Basic Income*, 5.

181 **At the World Government Summit:** Kathleen Pender, "Why Universal Basic Income Is Gaining Support, Critics," *San Francisco Chronicle*, July 15, 2017, accessed January 9, 2019, www.sfchronicle.com/business/article/Why-universal -basic-income-is-gaining-support-11290211.php.

181 **The *San Francisco Chronicle*:** Pender, "Why Universal Basic Income Is Gaining Support."

181 **In a Harvard University commencement:** "Mark Zuckerberg's Commencement Address at Harvard," *The Harvard Gazette*, May 25, 2017, accessed January 9, 2019, news.harvard.edu/gazette/story/2017/05/mark-zuckerbergs -speech-as-written-for-harvards-class-of-2017.

183 **From the right, Charles Murray:** Charles Murray, *In Our Hands: A Plan to Replace the Welfare State* (Washington, D.C.: AEI Press, 2016).

183 **Murray's succinct summary:** Murray, *In Our Hands*, 10.

185 **In April 2018, MMT's leading lights:** L. Randall Wray, Flavia Dantas, Scott Fullwiler, Pavlina R. Tcherneva, and Stephanie A. Kelton, "Public Service Employment: A Path to Full Employment," Levy Economics Institute of Bard College, April 2018, accessed January 9, 2019, www.levyinstitute.org/publications/ public-service-employment-a-path-to-full-employment.

185 **"We propose the creation of a":** Wray et al., "Public Service Employment," 1.

CHAPTER SIX: THE MAR-A-LAGO ACCORD

191 **"How often do we hear"**: Judy Shelton, "The Case for a New International Monetary System," *Cato Journal* 38, no. 2 (Spring/Summer 2018): 379, accessed January 9, 2019, www.cato.org/cato-journal/springsummer-2018/case-new-international-monetary-system.

198 **"I view gold as the primary"**: Interview with Alan Greenspan, "Gold: The Ultimate Insurance Policy," *Gold Investor*, February 2017, accessed January 9, 2019, www.gold.org/goldhub/research/gold-investor/gold-investor-february-2017.

198 **"Global debt is at an all-time high"**: Christine Lagarde, "Transcript of Managing Director's Press Briefing," International Monetary Fund, Washington, D.C., April 19, 2018, accessed January 9, 2019, www.imf.org/en/News/Articles/2018/04/19/tr041918-transcript-of-managing-directors-press-briefing?cid=em-COM-123-36937.

199 **The call for a new international:** Shelton, "The Case for a New International Monetary System," 379.

204 **"The IMF was a more formal"**: Timothy F. Geithner, *Stress Test: Reflections on Financial Crises* (New York: Broadway Books, 2014), 73.

208 **"IMF managing director"**: Dong He, "Monetary Policy in the Digital Age," *Finance & Development*, June 2018, International Monetary Fund, Washington, D.C., accessed January 9, 2019, www.imf.org/external/pubs/ft/fandd/2018/06/central-bank-monetary-policy-and-cryptocurrencies/he.pdf.

219 **"Untermyer: I want to ask you"**: "Testimony of J. P. Morgan Before the Bank and Currency Committee of the House of Representatives, at Washington, D.C.," December 18–19, 1912, 48, accessed, January 9, 2019, lcweb2.loc.gov/service/gdc/scd0001/2006/20060517001te/20060517001te.pdf.

CHAPTER SEVEN: GODZILLA

223 **"A finite time singularity"**: Geoffrey West, *Scale: The Universal Laws of Growth, Innovation, Sustainability, and the Pace of Life in Organisms, Cities, Economies, and Companies* (New York: Penguin Press, 2017), 413.

225 **"Consider increasing the height"**: West, *Scale*, 42.

232 **One model, developed by:** Leonard Beeghley, *The Structure of Social Stratification in the United States, Fifth Edition* (New York: Routledge, 2016).

233 **Another ontology is offered:** William E. Thompson, Joseph V. Hickey, Mica L. Thompson, *Society in Focus: An Introduction to Sociology, Eighth Edition* (Lanham, Md.: Rowman and Littlefield, 2017).

233 **Finally, Dennis Gilbert offers:** Dennis Gilbert, *The American Class Structure in an Age of Growing Inequality, Ninth Edition* (Thousand Oaks, Calif.: SAGE Publications, Inc., 2015).

242　**Walter Scheidel's book:** Walter Scheidel, *The Great Leveler: Violence and the History of Inequality from the Stone Age to the Twenty-first Century* (Princeton, N.J.: Princeton University Press, 2017).

243　**"After I arrived, I was ushered":** Douglas Rushkoff, "Survival of the Richest— The Wealthy Are Plotting to Leave Us Behind," *Medium Magazine,* July 5, 2018, accessed January 9, 2019, medium.com/s/futurehuman/survival-of-the-richest -9ef6cddd0cc1.

CHAPTER EIGHT: AFTERMATH

249　**"Reduced to essentials":** Walter Scheidel, *The Great Leveler: Violence and the History of Inequality from the Stone Age to the Twenty-first Century* (Princeton, N.J.: Princeton University Press, 2017).

263　**"In addition to structural":** Andrew Sheng and Xiao Geng, "Managing China's Global Risks," Project Syndicate, May 29, 2018, accessed January 9, 2019, www.project-syndicate.org/commentary/china-global-risks-trump-trade-war -by-andrew-sheng-and-xiao-geng-2018-05.

264　**In a closed-door meeting:** The Lighthizer actions and conversations described in the following pages were related to the author in a conversation on April 20, 2018, with one of Robert Lighthizer's closest associates, who had firsthand knowledge.

277　**Yet here's an interesting bit of math:** This example was first presented in similar form in B. J. Campbell, "The Surprisingly Solid Mathematical Case of the Tin Foil Hat Gun Prepper," *Medium Magazine,* April 20, 2018, accessed January 9, 2019, medium.com/s/story/the-surprisingly-solid-mathematical-case -of-the-tin-foil-hat-gun-prepper-15fce7d10437.

CONCLUSION

279　**"The essence of dramatic tragedy":** Alfred North Whitehead, *Science and the Modern World* (New York: Cambridge University Press, 2011), 13.

279　**"In his embarrassment":** Lionel Shriver, *The Mandibles: A Family, 2029–2047* (New York: Harper, 2016).

292　**The best depiction of life:** Shriver, *The Mandibles.*

295　**"All those pension funds":** Shriver, *The Mandibles,* 145.

SELECTED SOURCES

ARTICLES

Burger, Albert E. "The Monetary Economics of Gold." Federal Reserve Bank of St. Louis, January 1974.

Case, Anne, and Angus Deaton. "Mortality and Morbidity in the 21st Century." Brookings Papers on Economic Activity, Spring 2017.

Henrikkson, Roy D., and Robert C. Merton. "On Market Timing and Investment Performance. II. Statistical Procedures for Evaluating Forecasting Skills." *The Journal of Business* 54, no. 4 (October 1981).

Hewes, Henry. "Eliot on Eliot: 'I Feel Younger Than I Did at 60.'" *Saturday Review*, September 13, 1958.

Lorenz, Edward N. "Deterministic Nonperiodic Flow." *Journal of the Atmospheric Sciences* 20 (January 7, 1963).

Merton, Robert C. "On Market Timing and Investment Performance. I. An Equilibrium Theory of Value for Market Forecasts." *The Journal of Business* 54, no. 3 (July 1981).

Mundell, R. A. "Capital Mobility and Stabilization Policy under Fixed and Flexible Exchange Rates." *The Canadian Journal of Economics and Political Science* 29, no. 4 (November 1963).

Rickards, James. "Economic Security and National Security: Interaction and Synthesis." *Strategic Studies Quarterly* 3, no. 3 (Fall 2009).

Thaler, Richard, and Sherwin Rosen, "The Value of Saving a Life: Evidence from the Labor Market." In *Household Production and Consumption*, edited by Nestor E.

Terlecky (Cambridge, Mass.: National Bureau of Economic Research, 1976, 265–302).

Thaler, Richard H., Cass R. Sunstein, and John P. Balz. "Choice Architecture." Social Science Research Network, April 2, 2010.

Wray, L. Randall, Stephanie A. Kelton, Pavlina R. Tcherneva, Scott Fullwiler, and Flavia Dantas. "Guaranteed Jobs Through a Public Service Employment Program." Levy Economics Institute of Bard College, Policy Note 2018/2.

BOOKS

Ackerman, Kenneth D. *The Gold Ring: Jim Fisk, Jay Gould, and Black Friday, 1869.* Falls Church, Va.: Viral History Press, 2011.

Akerlof, George A. and Rachel E. Kranton, *Identity Economics: How Our Identities Shape Our Work, Wages, and Well-Being.* Princeton, N.J.: Princeton University Press, 2010.

Beeghley, Leonard. *The Structure of Social Stratification in the United States, Fifth Edition.* New York: Routledge, 2016.

Boethius, Anicius. *The Consolation of Philosophy.* New York: Penguin Books, 1999.

Boghossian, Paul. *Fear of Knowledge: Against Relativism and Constructivism.* New York: Oxford University Press, 2006.

Bostrom, Nick. *Superintelligence: Paths, Dangers, Strategies.* Oxford, U.K.: Oxford University Press, 2014.

Bowles, Samuel. *The Moral Economy: Why Good Incentives Are No Substitute for Good Citizens.* New Haven, Conn.: Yale University Press, 2016.

Brill, Steven, *Tailspin: The People and Forces Behind America's Fifty-Year Fall—and Those Fighting to Reverse It.* New York: Alfred A. Knopf, 2018.

Clearfield, Chris, and András Tilcsik. *Meltdown: Why Our Systems Fail and What We Can Do About It.* New York: Penguin Press, 2018.

Cohen, Stephen F. *War with Russia? From Putin & Ukraine to Trump & Russiagate.* New York: Hot Books, 2019.

Cohen, Stephen S., and J. Bradford DeLong. *Concrete Economics: The Hamilton Approach to Economic Growth and Policy.* Boston, Mass.: Harvard Business Review Press, 2016.

Dam, Kenneth W. *The Rules of the Game: Reform and Evolution in the International Monetary System.* Chicago, Ill.: The University of Chicago Press, 1982.

Duke, Annie. *Thinking in Bets: Making Smarter Decisions When You Don't Have All the Facts.* New York: Portfolio, 2018.

Eberstadt, Nicholas. *Men Without Work: America's Invisible Crisis.* West Conshohocken, Pa.: Templeton Press, 2016.

Edwards, Sebastian., *American Default: The Untold Story of FDR, the Supreme Court, and the Battle over Gold.* Princeton, N.J.: Princeton University Press, 2018.

Eliot, T. S. *Collected Poems 1909–1962*. New York: Harcourt, 1991.

Erixon, Fredrik, and Björn Weigel. *The Innovation Illusion: How So Little Is Created by So Many Working So Hard*. New Haven, Conn.: Yale University Press, 2016.

Fisher, Irving. *The Money Illusion*. New York: Adelphi Company, 1929.

Foer, Franklin. *World Without Mind: The Existential Threat of Big Tech*. New York: Penguin Press, 2017.

Friedman, Milton, and Anna Jacobson Schwartz. *A Monetary History of the United States, 1867–1960*. Princeton, N.J.: Princeton University Press, 1993.

Geithner, Timothy F. *Stress Test: Reflections on Financial Crises*. New York: Broadway Books, 2014.

Ghilarducci, Teresa, and Tony James. *Rescuing Retirement: A Plan to Guarantee Retirement for All Americans*. New York: Columbia University Press, 2018.

Gilbert, Dennis. *The American Class Structure in an Age of Growing Inequality, Ninth Edition*. Thousand Oaks, Calif.: SAGE Publications, Inc., 2015.

Gordon, Robert J. *The Rise and Fall of American Growth: The U.S. Standard of Living Since the Civil War*. Princeton, N.J.: Princeton University Press, 2017.

Grant, Michael, editor, *T. S. Eliot—The Critical Heritage*, vols. 1 and 2. London, U.K.: Routledge & Kegan Paul, 1982.

Hemingway, Ernest. *The Sun Also Rises*. New York: Scribner, 2006.

Hudson, Michael. . . . *And Forgive Them Their Debts: Lending, Foreclosure and Redemption From Bronze Age Finance to the Jubilee Year*. Dresden, Germany: ISLET-Verlag, 2018.

Hume, David. *Selected Essays*. New York: Oxford University Press, 2008.

Kahneman, Daniel. *Thinking, Fast and Slow*. New York: Farrar, Straus and Giroux, 2011.

Kahneman, Daniel, and Amos Tversky, eds., *Choices, Values and Frames*. New York: Cambridge University Press, 2000.

Kahneman, Daniel, Amos Tversky, and Paul Slovic, eds. *Judgment Under Uncertainty: Heuristics and Biases*. New York: Cambridge University Press, 1982.

Kelly, Robert E. *The National Debt of the United States, 1941 to 2008, Second Edition*. Jefferson, N.C.: McFarland & Company, 2008.

Knapp, George Friedrich. *The State Theory of Money*. Eastford, Conn.: Martino Fine Books, 2013.

Lavoie, Marc. *Post-Keynesian Economics: New Foundations*. Northhampton, Mass.: Edward Elgar Publishing, 2014.

Lind, Michael. *Land of Promise: An Economic History of the United States*. New York: Harper, 2012.

Mandelbrot, Benoit, and Richard L. Hudson. *The (Mis)behavior of Markets: A Fractal View of Risk, Ruin, and Reward*. New York: Basic Books 2004.

McCarthy, Cormac. *The Road*. New York: Alfred A. Knopf, 2006.

McMahon, Dinny. *China's Great Wall of Debt: Shadow Banks, Ghost Cities, Massive

Loans, and the End of the Chinese Miracle. New York: Houghton Mifflin Harcourt, 2018.

Mitchell, Rodger Malcolm. *Free Money Plan for Prosperity.* Wilmette. Ill.: PGM Worldwide, 2005.

Murray, Charles. *In Our Hands: A Plan to Replace the Welfare State.* Washington, D.C.: AEI Press, 2016.

Mussa, Michael, James M. Boughton, and Peter Isard, eds. *The Future of the SDR in Light of Changes in the International Monetary System.* Washington, D.C.: International Monetary Fund, 1996.

Navidi, Sandra. *Superhubs: How the Financial Elite & Their Networks Rule Our World.* Boston, Mass.: Nicholas Brealey Publishing, 2017.

Noah, Timothy. *The Great Divergence: America's Growing Inequality Crisis and What We Can Do About It.* New York: Bloomsbury Press, 2012.

Parijs, Philippe Van, and Yannick Vanderborght. *Basic Income: A Radical Proposal for a Free Society and a Sane Economy.* Cambridge, Mass.: Harvard University Press, 2017.

Platt, Stephen R. *Imperial Twilight: The Opium War and the End of China's Last Golden Age.* New York: Alfred A. Knopf, 2018.

Polanyi, Karl. *The Great Transformation: The Political and Economic Origins of Our Time.* Boston, Mass.: Beacon Press, 2001.

Reinhart, Carmen, and Kenneth S. Rogoff. *This Time Is Different: Eight Centuries of Financial Folly.* Princeton, N.J.: Princeton University Press, 2009.

Ricardo, David. *The Principles of Political Economy and Taxation.* Mineola, N.Y.: Dover Publications, 2004.

Rickards, James. *Currency Wars: The Making of the Next Global Crisis.* New York: Portfolio/Penguin, 2011.

———. *The Death of Money: The Coming Collapse of the International Monetary System.* New York: Portfolio/Penguin, 2014.

———. *The Road to Ruin: The Global Elites' Secret Plan for the Next Financial Crisis.* New York: Portfolio/Penguin, 2016.

Saint-Paul, Giles. *The Tyranny of Utility: Behavioral Social Science and the Rise of Paternalism.* Princeton, N.J.: Princeton University Press, 2011.

Scheidel, Walter. *The Great Leveler: Violence and the History of Inequality from the Stone Age to the Twenty-First Century.* Princeton, N.J.: Princeton University Press, 2017.

Schweizer, Peter. *Clinton Cash: The Untold Story of How and Why Foreign Governments and Businesses Helped Make Bill and Hillary Rich.* New York: Harper, 2016.

Shriver, Lionel. *The Mandibles: A Family, 2029–2047.* New York: Harper, 2016.

Smith, Adam. *The Wealth of Nations.* New York: Modern Library, 1994.

Steil, Benn. *The Battle of Bretton Woods: John Maynard Keynes, Harry Dexter White, and the Making of a New World Order.* Princeton, N.J.: Princeton University Press, 2013.

Streeck, Wolfgang. *How Will Capitalism End?* Brooklyn, N.Y.: Verso, 2016.

Strogatz, Steven. *SYNC: The Emerging Science of Spontaneous Order.* New York: Hyperion, 2003.

Subacchi, Paola. *The People's Money: How China Is Building a Global Currency.* New York: Columbia University Press, 2017.

Sunstein, Cass R. *The Ethics of Influence: Government in the Age of Behavioral Science.* New York: Cambridge University Press, 2016.

Suskind, Ron. *Confidence Men: Wall Street, Washington, and the Education of a President.* New York: Harper, 2011.

Thaler, Richard H. *Misbehaving: The Making of Behavioral Economics.* New York: W. W. Norton & Company, 2015.

Thaler, Richard H., and Cass R. Sunstein. *Nudge: Improving Decisions About Health, Wealth and Happiness, Revised and Expanded Edition.* New York: Penguin Books, 2009.

Thompson, William E., Joseph V. Hickey, Mica L. Thompson. *Society in Focus: An Introduction to Sociology, Eighth Edition.* Lanham, Md.: Rowman and Littlefield, 2017.

Tooze, Adam. *Crashed: How a Decade of Financial Crises Changed the World.* New York: Viking, 2018.

———. *The Deluge: The Great War, America and the Remaking of the Global Order, 1916–1931.* New York: Penguin Books, 2014.

———. *The Wages of Destruction: The Making and Breaking of the Nazi Economy.* New York: Penguin Books, 2006.

Turner, Adair. *Between Debt and the Devil: Money, Credit, and Fixing Global Finance.* Princeton, N.J.: Princeton University Press, 2016.

Vogl, Joseph. *The Ascendancy of Finance.* Malden, Mass.: Polity Press, 2017.

Volcker, Paul A., with Christine Harper. *Keeping At It: The Quest for Sound Money and Good Government.* New York: Public Affairs, 2018.

West, Geoffrey. *Scale: The Universal Laws of Growth, Innovation, Sustainability, and the Pace of Life in Organisms, Cities, Economies, and Companies.* New York: Penguin Press, 2017.

Whitehead, Alfred North. *Science and the Modern World.* New York: Cambridge University Press, 2011.

Wray, L. Randall. *Modern Money Theory: A Primer on Macroeconomics and Sovereign Monetary Systems.* New York: Palgrave Macmillan, 2012.

Zatarian, Lee Allen. *Tanker War: America's First Conflict with Iran, 1987–1988.* Philadelphia, Penn.: CASEMATE, 2008.

Zelizer, Viviana A. *The Social Meaning of Money: Pin Money, Paychecks, Poor Relief, & Other Currencies.* Princeton, N.J.: Princeton University Press, 2017.

INDEX

Jackson, Andrew, 47, 59

Japan: and current global risks, 276; debt-to-GDP ratio, 182–83; and global wealth gap, 245; and investing strategies for gold-backed currencies, 221; "lost decade," 85, 270; and the Malaysia Plan, 217; and monetary conferences, 191–92; and North Korea nuclear negotiations, 286; and risk of high debt-to-GDP ratios, 157–58, 162; trade negotiations with China, 266

Jarrett, Valerie, 73

Jefferson, Thomas, 15, 59

John Paul II, Pope, 16

Johnson, Lyndon, 46, 63, 69, 72, 171, 179

JPMorgan, 143, 230, 232, 238

J. P. Morgan & Co., 219

Judgment Under Uncertainty (Kahneman and Tversky), 92

Kahneman, Daniel, 87, 92–95, 113–14, 118–19

Kalecki, Michal, 164

Kaufman, Henry, 203

Kazakhstan, 41, 44

Kelleher, Colm, 252, 255, 256

Kelton, Stephanie, 11, 166–70, 172, 175, 185–86, 269–70

Kennedy, John F., 45, 63

Keynesian economics: definition of depression, 14; and global monetary reset proposal, 199; and history of U.S. debt, 62; and international monetary conferences, 195; and investing strategies for mercantilist world, 52; and liquidity trap concept, 3; and modern schools of economic thought, 163–64, 167; and risk of high debt-to-GDP ratios, 156–57; and risk of passive trading strategies, 146–47

Kim Jong Un, 286, 287

"King Dollar" policy, 196–97

Kissinger, Henry, 271

Kiss of Death, 24–25

kleptocracy, 272

Knapp, Georg Friedrich, 167

Korean War, 64, 171

Korea-United States trade deal (KORUS), 285

Kovner, Bruce, 129–33, 135, 150

Krugman, Paul, 159–62, 164

Kudlow, Larry, 9, 74, 264, 282

Labor Force Participation Rate (LFPR), 176–77, 178

Lacqua, Francine, 253

Laffer, Art, 9, 74, 282

Laffer Curve, 9, 75, 285

Lagarde, Christine, 198–99, 208

Landry, John R., 37–38, 40

Lapidus, Morris, 28

Latin America, 50, 271, 272

Lehman Brothers, 4, 231, 237, 281, 288

leverage, 6, 49–50, 148, 261, 269, 283

Levine, Matt, 148–49

Levy Economics Institute, 177

libertarian paternalism, 95, 100

Liberty Bonds, 61

Lighthizer, Robert E., 264, 266, 268

Lincoln, Abraham, 15, 59

Lipsky, John, 200–205

liquidity, 3, 7, 13, 130, 202, 255, 273

Liu Hu, 116

London Clearing House, 255

London School of Economics, 163

Long-Term Capital Management (LTCM), 129–30, 131, 151, 272–73

loss limits, 131–32

lost decades, 85, 270

Louvre conference, 146, 191–92, 197

M1 money supply, 169, 221

Maastricht Treaty, 69, 159

machine trading, 144–45

Mack, John, 238

Madison, James, 59

Madoff, Bernie, 258–62

Mahathir bin Mohamad, 214–15

Malaysia, 215–19, 272

Malpass, David, 74

The Mandibles (Shriver), 279, 292–96

Mar-a-Lago conference (proposal), 199, 205–6, 266

marginal propensity to consume (MPC), 188

Markopolos, Harry, 259–60

Mattis, James, 50

May, Theresa, 191

McCarthy, Cormack, 291

McCulley, Paul, 173

McKee, Michael, 253

McKinley, William, 60

McMaster, H. R., 50

Medicare and Medicaid, 72, 78, 183

Menendez, Robert, 36

mercantilism, 22, 52–53